THE
DESERT FOX
IN NORMANDY

Field Marshal Erwin Rommel, the "Desert Fox." (U.S. National Archives)

THE
DESERT FOX
IN NORMANDY

Rommel's Defense
of Fortress Europe

Samuel W. Mitcham, Jr.

First Cooper Square Press edition 2001

This Cooper Square Press paperback edition of *The Desert Fox in Normandy* is an unabridged republication of the edition first published in Westport, Connecticut in 1997. It is reprinted by arrangement with Greenwood Publishing Group, Inc.

Published by Cooper Square Press
An Imprint of the Rowman & Littlefield Publishing Group
150 Fifth Avenue, Suite 817
New York, New York 10011

Distributed by National Book Network

Library of Congress Cataloging-in-Publication Data

Mitcham, Samuel W.
    The Desert Fox in Normandy : Rommel's defense of fortress Europe / Samuel
W. Mitcham, Jr.—1st Cooper Square Press ed.
        p. cm.
    Originally published: Westport, Conn. : Praeger, 1997.
    Includes bibliographical references and index.
    ISBN 0-8154-1159-6 (pbk. : alk. paper)
        1. World War, 1939-1945—Campaigns—France—Normandy. 2. Rommel,
Erwin, 1891-1944 3. Normandy (France)—History, Military. I. Title.

D756.5.N6 M496 2001
940.54'21421—dc21

                                                        2001028682

⊖™ The paper used in this publication meets the minimum requirements of
American National Standard for Information Sciences—Permanence of
Paper for Printed Library Materials, ANSI/NISO Z39.48–1992.
Manufactured in the United States of America.

This book is dedicated to
Gavin Kurt Ryne Mitcham
my one-year-old son,
and to his mother

Also by SAMUEL W. MITCHAM JR.

Hitler's Field Marshals and Their Battles

Eagles of the Third Reich: The Men Who Made the Luftwaffe

*Hitler's Commanders: Officers of the Wehrmacht, the Luftwaffe,
the Kriegsmarine, and the Waffen-SS*

Hitler's Legions: The Germany Army Orders of Battle, World War II

Men of the Luftwaffe

Retreat to the Reich: The German Defeat in France, 1944

Rommel's Desert War: The Life and Death of the Afrika Korps

*Rommel's Greatest Victory: The Desert Fox and the
Fall of Tobruk, Spring 1942*

The Battle of Sicily, 1943

Triumphant Fox: Erwin Rommel and the Rise of the Afrika Korps

Why Hitler?: The Genesis of the Nazi Reich

CONTENTS

Photo essay follows page 128

ILLUSTRATIONS

ACKNOWLEDGMENTS

First of all, I thank my long-suffering wife Donna for proofreading and helpful suggestions. I also thank Frank Tugwell (who has a true understanding of Hitler and the Third Reich) for his help with computer operations and the final production of the manuscript. Thanks also to Dr. John C. Lewis for his help and advice. Special thanks to my in-laws, Don and Wanda Pounds of Nashville, Arkansas, for letting me use their "summer house," where I could work in isolation. I also express my gratitude to Dr. Gene Mueller of Henderson State University, to Dr. John T. Morgan of Emory and Henry, and to Wayne D. Shows for their assistance in various projects, and to Friedrich von Stauffenberg for giving me his papers shortly before his death. I also thank Dr. Sidney Jumper, Dr. Charles S. Aiken, and the Department of Geography at the University of Tennessee; and Lieutenant Colonel Ernest Bruce, Department of Aviation, Northeast Louisiana University, for preparing me to work at this level. As usual, thanks to the United States Military History Institute at Carlisle Barracks, Pennsylvania, the Still Photo Division of the U.S. National Archives, and the staff of the Bundesarchiv/Kolbenz, for providing materials and/or photographs. Gratitude is also expressed to Princess Cruises, which gave me the opportunity to visit Normandy and the various landing beaches in the summer of 1994. Last but not least, thank you to Melinda Matthews, interlibrary loan librarian at Northeast Louisiana University, for the fine job she did in locating and obtaining materials, some of which were difficult to find.

INTRODUCTION

When I visited the United Kingdom and the European mainland in the summer of 1994, I was encouraged by several friends to write the story of the Normandy invasion from the German point of view. It certainly was not hard to convince me to do so, because I had done a book of a similar nature. (Twelve or more years ago I wrote a book entitled *Rommel's Last Battle*, but much has been written and uncovered since then.) This project quickly developed into one focusing on the generalship of Field Marshal Erwin Rommel, the Desert Fox, and the last 10 months of his incredible life.

To understand history, one must read biography—especially the biographies of famous leaders. This goes against the current fad in many American universities—where it is considered unfashionable or "politically incorrect" to study or write about "DWMs" (dead white males), a term usually muttered by leftist and largely socialist professors with a slight air of contempt, condescension, and perceived (and self-ordained) intellectual self-superiority. Unfortunately, these people write as they think, which is why so much garbage and so little of substance or importance is being produced by the vast majority of them. Like it or not, we owe our Western Civilization, our democratic and religious institutions, our values, and most things that make life worth living, to DWMs—not to affirmative action and similar scams.

DWMs have also produced a great deal of havoc and mischief. The worst one to appear in our century (with the possible exception of Stalin) was Adolf Hitler. Democratically elected (he garnered the same percentage of the popular vote as did Bill Clinton in 1992 and Abraham Lincoln in 1860), he quickly established himself as the master of Germany while simultaneously increasing his popularity and expanding German space—initially by peaceful means. When these methods failed and he went to war in 1939, he unquestionably had the full support of the German people and most of the military establishment—including Erwin Rommel.

Only gradually did things change. Although he retained the support of the German people ("The Fuehrer is always right"), by 1943 it was less enthusiastic than before and more likely to be the product of fear than love. It was, nevertheless, always there; the German people never did revolt or attempt to overthrow Hitler. Much of the senior military establishment, however, knew what the civilians did not know: that the war could no longer be won militarily, and some of these senior officers were ripe for rebellion. Into this situation walked Erwin Rommel, after two years of relatively isolated combat in the Sahara Desert. An acclaimed military genius, he was out of his element in the realm of power politics (he was always politically naive), but he was guided by his own strong moral values and a well-developed sense of justice and fairness. He made an interesting contrast with some of his peers.

At first, Rommel was given a relatively insignificant command in northern Italy. Then, at the end of 1943 he was given his most challenging and important assignment: Take charge of Army Group B and repel the great Anglo-Saxon invasion. Despite the fact that he knew the odds were heavily against him, he threw his entire being into his new task. An acknowledged master of mobile warfare, he developed a scheme of defense and fought a brilliant campaign—both of which were the antithesis of the blitzkrieg. In many ways, it was his most brilliant. His most noble battle, however, came against his former master. After a struggle of conscience, Field Marshal Erwin Rommel, the Desert Fox, decided to help depose Adolf Hitler.

Incidentally, another unfortunate trend has emerged in American historical thought in recent years: hero bashing. Any nonliberal is considered an appropriate target. Erwin Rommel, Douglas MacArthur, Ronald Reagan, George Washington, and Robert E. Lee (of all people!) have been among those bashed by these historians—some of whom call themselves "biographers." Many of them should be called novelists. Most of these works begin with a preconceived objective (to "discredit" a famous person who has achieved hero status) and then proceed from there. Unfortunately, in our sensation-seeking society, the books of such "bashers" and self-styled intellectuals are guaranteed a certain audience. This book is not for that audience. There were, in fact, heroes, despite what some people would have us believe; there still are.

CHAPTER I

THE ATLANTIC WALL

The genesis of the German defense of Normandy can be traced to the end of November 1943, when the High Command of the Armed Forces telephoned Field Marshal Erwin Rommel—the legendary Desert Fox—who was vacationing with his family at a villa in southwestern Germany and gave him a new assignment.

Military leaders of Erwin Rommel's caliber were rare even in Nazi Germany, which was noted for its brilliant commanders. Rommel's career had been meteoric. Born in Heidenheim, Swabia (a part of Wuerttemberg in southwest Germany), he was the son and grandson of schoolteachers. He enlisted in the Wuerttemberg 124th Infantry Regiment in 1910 as a *Fahnenjunker* (officer-cadet), attended the War School in Danzig, and was commissioned second lieutenant in 1912. He fought in Belgium, France, Romania, and Italy during World War I and emerged from the conflict with the *Pour le Mérite* (a decoration equivalent to the Congressional Medal of Honor) for capturing an Italian division with an *ad hoc* battalion-sized battle group in 1918. He remained in the Reichsheer (the 100,000 man army allowed by the Allies under the terms of the Treaty of Versailles) and by 1939, after 29 years' service, was a colonel, commanding the obscure infantry school at Wiener Neustadt in the Austrian Alps. World War II began on September 1, 1939. In the next three years, Rommel rose to field marshal, the highest rank in the German Army. (For a comparison of German and U.S. ranks, see Appendix I.) He had commanded the Fuehrer's bodyguard in Poland; the 7th Panzer Division in Luxembourg, Belgium, and France; and then the vaunted Afrika Korps, Panzer Army Afrika, and Army Group Afrika in Libya, Egypt, and Tunisia. Quick of decision and absolutely fearless, he always struck boldly, forcefully, and without hesitation—and usually where the enemy least expected him. Time after time he had smashed numerically superior Allied forces at places like Sidi Rezegh, Sollum, Gazala, Benghazi, Tobruk, and the Kasserine Pass. In the process his fame spread throughout the world, and his military genius became legendary. His numerically superior opponents both feared and respected him, for he had a well-developed sense of fairness and morality and waged war without hate, brutality, or criminality. His own men loved him, spoke of him with awe, and would follow him anywhere. After making the British Empire dance to his tune for more than a year, he was finally decisively defeated at El Alamein and correctly concluded that North Africa could not be held. He urged Hitler to abandon the unequal struggle, but this only earned him the label "defeatist," and, his health damaged by two years of warfare on the Sahara Desert, he was placed in "Fuehrer Reserve" (i.e., ordered home in semidisgrace) in March 1943. His Army Group Afrika was taken over by Colonel General Juergen von Arnim, a veteran of the Russian Front. Nine weeks later von Arnim was forced to surrender to the Allies. The 5th Panzer Army, the 1st German-Italian Panzer Army, and the elite Afrika Korps were all destroyed; 130,000 Axis soldiers, many of them Germany's best, marched off to prison camps. Italy rapidly became destabilized after this disaster. Soon the British and Americans invaded Sicily, the 6th Italian Army collapsed on the first day of the battle, Mussolini fell from power, the new government in Rome prepared to defect to the Allies, and the Mediterranean became an enemy lake. All of these developments, plus the loss of 230,000 Axis soldiers at Stalingrad, temporarily shook Hitler's faith in his own infallibility. "I should have listened to you," the former sidewalk artist confessed to Rommel as German resistance in Tunisia disintegrated.[1] Hitler took him out of semiretirement and eventually gave him command of Army Group B in Italy, where he briefly shared hegemony with Field Marshal Albert Kesselring. Rommel had charge of northern Italy, where he thought the Allies might land; his competitor directed Axis forces in Sicily and the south.

It soon became obvious even to Hitler that his old political principle of "divide and rule" would not work in Italy. The military situation and both field marshals argued against it, when they were not arguing against each other. In the end, on November 21, 1943, Hitler picked Kesselring for the top assignment because Rommel advocated abandoning all of Italy south of the northern Apennines, whereas Kesselring promised to hold the boot of Italy despite the Allies' amphibious capabilities. For the second time in nine months, the Desert Fox was unemployed.

Erwin Rommel had something other than military matters on his mind in November 1943 as he flew from Italy to Wiener Neustadt. The war had transformed his old post from a quiet garrison town into an industrial center that specialized in the production of Messerschmitt fighter planes, and Rommel wanted to get his family out before the Allies bombed the place. (He was right: The Allies leveled Wiener Neustadt in 1945, and the former Rommel home was totally destroyed by Allied bombs.) He told Lucie, his wife of 26 years, and his only child, 14-year-old Manfred, to pack their belongings, and he shipped them off to the village of Herrlingen, near Ulm, in his native Swabia. Here they temporarily lived at the villa of Frau Laibinger, the widow of an Ulm brewer, until Rommel's own new home could be made ready.[2] The field marshal and Frau Rommel celebrated what turned out to be their last wedding anniversary on November 27. Erwin Rommel was a devoted family man who had fallen hopelessly in love with his wife when he was an officer candidate at Danzig in 1911. Time had not weakened his affection one degree, and he apparently never considered being unfaithful to her, even though he was a hero of Nazi Germany and could have had his pick of dozens of beautiful women if he had wished. In fact, the legendary panzer commander was slightly henpecked! This time, however, their vacation was destined to be very short. At the end of the month the High Command called; Rommel had a new assignment.

Adolf Hitler was looking for something for Rommel to do, although he did not intend to permanently assign him to the Western Front when he asked the field marshal to conduct an inspection of the Atlantic Wall in late 1943. The Fuehrer had earmarked his former desert commander for a post on the Eastern Front, which promised to take some very heavy blows in 1944. In the meantime, Hitler felt that Rommel could do a useful job by assessing the state of German defenses in Denmark, the Netherlands, Belgium, and France. His skeleton staff from Italy, designated Army Group B z.v.B. ("for Special Purposes"), would accompany him on the tour.

The reason Hitler gave Erwin Rommel this new task was obvious. Everyone knew that the Western Allies would mount their cross-channel invasion sometime in 1944, and that it would be the greatest amphibious assault in history. This invasion represented both the greatest threat to and the greatest opportunity for Nazi Germany. If the Reich could repel it, the Western Allies would be unable to launch another attempt for at least a year. Dozens of divisions, including several elite panzer units, would be released for service on the Eastern Front. With these men, the Russians could perhaps be defeated or at least halted short of the German border. If Germany could not regain her military superiority in Europe, she could at least reestablish the balance of power and perhaps force the Allies to accept a negotiated peace. Even if this failed, German scientists would have another year to perfect their "miracle weapons," which included new and more dangerous U-boat models, guided rockets, remote-controlled tanks, jet airplanes, and atomic bombs. On the other hand, if the invasion succeeded, Adolf Hitler's empire was doomed. This is why Hitler sent his best commander to evaluate the strength of this, his most critical sector.

The "Atlantic Wall" was an all-inclusive term for the German defensive network in Western Europe. Rommel was instructed to examine the dispositions, mobility, and combat readiness of all units in the zone, with particular emphasis on the reserves. He was authorized to prepare defense and counterattack studies and to make recommendations concerning the employment of tank forces in the potential zone of operations.[3] Hitler promised to give him a tactical command when the battle started but made no mention of this promise to Field Marshal Gerd von Rundstedt, who was in overall command of the Western Front. The 69-year-old Rundstedt was beside himself with anger anyway. A Prussian aristocrat who had entered the Kaiser's army in 1892—when Erwin Rommel was one year old—he was a patrician of the Old School, the direct opposite of the Desert Fox. To many, Rundstedt represented the symbol of a better, bygone era, when it was possible for German officers to serve their country without running the risk of becoming criminals. Erwin Rommel, on the other hand, was perceived as the propaganda version of the National Socialist officer: tough, blunt, demanding, energetic, and fanatically loyal to the Fuehrer. Rundstedt, who had become a general while Rommel was a captain and who had commanded an army group before Rommel even led a division, bitterly referred to his new rival as "Marschall Bubi"—roughly, Marshal Laddie—and even asked Field Marshal Wilhelm Keitel, Chief of the *Oberkommando des Wehrmacht* (the High Command of the Armed Forces or OKW) if Rommel was being earmarked as his successor.[4]

Meanwhile, Erwin Rommel was driving down the North Sea coast and was not impressed by what he saw. He told his chief engineer officer, Lieutenant General Doctor Wilhelm Meise,[5] that when the invasion began, enemy air superiority would make it impossible for the Germans to bring up tanks, guns, and supplies. Their only possible chance for victory, he declared, was to stop the enemy on the beaches, when and where he would be the weakest. Then Rommel got down to specifics. Meise listened in fascination as Rommel described his plans for the defense of the West. He would turn the Atlantic Wall into an El Alamein line, very much like the one he used to hold up General Sir Bernard Law Montgomery's numerically superior British 8th Army for two terrifying weeks in North Africa. He demanded tens of thousands of mines of a multiplicity of types, including antipersonnel mines, antitank mines, antiparatroop mines, anti-landing craft mines, and nonferrous mines, which would not register on enemy mine detectors. He wanted mines activated by trip wires, remote-controlled mines, and mines that could be detonated by interrupting a beam of light. As he spoke, Rommel drew diagrams to illustrate what he had in mind.

Quite aside from his greatness as a general, Meise said later, he was the greatest engineer of World War II. "There was nothing I could teach him. He was my master."[6]

There was much that was still to be done, and a great deal of valuable time had been lost. The defense of occupied Western Europe had been of little interest to the Third Reich during its expansion period. When Field Marshal Erwin von Witzleben, the first German Commander-in-Chief, West, requested that the army begin work on permanent defensive fortifications, OKH (*Oberkommando des Heer*, the High Command of the Army) refused to give him a single construction battalion. Needless to say, no progress was made.

The High Command began taking notice of their vulnerable position in the West only after March 1942, when 600 British commandos did irreparable damage to the Normandy Dock at St. Nazaire, at the mouth of the Loire River in France. Although fewer than half of the raiders returned and the U-boat pens were not damaged, Hitler was furious and the weaknesses of the Atlantic defenses were dramatically demonstrated. The chief of staff to the Commander-in-Chief, West, Lieutenant General Carl Hilpert, was immediately sacked and replaced by the energetic Major General Kurt Zeitzler, the future chief of the General Staff. Construction efforts were quickly intensified.[7] Organization Todt (Hitler's construction and labor force) tripled the amount of concrete poured in Western Europe from 100,000 to 300,000 cubic meters per month.[8] The same month as the St. Nazaire raid, Hitler used Witzleben's health as a pretext to retire him. (The field marshal, who held Hitler in contempt and who wanted to overthrow Nazism via a military coup, had gone on leave to undergo a hemorrhoid operation.) He was replaced by von Rundstedt. This distinguished but aging and energy-deficient commander was not an advocate of the strong fortification theory and therefore did little to improve the overall situation along the coast. Hitler himself provided much of the added impetus to the construction program during 1942 and 1943. On August 13, 1942, he ordered that the western coast of Europe be turned into an impenetrable fortress. He wanted 15,000 permanent defensive positions constructed by the end of spring 1943. He wanted 20 positions built per kilometer of coastline (about 30 per mile), although he said that 10 per kilometer might be tolerable. The positions were to be manned by 300,000 combat troops, backed up by 150,000 reserves. He felt that 450,000–500,000 men could hold the Atlantic Wall against anything the Allies could muster.[9]

The leaders of Organization Todt, the Reich's labor service in charge of military construction, were horrified. They estimated that they could have only 40 percent of Hitler's program completed by the deadline. They were right: When the target date arrived, construction was not even close to half finished. OT simply lacked the resources and personnel to accomplish such an ambitious task. In addition, Hitler's own order of priorities for coastal defense work further deflected attention away from the beaches on which Eisenhower's men would eventually land. The protection of U-boat bases received top priority, followed by harbor defense for coastal traffic, harbor defense against enemy landings, and the defensive works on the Channel Islands. The defense of the open beaches was listed as the last priority. Hitler himself apparently never attached great importance to the Atlantic Wall, either. Although his propaganda machine made a big to-do over it and he boastfully described it as "the greatest line of fortifications in history,"[10] his remarks were aimed at giving the German people a greater sense of security. Except for an early morning trip to Paris shortly after its fall in the summer of 1940, the Fuehrer did not return to France until after D-Day. He never set eyes on the Atlantic Wall in his life.

OB West (the German abbreviation for *Oberbefehlshaber West*, the Commander-in-Chief, West, or his headquarters) did not help matters by unevenly distributing the resources that were available. During 1942, for example, it allocated four times as much concrete to the left corps of the 15th Army (in northwestern France) as it did to the LXXXIV Corps of the 7th Army in Brittany and Normandy. By May 1943 the 15th Army had almost three times as many men as did the 7th Army to the south, in whose zone the Allies would eventually strike. The Atlantic Wall was further weakened by the demands of the Eastern Front. In September 1942 most of OB West's 28 infantry and seven panzer or panzer grenadier divisions had three regiments. By September 1943, von Rundstedt had 34 infantry and six mobile divisions, but only a few of them had their full contingent of regiments, because most of the third regiments had been dissolved due to casualties suffered on the Russian Front. In short, the number of divisions in the West had increased slightly, but their power had declined substantially.[11]

The prevalent attitude at Rundstedt's headquarters did not improve the situation. In 1943 German Vice Admiral Friedrich Ruge found "a fatalistic acceptance of the deteriorating situation, and a lack of alertness in looking for possible improvements."[12] Even Rundstedt's friend and fellow aristocrat, General of Panzer Troops Baron Leo Geyr von Schweppenburg, admitted that Rundstedt was one of the officers who did not keep abreast of the developments in his profession. "Of all the German generals, Field Marshal von Rundstedt knew the least of panzer tactics," he told his interrogators in 1947. "He was an infantryman of the last generation. He and his staff were armchair strategists who didn't like dirt, noise and tanks in general—as far as I know, Field

Marshal von Rundstedt was never in a tank. Do not misunderstand me, however," he added, "I have the greatest respect for von Rundstedt, but he was too old for this war."[13]

OB West was further handicapped by its chief of staff, Lieutenant General Guenther von Blumentritt, who, as General von Geyr stated, was "unsuitable [for the post] in ability or character."[14] Blumentritt, in fact, thought that the entire invasion might well be a colossal bluff that might not take place at all.[15]

Erwin Rommel, who was in for an education, began his inspection at Copenhagen, Denmark, on December 11, 1943. He had believed the Propaganda Ministry's reports concerning the great strength of the Atlantic Wall but soon saw through the curtain of deception. Rommel then denounced the wall as a farce—a "figment of Hitler's *Wolkenkuckucksheim* (cloud cuckoo land)."[16] He called it an "enormous bluff . . . more for the German people than for the enemy . . . and the enemy, through his agents, knows more about it than we do."[17]

Rommel rapidly toured the front from the North Sea to the Pyrenees Mountains on the Spanish frontier. On December 14 he arrived at Fontainebleau, his new headquarters, which had been allocated to him by OB West. This luxurious little chateau had once belonged to the notorious Madame de Pompadour, the mistress of Louis XIV. In keeping with his simple, puritanical tastes, he did not like it but "made do" and eventually got used to it. The next day he had a pleasant lunch with Field Marshal von Rundstedt. Prior to this meeting, Rundstedt had been warned about Rommel by Wilhelm Keitel, Hitler's chief military lackey, that Rommel was "a tiresome person because he doesn't like taking orders from anybody."[18] Contrary to the expectations of Hitler and OKW, however, the Desert Fox and von Rundstedt quickly developed an understanding and even a faint liking for one another. This was particularly surprising, considering their opposing attitudes and backgrounds. The elder marshal, however, recognized Rommel's leadership abilities and listened to his opinions, even if he did not always agree with them. Rommel, on the other hand, respected von Rundstedt's age and seniority, although—as in North Africa—the opinions of others would have no influence on him after he made up his mind on a particular question. Neither of the men liked the terms of Rommel's current assignment. To Rundstedt, it was like having a spy whom he could not control roaming freely about in his territory. To Rommel, it was an equally frustrating experience. He, the Desert Fox, always a man of action, had no forces under his command and could not influence the campaign that promised to be the decisive engagement of the Second World War. The two marshals no doubt discussed this intolerable arrangement at their lunch, for Rundstedt would forward a plan to remedy it about two weeks later.

First, however, Erwin Rommel had a report to write. He finished his whirlwind inspection in late December and was greatly disturbed by what he saw. He found the army's forces "barely adequate" for a vigorous defense, and the Navy and Luftwaffe were too weak to be of substantial help. There were no defense plans except for around major ports, and even here not all the necessary measures had been carried out. The army was severely hindered by a lack of mobility and a shortage of land mines. Rommel concluded that almost every commander had a different idea for defending his own coastal sector and had no overall policy to guide him.[19] As to where the Allies would land, the Desert Fox told Hitler that he believed the Allies would probably land in the Pas de Calais sector, in the zone of the 15th Army.[20] In making this prediction, which he later retracted, Rommel underestimated Allied shipping capacity and over-estimated the effect the V-1 and V-2 rockets would have on the Allied High Command. True, the rockets would cause great panic and destruction in England, but not enough to force them to change the target of their attack. They would eventually land on the Cotentin Peninsula in Normandy, far south of the Pas de Calais.

Rommel also predicted in this report that the enemy would launch his invasion with aerial bombings, naval bombardments, and airborne assaults, followed by the actual seaborne landings. He did not believe the coastal defenses would hold. He felt that after the coast was penetrated, only a rapid counterattack by the mobile infantry and panzer divisions could defeat the Allies and throw them back into the sea. These units would have to be moved close to the coast, he wrote, so that they would be in position to deliver the decisive blow.[21]

On this critical issue he disagreed with Rundstedt, who felt that the decisive battle should be fought somewhere in the interior of France, well out of range of the heavy guns of the British and American battleships.

Despite their differences over how the decisive battle should be fought, Rundstedt recommended that Rommel's Army Group B head-quarters be subordinated to OB West. On December 30 he proposed that the 7th and 15th armies, along with the Armed Forces Commander of the Netherlands, be placed under Rommel's command. It is not known which of the field marshals originated the idea, but it was clearly acceptable to both from the beginning. Hitler was not enthusiastic about it but finally agreed to go along with it, although he reserved the right to transfer the army group headquarters (i.e., Rommel and his immediate staff) to the Russian Front if he deemed it necessary. Rundstedt agreed to this provision, and Erwin Rommel received his largest and last command. Map 1.1 shows Rommel's general area of responsibility.

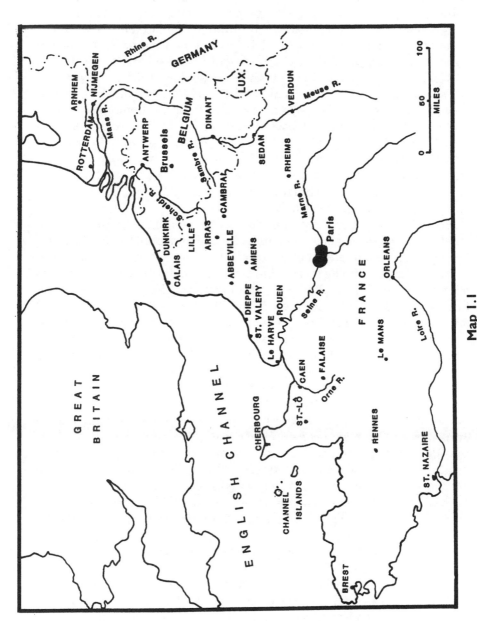

Map 1.1
ROMMEL'S GENERAL AREA OF RESPONSIBILITY

At Fontainebleau, Rommel went about the process of converting his skeleton staff into a true army group headquarters. He initially appointed Lieutenant General Alfred Gause chief of staff, but they had a personal falling-out in mid-April, and Rommel replaced him with Lieutenant General Doctor Hans Speidel.[22] Like his commander, Dr. Speidel was a Swabian. They had met in the Argonne Forest battles of 1915 and had later served together in the 13th Wuerttemberg Infantry Regiment. Also, both men were the sons of teachers. Here the similarity ended, however, for Hans Speidel was a career staff officer. Before the war he had been chief of Section "West" of the General Staffs Foreign Armies Department. From July 1940 until March 1942 he had been chief of staff to the German military governor of France, before spending two years on the Russian Front, successively serving as chief of staff, V Corps; chief of staff, Army Detachment Lanz; and chief of staff, 8th Army. He joined Rommel in April 1944.

Speidel was an anti-Nazi and much more politically adroit than his chief, who was naive about such matters. He undoubtedly helped influence Rommel to support the conspiracy against Hitler, which was now growing into a full-blown resistance group, unofficially led by the dynamic Colonel Count Claus von Stauffenberg. The count had served briefly with the 10th Panzer Division on the North African Front in 1943 and had lost an arm and an eye when his car was strafed by an Allied fighter-bomber. He awoke from his coma convinced that God had spared him for a reason—to rid the world of Adolf Hitler, whom Stauffenberg considered to be the anti-Christ. "Men are not guaranteed a civilized existence by a state without religious background," he correctly proclaimed.[23] With grim determination, the iron-willed Stauffenberg rehabilitated himself, returned to active duty, and in 1944 was named chief of staff to the Commander-in-Chief of the Replacement Army, headquartered in Berlin. Here this human dynamo spun a web of intrigue and began hatching a plot to remove Adolf Hitler and save Germany from occupation, complete brutalization, or both.[24] Among the men whom he needed on his side was Erwin Rommel—so General Speidel and others went to work convincing his boss to act against the leader the Desert Fox had once admired.

Rommel picked Vice Admiral Friedrich Ruge as his naval advisor.[25] Prior to being assigned to Rommel's staff (on the recommendation of General Gause), Ruge had been commander of the German naval forces in Italy, such as they were. He and the field marshal immediately became good friends and were to have many long walks and private conversations together in the rose garden.

The remaining members of Rommel's staff were also talented, capable professionals. The handsome Colonel Hans-Georg von Tempelhoff was Chief of operations (abbreviated Ia—see Appendix II); Colonel Anton

Staubwasser, intelligence chief (Ic); and Colonel Freyberg, adjutant. Rommel's technical staff was small but also capable and included Colonel Hans Lattmann, artillery advisor; Lieutenant Colonel Wolfgang Queisner, Luftwaffe General Staff officer; Colonel Heckel, quartermaster; several clerks; and a few war reporters and historians. The army group quartermaster department was abolished shortly before the invasion, and its responsibilities were assumed by the Quartermaster General of France. Despite regulations requiring one, Rommel did not appoint a National Socialist Guidance Officer. The result of these appointments, according to Speidel, was "outer and inner harmony and mental balance; the officers were free, in so far as possible, to use their own initiative."[26]

Rommel's entourage grew by two more members on January 21, 1944, when members of the Organization Todt presented him with two dachshunds, one a year old and one a three-month-old puppy. The puppy was quite affectionate, and Rommel fell in love with it almost immediately. He had always been fond of dogs but seems to have become particularly attached to this one. He named it Elbo, and it was soon sleeping in his room, underneath his luggage stand. Rommel later sent the older, less energetic dog home to Germany, where it was killed by a car. The Todt people must have heard about its death, because they replaced it with a big, brown, smooth-haired hunting dog.[27]

It was good that Rommel could enjoy at least one aspect of domestic life, for elsewhere the war closed in. On January 6, 1944, his 14-year-old son was drafted. His family was now completely broken up, and Germany looked to him to defeat the invasion, which promised to strike soon and in overwhelming force. Despite his growing distaste for the Nazi dictatorship, Erwin Rommel threw his entire being into the task.

The Desert Fox had a formidable task ahead of him, and he knew it. He was shocked over the lethargy he found at Rundstedt's headquarters and indeed throughout the Western Front. "To me, things look black," he commented.[28] The confidence of the frontline soldiers had to be restored, and, with that intangible gift he had for instilling a fighting spirit in his men, Rommel hurled himself into his work. The arrival of the Desert Fox immediately boosted the self-confidence of the men of the Western Front. The U.S. Army's official history of the campaign recorded: "Rommel's reputation in combat was a stimulant and a dramatization of the new importance assigned to the west."[29] The rank and file, it seemed, were eager to serve under a leader of Rommel's caliber. Morale soared in both armies as they looked upon their leadership with renewed confidence.

When Rommel assumed his new responsibilities, OB West had four armies plus the Armed Forces Netherlands under its command. Rommel took over the two strongest armies, plus the Dutch command. As Commander-in-Chief, Army Group B, Field Marshal Rommel directed two armies with eight corps, 24 infantry divisions, and five Luftwaffe field divisions. The northernmost (Dutch) sector belonged to Luftwaffe General of Fliers Friedrich "Krischen" Christiansen, a tough seaman who had distinguished himself as a pioneer in the field of naval aviation but who did not possess the education or mental qualities to serve successfully as the Wehrmacht commander of the Netherlands.[30] He owed his appointment and continued tenure solely to his friendship with Reichsmarschall Hermann Goering. Lieutenant General Heinz Helmut von Wuehlisch, a former cavalryman and long-time General Staff officer now in the Luftwaffe, served as Christiansen's chief of staff and did much to offset the deficiencies of his boss.[31] In early 1944, Christiansen's command consisted of one corps: the LXXXVIII. It had three weak divisions: the 347th Infantry, the 719th Infantry, and the 16th Luftwaffe Field.[32]

The 15th Army under Colonel General Hans von Salmuth held the center of Rommel's coastal line and was where most of the German leaders expected the Allies to strike, for it defended the West European coastline nearest to the British Isles and covered the Ruhr, Germany's industrial heartland. On a clear day, German soldiers could actually see England at its closest point to the continent. The 15th Army leader was no stranger to responsibility, for he had already held a number of tough commands. Salmuth had been chief of staff to Field Marshal Fedor von Bock in the Dutch and French campaigns of 1940, and later commanded the XXX Corps in the Crimea and the 2nd Army on the Russian Front, where he had assisted the SS in the mass murders of the Jews; then he was unjustly relieved of his command in early 1943 for conducting an unauthorized breakout that saved his army. The Nazis eventually realized Salmuth had been right and returned him to active duty; nevertheless, they had incurred his undying hatred.[33]

The LXXXIX, LXXXII, LXVII, and LXXXI Corps were under the 15th Army. They had six infantry divisions along the coast: the 70th, 47th, 49th, 344th, 348th, and 711th, along with the unreliable 17th and 18th Luftwaffe Field divisions. Eight Army infantry divisions (the 64th, 712th, 182nd Reserve, 326th, 331st, 85th, 89th, and 346th) backed up the front. The 19th Luftwaffe Field Division was also part of the infantry reserve.[34]

The 7th Army held the western and southernmost sectors of Rommel's zone of operations and formed his left flank, which included the Brittany and Cotentin peninsulas. Rommel did not expect the Allied landings to come in this sector, but he eventually changed his mind and poured men and resources into the area, as we shall see. Colonel General Friedrich Dollmann, the commander of the 7th Army, was an experienced artillery and General Staff officer who knew how to play the political "angles" that exist in any army; as a result, he had been promoted beyond his capabilities. He possessed little field experience, was in poor health, and had trouble with his conscience, as he was deeply disturbed by the methods of the Nazi regime. He really should not have been in command of the 7th Army at that time.[35]

Dollmann's army included the LXXXIV, LXXIV, and LXX Corps. Its coastal or frontline units included the 716th, 352nd, 243rd, 319th, 266th, 343rd, and 265th Infantry divisions, with the 84th Infantry, 353rd Infantry, and 91st Air Landing divisions in reserve. The II Parachute Corps, with the 3rd and 5th Parachute divisions, were later assigned to the 7th Army.[36]

Rommel's army group was not assigned a single panzer division when it became operational. These units were under the command of Panzer Group West, a headquarters created in November 1943 by von Rundstedt. It was officially activated on January 24, 1944.[37] The elder field marshal believed that the Allies could best be defeated by a massive armored counterattack, so he formed the panzer group to direct this stroke, as well as to train panzer soldiers and advise him on all matters pertaining to armored employment. He chose General of Panzer Troops Baron Leo Geyr von Schweppenburg, a veteran armored corps commander from the Eastern Front, to lead this special force.[38] Rommel had no authority over Geyr or any of his men.

General Geyr had two corps in his group: the I SS Panzer and the LXIII Panzer. Five panzer divisions were camped in the I SS area, north of the River Loire: the 1st SS Panzer "Leibstandarte Adolf Hitler"; the 12th SS Panzer "Hitler Jugend"; and the Army's 2nd, 21st, and 116th Panzer divisions. South of the river lay the LXIII Panzer Corps with the 9th and 11th Panzer divisions. The 2nd SS Panzer "Das Reich" and 17th SS Panzer Grenadier "Gotz von Berlichingen" divisions were also south of the Loire but were not assigned to a specific corps.

The total Atlantic coast frontage of OB West was 2,500 miles. Fifty-eight divisions manned this huge area, and most of them were semimobile or practically immobile and were made up of men from the older age groups who were by and large unfit for service on the Eastern Front. They were poorly equipped with foreign or obsolete material and weapons and lacked all forms of transportation, including horses and donkeys.

Rommel pointed out to Hitler that such units would be useless in modern warfare until they were provided with a proper number of vehicles. Hitler curtly rejected Rommel's conclusions and stated that it was a soldier's duty "to stand and die in his defenses," not to be "mobile."[39] Hitler had a point in this argument. Germany could not possibly have manufactured enough vehicles to supply these formations anyway and still meet its requirements on the Eastern Front. In any event, petroleum resources were too limited to have made mobile divisions of much value, even if they had been equipped as Rommel demanded.

Most of Rommel's divisions, though by no means all, had been reduced from normal 1939 strength of nine battalions to six understrength battalions by 1944. The authorized full establishment of the average German infantry division (called Table of Organization and Equipment or TOE in the U.S. Army) had been steadily reduced from 17,200 men in 1939-type divisions to 13,656 in 1943. The 1944-type divisions had a strength of 12,769 at full establishment, but very few were at 100 percent strength, and many were well below that. Many units had so few transport vehicles that they were classified as "static" (*"boden-staendig"*); they relied on horses and ox carts to haul supplies and even their artillery. The number of troops, size of area of responsibility, equipment, nationality, and organization of these static units varied remarkably. The 709th Infantry Division, for example, had 11 battalions under three regimental headquarters, while the 716th had six battalions and only one regimental HQ.[40] Some of these divisions were composed of men who had special disorders that prevented them from serving on or returning to the Russian Front. The 70th Infantry Division, for example, was composed largely of soldiers with stomach ailments and was nicknamed the "Whipped Cream" or "White Bread Division" because of its special diet. It fought extremely well, nevertheless, single-handedly holding up Montgomery's army group for nine days in the Battle of the Scheldt in November, but that is another story.

The Third Reich was nearing the end of its manpower reserves as it entered 1944, the fifth year of the war. In the West it faced a serious shortage of first-rate combat troops. Of the 4,270,000 men in the German Army in December 1943, more than 1,500,000 were over 34 years of age. Many of those below 34 were very young (17–19), or were victims of third-degree frostbite, or were ethnic Germans (*Volksdeutsche*), or were "Eastern Troops" (*"Osttruppen,"* or non-Germans recruited in occupied countries). The average age in the whole Nazi Army was 31.5 years, or four years older than the average age of the Kaiser's army in 1917, the year before the Second Reich lost World War I. It was more than six years older than the age of the average American soldier in 1943.[41]

The problem of age was more pronounced in some units than in others. The average age in the 709th Division, for instance, was 36. Gun-crew ages averaged as high as 45, and some of the men were over 55. Many of Rommel's men were not Germans or Volksdeutsche at all, but Russians. Most of them volunteered from POW camps when it looked as if Germany would win the war in the East—or to avoid starving to death. (Two-thirds of the Soviet prisoners captured by the

Wehrmacht died in captivity.) By 1943 the Red Army was advancing on all fronts, and these men were reconsidering their decisions. To preserve their "loyalty" to the Reich, the High Command transferred most of them to France, where their arrival released German units for the Russian Front. By May 1944 the 7th Army had 23 *Osten* (Eastern) infantry battalions, which represented about one-sixth of all the infantry battalions in that army. In the LXXXIV Corps, which defended Normandy, 8 of 42 rifle battalions were made up of Osttruppen.[42]

The Eastern Front was taxing Hitler's empire almost to the breaking point, so little could be spared for the defense of the West prior to 1944. In 1943, German losses in Russia reached 2,086,000, of which 677,000 were permanent (killed, missing, captured, or permanently incapacitated). Of the 151 German divisions fighting on this front, 10 panzer and 50 infantry divisions were classified as "fought out." The abbreviation "KG" now appeared on German Order of Battle lists with alarming frequency. It stood for *Kampfgruppe* ("battle group") and when used in connection with a particular division, it indicated that the division had been reduced by casualties to the combat value of a regimental-size battle group. Rommel would become very familiar with the term in the weeks ahead.

To meet this drain of manpower, plus the demands of the new Italian Front, Adolf Hitler called on units stationed in France, Belgium, and the Netherlands. By October 1943, 36 infantry and 17 mobile divisions had been transferred from OB West to other fronts. Almost all these units ended up in Russia. Despite these reinforcements, the Third Reich's strategic situation in the U.S.S.R. verged on the critical. In the spring of 1944, despite astronomical losses, Russia still fielded more than 5,000,000 troops in 300 divisions, as opposed to Germany's 2,000,000 soldiers in less than 200 divisions.[43] Table 1.1 shows the dispositions of Germany's divisions by theater on June 1, 1944, and clearly indicates the drain caused by the Eastern Front.

Rommel found that many of his new units were formations previously mauled in the East. They were in France primarily to recuperate from their exhausting campaigns and in many cases needed to be refitted or completely rebuilt. Unfortunately for Germany, Army Group B simply did not have the resources to carry out a project of this magnitude.

If the manpower drain to the East was serious in itself, it became catastrophic when coupled with the material requirements of that theater. First priority of equipment was to the East until January 1944, and with good reason, for tank losses in Russia were tremendous. Between October and December 1943, 979 Panzer Mark IIIs and IVs were lost, along with 444 assault guns and tons of other equipment. In the last six months of 1943, Germany lost 2,235 field guns and 1,692 antitank guns on the Russian Front alone.[44]

Table 1.1
German Dispositions of Divisions by Theater
June 1, 1944

Theater	Army	LwField	SS	Total
Eastern	149	—	8	157
Finland	6	—	1	7
Norway-Denmark	15	—	—	15
Western	47	3	4	54
Italy	23	3	1	27
Balkans	8	—	7	15
Totals	258	6	21	285

Source: Seaton, The Russo-German War, 1941–45 (New York: Frederick A. Praeger, 1971), p. 458.

Hitler's industrial program emphasized massive output of new panzers instead of a balanced program of production. As a result, a critical spare-parts shortage developed that nullified all the gains of the German war industries. In June 1943, the German Army had 3,032 tanks. Only 463 of these, or 15 percent, were nonoperational. By February 1944, the Reich had 3,053 tanks, but 1,534—or more than 50 percent—were in need of major repair. This meant that more than half of the tanks of an army that depended on its mobility for its survival were inoperable because of a lack of spare parts! In that month, only 145 damaged tanks were repaired and sent back into combat. Colonel General Heinz Guderian, inspector-general of panzer troops, estimated that tanks and assault guns awaiting repair in early 1944 equaled about nine months of new production. By the end of March the situation had not improved. The number of operational panzers in Hitler's armies continued to decline, despite increasing industrial productivity.

By February 1944, the threat in the West became real enough for the High Command to warrant an increase in tank delivery to Rundstedt and his subordinates. Although the bulk of the new Panzer Mark VI (PzKw VI or "Tiger") production still went east, PzKw V ("Panther") output was largely sent to France. (For a description of German and Allied armor, see Appendix III.) By the end of April, OB West had 1,608 German-made tanks and assault guns, of which 674 were PzKw IVs and 514 were Panthers.[45] This still fell far short of the great concentrations in Russia. At the Battle of Kursk in July 1943, for example, Hitler's forces lost almost 2,000 tanks. On June 1, 1944—at approximately its peak strength—OB West mustered an overall strength of 1,552 panzers.[46]

The Wehrmacht was not only short of tanks in 1944, it was short of practically everything else as well. As a result, Rommel's battalions were forced to improvise and were equipped with the most astonishing array of obsolete, foreign, and captured equipment imaginable. One division's artillery regiment had so many different types of obsolete and foreign guns that it called itself "the travelling artillery museum of Europe." The 7th Army had 92 different kinds of artillery pieces, which used 252 types of ammunition, of which 47 varieties were no longer manufactured.[47] Rommel's trucks were of German, French, Italian, Russian, or even of Czech manufacture, and quite a few of his "mobile" regiments travelled by bicycle. The 243rd Infantry Division was a real hybrid—one of its regiments was motorized, one used bicycles, and the third marched; its artillery and supply trains were horse-drawn.

Field Marshal Rommel always liked to be near the front and always felt that Fontainebleau was too far from the coast and thus too far from the likely invasion sector. On March 9 he moved his headquarters to Chateau La Roche-Guyon, 40 miles downstream from Paris, on the north bank of the Seine, near the town of Nantes. The beautiful chateau/castle had been the seat of the dukes de la Rochefoucauld for centuries. The site was not chosen by Rommel, who had a well-deserved reputation from indifference to physical comfort, and was probably selected by his headquarters company commander. The field marshal allowed the ducal family to remain and chose for his own quarters a small apartment on the ground floor, adjacent to a rose terrace. His office had a high ceiling with a faded Gobelin tapestry on one wall and an ancient portrait of Duke François de la Rochefoucauld on the other. His desk was the same one upon which Louis XIV's minister of war signed the Edict of Nantes. Nothing in the room belonged to Rommel. He brought in no photographs of his family, no souvenirs, no mementos from his Afrika Korps days—nothing. He could have walked out of the place at any moment, and there would have been no evidence that he had ever been there.[48]

The Desert Fox was not the sort of man to concede easily. The ordinary mortal might shrink in the face of odds weighted so heavily against him; Rommel's reaction was the opposite: The greater the odds, the more energetic and ingenious his response became. Rather than try to share or shirk his huge responsibilities, Rommel assumed more and insisted that everyone else do the same. His job was to defeat the enemy, and that was precisely what he intended to do, despite the enemy's huge margin of superiority in every conceivable category. Soon Rommel was shouldering a greater burden than anyone on the Western Front. The U.S. Army's official history reports:

The evidence indicates that Rommel had an energy and strength of conviction that often enabled him to secure Hitler's backing, whereas Rundstedt, who was disposed whenever possible to compromise and allow arguments to go by default, seems to have relaxed command prerogatives that undoubtedly remained formally his. It is possible, of course, that he too came under Rommel's influence and because he was content to allow Rommel to assume the main burden of responsibility. In any case the clear fact is that after January, 1944, Rommel was the dominant personality in the west with an influence disproportionate to his formal command authority.[49]

The Atlantic Wall was little more than a joke when Rommel took over in early 1944. The length of the coast permitted only the erection of a system of strong points, not a continuous line of fortifications. However, not even that had been accomplished by January 1944. France had become a giant recuperation center for the wounded and frostbitten veterans limping back from the Russian Front. Rommel immediately made his position known beyond any possible misunderstanding. Preparation for Eisenhower's invasion, not recuperation from the winter war, was now the mission of Army Group B. The men had rested long enough; now the work would begin in earnest.

Colonel General Hans von Salmuth was among the first to feel the sharp edge of Rommel's tongue. The Desert Fox first inspected the 15th Army in December 1943 and told von Salmuth that he wanted hundreds of thousands of mines laid all along the Atlantic coast. Less than a month later Rommel paid another visit to the coast of northern France and Belgium and was not satisfied with the progress being made. He visited von Salmuth's headquarters, a luxurious chateau near Tourcoing, and ordered him to increase the amount of time each soldier spent laying mines, even if training time had to be sacrificed.

The 15th Army commander looked down his nose on Rommel, whom he apparently considered a Swabian commoner who had gotten lucky. He loftily told Rommel that he wanted to go into battle with well-trained and rested soldiers—not physical wrecks.

The Desert Fox accepted the challenge. "Evidently you don't intend to carry out my orders," he snapped.

Salmuth scoffed and advised Rommel that his program could not be carried out in less than a year. Anyone who tried to tell Rommel any different, according to von Salmuth, was either "trying to flatter you or he's a pig idiot."[50] His tone and condescending manner made it clear that he felt he knew more about military matters than Rommel, to whom he felt superior in all areas except rank.

The marshal's face betrayed no emotion and he said nothing, although the atmosphere had clearly become tense. Rommel waited until it was time to depart. Then, as soon as his staff officers had gotten into their cars and shut the doors, Rommel pulled the colonel general aside, spoke to him in private, and gave him the dressing down of his life. Salmuth's face was red when he escorted the marshal back to the car, and his manner had changed completely. Rommel bade him farewell as if nothing had happened. As they drove away, the Desert Fox winked at Admiral Ruge and said: "He is a thoroughly rude fellow and has to be treated the same way!" But Rommel never held grudges, and the commander of the 15th Army had gotten the message. Minefield and obstacle construction in Salmuth's zone picked up considerably after this outburst, and Rommel had his complete and comradely support—and everyone knew who was the boss.[51] Word soon got around that Rommel meant business. It was as if a cold wind had blown through the comfortable headquarters throughout France. The staffs did not like it, but there was nothing they could do about it. Work and anti-invasion preparations picked up with a vengeance.

Rommel found that the coast of Normandy had been particularly neglected, but things were almost as bad elsewhere. Between Dieppe and St. Nazaire, a distance of 600 miles of coastline, only 11 batteries existed, with a total combined strength of 37 guns. Only the Channel Islands, the Cape Gris Nez, and Brest were properly fortified. The entire defensive system lacked materiel, leadership, and an overall plan.[52] Rommel now provided two of the three essential elements.

The Atlantic Wall was short not only of fortifications and minefields, it was short of defenders as well. The average defensive sector of a division on the Western Front ranged from 50 miles of frontage in the 15th Army to 120 miles in the 7th Army's sector. This compared to an average corps frontage of 32.5 miles (for three divisions) on the Russian Front.[53] Lieutenant General Karl Wilhelm von Schlieben's 709th Infantry Division, which would be decisively engaged on D-Day, had to defend a 40-mile front with only two regiments. At that time, a division could hope to defend successfully only six miles of frontage against a determined assault.

Rommel's solution to Schlieben's problem was the answer he had to everybody's problem: obstacles and minefields. His defense of France would be his defense of El Alamein on a larger scale. At El Alamein, he had held up the enemy for two weeks, despite their overwhelming ground, air, and naval superiority. If he could delay them on the French coast for just a few hours and simultaneously inflict heavy casualties on them, the panzer reserves might be able to counterattack and push them back into the sea. This was Germany's only remaining chance to avoid losing the war. Admiral Ruge wrote: "He [Rommel] knew that there was no hope of winning [the war], but hoped that the war could be brought to a tolerable end. . . . So he looked for a way to defeat the landing on the beach, and to win a respite which could be exploited politically."[54]

The Desert Fox had several ideas for strengthening the Atlantic Wall. First, to provide depth to the defense, the mined and fortified zone had to be extended five to six miles inland. The number of strong points at and near the coast had to be increased, along with the number of antitank guns and heavy machine guns in the forward sectors. Finally, the principal mobile reserves had to be brought up from far inland so that they would be close enough to launch a major counterattack on the first or second day of the invasion.

Rommel believed that the battle would be decided at the water's edge, because the enemy would be weakest just after he landed. He would be short of or without tanks, heavy weapons, and artillery, and his troops would be unsure of themselves—possibly even seasick. That was the moment to strike them and defeat them, he declared.[55]

The Desert Fox was quick to put his talent for improvisation to work in his new environment. There was much to be done. Because Rundstedt believed that the decisive battle would be fought well inland, he had not put the French coast into shape for the defense. Not even the existing strong points were protected by mines. In three years only 1,700,000 mines had been laid. The beach obstacles were extremely primitive and useless against tanks. Because Organization Todt was almost fully committed with port fortifications and railroad repair and maintenance, the Desert Fox concluded that he would have to put the soldiers themselves to work, laying barriers, obstacles, antitank devices, and minefields. On January 13 Rommel made his initial request for mines to the visiting Colonel General Alfred Jodl, the chief of operations at OKW. He wanted 2,000,000 mines per month,[56] which means that he intended to lay more mines every 30 days than his predecessors had laid in 3 1/2 years. Shortly afterward he increased this figure when he wrote General Meise and told him that he wanted a mine laid every 10 yards for a 1,000-yard-wide stretch all along the French coast. This would require 20,000,000 mines. Then phase two could begin. This would involve laying a mine every 10 yards for a distance of 8,000 yards inland, and more at strategic spots, requiring another 20,000,000 mines.

Rommel was seldom happy with the progress of his subordinates' mine-laying efforts. Four years had been wasted, and Rommel was feverishly trying to make up for lost time. In mid-January, when General of Panzer Troops Adolf Kuntzen, the commander of LXXXI Corps informed him that General von Salmuth was requiring each sapper to lay ten mines a day, Rommel tersely replied, "Make that twenty."[57] This was one of the orders that led to the chewing out of the 15th Army commander a few days later.

Up to May 20, 1944, as many as 4,193,167 mines had been laid along the channel, most of them since the end of March. Numerous obstacles had been laid under the surface of the water, to act as artificial reefs to destroy shore-bound ships and personnel carriers. Some of these were stakes carrying an antitank mine at the tip; others were concrete tetrahedrons, equipped with either steel blades or antitank mines.

Various other devices were employed, such as Rommel's "nutcracker mine," which consisted of a stake protruding from a concrete housing containing a heavy shell. A landing craft striking the stake would cause the shell to detonate.[58]

Rommel envisioned four belts of underwater obstacles:

1. A belt in 6 feet of water at mean high tide
2. A belt in 6 feet of water at half tide of a 12-foot tide
3. A belt in 6 feet of water at low tide
4. A belt in 12 feet of water at low tide

Rommel felt that the Allies would come at high tide to minimize the distance of open beach over which their soldiers would have to run for cover. By D-Day, only the first two belts had been completed in most sectors. Up to May 13 a total of 517,000 foreshore obstacles were laid, of which 31,000 were armed with mines.

The Field Marshal also emphasized the construction of antiaircraft obstacles. These poles, nicknamed "Rommel asparagus," consisted of stakes approximately 10 feet high driven into the ground at 100-foot spacings. They were designed to break up gliders and to cause them to flip over, smashing equipment and causing heavy casualties in the process.[59] Shells were to be attached to them with interconnecting wires. Troops aboard any glider landing in these areas would suffer heavy casualties. However, owing to the inefficiency of the Nazi bureaucracy, Rommel only received the shells in early June—too late to install them before D-Day. Nevertheless the stakes were dangerous and caused a number of gliders to pile up on June 6.

The Desert Fox also emphasized the construction of dummy positions and, in fact, wanted one dummy position constructed for every real position. "Dummy batteries (*Scheinbatterien*) attracted a great many Allied air attacks and helped the real guns to survive," Admiral Ruge wrote later. By nightfall of June 5 the U.S. and Royal Air Forces had destroyed only 16 German guns—8 in the Pas-de-Calais area, 5 in the Seine-Somme region, and 3 in Normandy.[60]

Rommel's program also called for the construction of naval minefields in the English Channel. The German Navy, however, proved unequal to the task and was at first uncooperative as well. It had done very little to infest the Channel with mines in the previous five years and did little to improve its poor performance in 1944, largely because it had few vessels left with which to perform the mission.

The U.S. Army's official history summed up Rommel's efforts well when it reported: "In all these ways Rommel sought to make the expected invasion physically impossible. The Allied force entangled in the spider web of obstacles would be given the paralyzing sting by the German Army waiting at the water's edge."[61]

"About all that was missing from Rommel's medieval arsenal of weapons were crucibles of molten lead to pour down on the attackers," Cornelius Ryan wrote, "and in a way he had the modern equivalent: automatic flame throwers." He even concealed kerosene tanks along approaches leading off the beaches. The push of a button would engulf advancing troops in flame.[62]

Under Rommel, the 7th and 15th armies laid three times as many mines in France in six months as all the German armies had buried in almost four years. Still it did not satisfy him. A few weeks before the invasion, he ordered all coastal units to cease training and to devote all of their time to obstacle construction, pointing out that it was on the beaches that the fate of the invasion would be decided and—furthermore—it would be decided within the first 24 hours.[63]

Rommel spent his days inspecting and monitoring the progress of his program. "I have only one real enemy now and that is time," he told his aide, Captain Hellmuth Lang. The two of them were usually on the road by 4:30 A.M., heading for an inspection that might be in Holland or in Brittany.[64] After the war, Admiral Ruge described a typical day with Rommel to Brigadier Desmond Young. "He got up early, traveled fast, saw things very quickly and seemed to have an instinct for places where something was wrong," Ruge said.

On one typical winter inspection we arrived at Perpignan late one night. We left at 6:00 a.m. next morning, without breakfast. Driving through snow and rain, we reached Bayonne at 2:00 p.m. An hour later, having received the report of the local commanding general, we left, without luncheon, for St. Jean-de-Luz, on the Spanish frontier. There we inspected batteries. We arrived at Bordeaux at 7:00 p.m. and conferred with [Colonel] General von Blaskowitz. At 8:00 p.m. we had an hour off for supper, the first meal of the day. We settled down to work again at 9:00 p.m., but fortunately the engineer-general fell asleep over the table.[65]

General Speidel recorded similar experiences. On a typical day, he wrote, Rommel ate an early breakfast with his chief of staff. Between 5:00 A.M. and 6:00 A.M. he left on his inspection tours, accompanied only by Captain Lang and sometimes Admiral Ruge. During these inspections, he would frequently insist that his men obey the laws of humanity to the letter. This antagonized Hitler, who regarded these demands as a sign of weakness. Rommel was usually gone from La Roche-Guyon until evening. The headquarters conferences would begin immediately upon his return.

As in the desert, Rommel still ate a simple supper, usually from a field kitchen, as he had always done, but instead of eating alone (as in

Africa), he dined with the ten or twelve officers who worked most closely with him. He would discuss any subject brought up during the meal. Also, he was not a person determined to dominate every conversation, as Hitler was; Rommel knew how to listen and had a sense of humor, even when the joke was at his expense. However, he did not like off-color or "dirty" jokes and would not tolerate people telling them in his presence. He did like to talk about his campaigns, but never in a boastful way, and freely discussed his mistakes and the lessons that could be learned from them. He always wanted to keep human casualties to a minimum. "Despite his fame," Friedrich Ruge recalled, Rommel "had remained a modest human being with an engaging personality."[66] After dinner, Rommel would go on an evening walk with Ruge and Speidel. Then further conferences occupied his night until bedtime, which was usually early.[67] He never smoked and almost never drank.

The Desert Fox preferred to eat the same rations as his troops, especially on visits or on inspection trips. This did not always happen, because certain of his aides would occasionally telephone ahead and make additions to the menu, in order to improve their own rations. "To what extent Rommel noticed this is hard to say," a member of his staff recalled. "He was a sharp observer . . . but did not always remark on what he had seen. It was not in his nature to waste time with trifles."[68]

Sometimes Rommel's physical ailments, most of which he had acquired in North Africa, continued to plague him in the winter of 1943–1944, and were no doubt aggravated by the demands that he made upon himself. The Desert Fox, after all, was no longer a young man; he was 52 years old and had recently spent two years in the brutal environment of the Sahara Desert. In January, for instance, lumbago attacks caused him severe pain, but he continued his inspection of the Normandy coast as if nothing were wrong. At least his desert sores, which caused him such agony in early 1943, were gone now. The Desert Fox never slowed down. He spent December 20–24 inspecting parts of the 15th Army's zone. Christmas Day was spent catching up on paperwork. The last week in December was devoted to more planning sessions and inspections, except for a December 27 conference with von Rundstedt. He celebrated New Year's Eve in his typical puritan fashion: he consumed two small glasses of claret. Early January was spent in the same manner. Rommel inspected the coastal defenses of the Netherlands and Belgium from January 2 to 5. He did not really expect the Allies to land here, because of the swampy nature of the terrain and the innumerable streams, rivers, and canals that marked the countryside, but then one never knew. He was in a bitter mood when he examined the interior of these two occupied countries, and he clearly expressed his dislike for the civilians who lived there in his letters to his wife.[69] Despite his contempt for the French, Dutch, and Belgian civilians, however, Rommel never inconvenienced or punished them, except out of military necessity. He continued to work even harder. From February 7 to 11 he drove 1,400 miles and inspected the 1st and 19th armies from the Bay of Biscay to the Mediterranean Sea in an attempt to confuse Allied intelligence as to what his area of responsibility really was. A few days later he attended a major war game, conducted by Geyr von Schweppenburg in Paris. All the inspecting and planning took its toll, however, and on February 22 an exhausted Rommel left France for a ten-day rest. The brief furlough seems to have recharged Rommel's batteries. As soon as he returned to Army Group B, he made another inspection of Normandy with General of Artillery Erich Marcks, whose LXXXIV Corps included the 709th and 243rd Infantry and 91st Air Landing divisions. This was followed by an inspection of the XXV Corps in Brittany, where he inspected the 3rd Parachute Division and the 266th Infantry Division, which included five Eastern battalions and was of little value. He also inspected the 155th Reserve Panzer Division.[70] March 9 and 10 were devoted to setting up shop at La Roche-Guyon (see above), and he was off again on March 11, inspecting the sector from the mouth of the Somme to Calais. He was back at HQ for a commanders' conference on the 13th, but the next day was on the road again, inspecting the LXXXI Corps and the 245th Infantry and 17th Luftwaffe Field divisions east of Le Havre. March 15 was spent with the 346th and 84th Infantry divisions, before returning to La Roche-Guyon for a fruitless conference with General von Geyr. He traveled to Paris on the evening of March 17, spent the night on a special train, and was carried to Berchtesgaden for two days of conferences on March 19 and 20. He returned to La Roche-Guyon the following day.

Not even Rommel's energy and personal supervision could entirely make up for all the deficiencies in the German defensive system. The worst problem, which was never really solved, was that of command fragmentation. Winston Churchill put it well when he told the House of Commons: "The German command has passed from the expert hands of the General Staff to those of a lance corporal."[71] Adolf Hitler, the consummate politician and military illiterate, practiced the political principle of "divide and rule" in the military sphere and never allowed a unified command to develop on either major front, a system that violated every dictate of military science and common sense. General Speidel later described the German civil-military organization and chain of command as "somewhere between confusion and chaos."[72] By 1944 the command system was fouled up beyond belief. At the top, OKH under General Zeitzler, the chief of the General Staff, directed the war on the Eastern Front, while OKW—which was mainly supervised by its operations officer, Colonel General Jodl—was responsible for all other theaters. These included France, Belgium, the Netherlands, Denmark, North Africa (until General von Arnim was forced to surrender in May 1943), Italy, the Balkans, and Scandinavia. "This division in the Supreme Command led to daily friction and seriously damaged the conduct of the whole war," Rommel's chief of staff wrote later. It got to the point where, when Jodl or his deputy, General of Artillery Walther Warlimont, began discussing "OKW fronts," such as Norway or Italy, Zeitzler and his staff would get up and walk out.[73]

The fact that the interests of the Navy, the Luftwaffe, and the SS and other party organizations conflicted with those of the Army and with each other only added fuel to the flames. In the West, von Rundstedt had no control over the Luftwaffe or the Navy in his area. He might ask Field Marshal Hugo Sperrle, the commander of the 3rd Air Fleet, for his cooperation, but Sperrle was subordinate only to Hermann Goering's OKL (the High Command of the Luftwaffe) and likely as not would ignore OB West's requests. Admiral Theodor Krancke, the pro-Nazi commander of Naval Group West, was also independent of Rundstedt and reported directly to Grand Admiral Karl Doenitz and the OKM (High Command of the Navy).[74] The military governors of France (General of Infantry Carl-Heinrich von Stuelpnagel),[75] Northern France and Belgium (General of Infantry Alexander von Falkenhausen),[76] and the Netherlands (General Christiansen) were subordinate to OB West in tactical matters but not in administrative matters nor in the internal affairs of their territories, for which they were responsible directly to OKW. In addition, SS forces received orders from Reichsfuehrer Heinrich Himmler, and the Todt Organization worked directly for Albert Speer, the Reichsminister of Armaments and Munitions.

The fragmentation of command debilitated the German armed forces right down to the tactical level. The naval coastal guns, for example, would remain under naval control even while the Anglo-American amphibious vessels were on their approach runs to the coast. The moment they landed, however, command of the coastal batteries reverted to the Army. If there was ever an order changing horses in midstream, this was it. Hitler, in short, exercised the principle of divide and rule, just as he had in his election campaigns prior to his "seizure of power" in 1933. It worked well then, but it proved disastrous in the military arena.

The main question the chain of command had to answer was the issue of how to employ the strategic reserves. Rundstedt's concept was that of the old school. He wanted to hold his reserves southeast of Paris and use them against the Allies as they approached the French capital, long after the landings. He believed that in this way he could bring the German tank superiority to bear against Eisenhower's forces and decisively defeat them in open battle. What he failed to notice was that

German armored superiority no longer existed. True, the Panther might be superior to the Allies' Sherman tank, but it was not superior to the fighter-bomber or the heavy bomber. Rundstedt had not yet learned the value of the Allied tactical air forces, as Rommel had in North Africa. He was in for a rude awakening.

Rommel's concept was diametrically opposite to von Rundstedt's. He wanted to group the reserves near the expected points of invasion and deal the attackers a crushing defeat on the beaches. He said, "If we cannot get at the enemy immediately after he lands, we will never be able to make another move, because of his vastly superior air forces. . . . If we are not able to repulse the enemy at sea or throw him off the mainland in the first 48 hours, then the invasion will have succeeded and the war will be lost."[77]

Although Rommel was the dominant personality in the western armies, he was not unchallenged on the issue of the strategic reserves. In fact, he stood almost alone, for of all the major commanders only he had experienced firsthand the awesome effect of Allied aerial domination. He also realized that Eisenhower's air armada would vastly exceed anything that supported the British 8th Army when it virtually annihilated his Panzer Army Afrika in late 1942. He also realized that if the Wehrmacht allowed the Anglo-Saxons to secure themselves on the beaches of France, nothing would ever be able to dislodge them. Rommel argued, but his contemporaries did not really believe him, because they had not shared the experiences of El Alamein, Alma Halfa, and Tunisia. They simply could not grasp what Rommel was telling them. In many cases, their thinking was colored by 1940—the last time they had met the British in battle—when the Wehrmacht had smashed the British Expeditionary Force and sent it fleeing across the Channel in any available boat, minus all of its tanks, artillery, vehicles, and heavy equipment. Rommel, who had fought them from 1940 to 1943, knew how much they had learned and had developed professionally and that they would be a much more formidable foe indeed than they had been four years earlier. General von Geyr led the opposition to Rommel's theories, insisting that the decisive engagement must be fought inland. Like many other German commanders, he did not realize that the days of the blitzkrieg were over. Part of Geyr's opposition stemmed from the fact that he was an aristocrat, with a long family history of military service, whereas Rommel was "only" a commoner and was the son and grandson of schoolteachers. Many of Geyr's contemporaries (especially von Rundstedt) also underestimated the ability of the Anglo-Americans to wage mobile warfare. The U.S. forces were particularly suspect, for it was not yet clear to most German generals how well they had learned the lessons of Kasserine Pass, where the Desert

Fox had dealt them a major defeat the year before. Rommel, who did not mistake local incompetence for national ineptitude, rated their fighting abilities much more highly (and much more realistically) than did the average German officer.

The more Rommel insisted that his minefields and obstacles were not only the best defense for the Reich but its only defense, the more opposition he inspired. Even Colonel General Heinz Guderian joined those supporting the Rundstedt-Geyr school of thought. He visited Rommel on April 27, 1944. The inventor of the blitzkrieg had a healthy respect for the Desert Fox, with whom he had maintained friendly contacts since before the war. He called Rommel "an open, upright man and a brave soldier . . . [who] possessed energy and subtlety of appreciation; he had great understanding of his men and, in fact, thoroughly deserved the reputation that he had won for himself." Guderian tried to intercede on behalf of Geyr and convert the Swabian marshal to their way of thinking. "I was . . . not surprised by Rommel's highly temperamental and strongly expressed refusal when I suggested that our armor be withdrawn from the coastal areas," he wrote later. "He turned down my suggestion at once, pointing out that as a man from the Eastern Front I lacked his experiences of Africa and Italy; that he knew, in fact, far more about the matter in hand than I did and that he was fully convinced that his system was right." The colonel general seems to have known his friend quite well, for he continued: "In view of this attitude of his, an argument with Rommel . . . promised to be quite fruitless."[78] Hence he dropped the subject. The conference ended without achieving any tangible results. General Georg von Sodenstern, the commander of the 19th Army (in southern France),[79] caustically, though privately, expressed his fears that German generalship would exhaust itself building masses of concrete. "As no man in his senses would put his head on an anvil over which the smith's hammer is swung, so no general should mass his troops at the point where the enemy is certain to bring the first powerful blow of his superior materiel," he commented.[80]

Of remarks of this nature, Rommel said,

Our friends from the East cannot imagine what they're in for here. It's not a matter of fanatical hordes to be driven forward in masses against our line, with no regard for casualties and little recourse to tactical craft; here we are facing an enemy who applies all his native intelligence to the use of his many technical resources, who spares no expenditure of materiel and whose every operation goes its course as though it had been the subject of repeated rehearsal.[81]

To his credit, the talkative General von Sodenstern kept an open mind and came around to Rommel's way of thinking. In early May he expressed displeasure with himself for not drawing the same conclusions on his own.

Hitler should have been the one to choose between Rommel's concept of operations and those of von Rundstedt, Guderian, and Geyr von Schweppenburg. Unfortunately for the German war effort, he was far too preoccupied with the war in Russia to even visit the Western Front. As a result, a sort of defense by compromise was adopted, without the total consent of any of the major commanders involved. Without an overall policy, Rommel and von Rundstedt had to depend on mutual agreement, despite their divergent theories. This resulted in the moving forward of some of the panzer units, but not nearly as many as Rommel demanded. The U.S. Army's official history put it this way:

In summary, the conflict between Rommel's and Rundstedt's theories of defense was never resolved definitely in favor of one or the other and led to compromise troop dispositions which on D-Day were not suitable for the practice of either theory. The pool of mobile reserves had been cut down below what would be needed for an effective counterattack in mass; it had been removed from OB West's control, and, as though to insure finally that it would not be employed in force, it had been divided among three commands. While the possibility of seeking a decision by counterattack had thus been whittled away, considerable forces were still held far enough from the coast so that, if Rommel's theories were correct, they would be unable to reach the battlefield in time to influence the action. In short, operational flexibility had been curtailed without achieving a decisive thickening of the coastal defense.[82]

In mid-March 1944 it appeared that Hitler had finally made up his mind to adopt a single strategy and philosophy of defense in the West. On March 20 he addressed the Commanders-in-Chief of the three services in France (Sperrle, Krancke, and von Rundstedt), along with their top subordinates, and told them that he believed that the most suitable places for the invasion were the two west coast peninsulas (Brittany and Cotentin). The Allies' initial strategic objective would probably be the port cities of Cherbourg or Brest. He then declared that the defeat of the Allied landing was more than a purely local matter—it would be the decisive battle of the whole war.[83] He also said, "The enemy's entire invasion operation must not, under any circumstances, be allowed to survive longer than hours, or at the most days." The invasion being defeated, Hitler said, the Allies would never be able to try again, because the defeat would crush British and American morale. This would release 45 divisions for employment in the East, which would fundamentally change the situation there as well.[84]

This speech clearly indicated that Hitler was leaning toward Rommel's concept of operations. As in battle, the Desert Fox lost no time in pressing his advantage. As a field marshal, he had the right to appeal directly to Hitler any time he saw fit. He met with the Fuehrer the next day, and the former corporal agreed with Rommel's opinion on the necessity of stationing strong reserves, including panzer and motorized divisions, near the coast. Rommel had won the great strategic political battle for the panzer reserves. Unfortunately for him, his victory lasted only 24 hours. Members of Hitler's entourage, led by Jodl and backed by a written protest from von Rundstedt, convinced the Nazi dictator that he should again reverse himself. The policy would remain as it was before, which was—no policy. Of Hitler at this time, Rommel snapped: "The last [person] out of his door is always right."[85]

At least Rommel did win some new units as a result of this encounter, for Hitler now felt compelled to compromise with him. The 2nd, 21st, and 116th Panzer divisions were transferred from the control of Panzer Group West to Army Group B. Three other panzer divisions (9th and 11th and 2nd SS) were earmarked for soon-to-be activated Army Group G under Colonel General Johannes Blaskowitz.[86] General von Geyr was allowed to keep only four of his original ten mobile divisions: the 1st SS and 12th SS Panzers, 17th SS Panzer Grenadier, and Panzer Lehr. This compromise satisfied no one. Of decisions like this one, Field Marshal von Rundstedt later bitterly remarked to a Canadian interrogator after the war, "As Commander-in-Chief West my one authority was to change the guard in front of my gate."[87] Nevertheless, Rommel kept his three panzer divisions, but even their areas of operations were dictated by OKW. Second Panzer Division was sent to the Somme area; 116th Panzer was posted north of the lower Seine; and 21st Panzer Division was assigned to the Orne River area near Falaise in Normandy. Rommel, who had come to suspect that the Allies would land in Normandy, objected but was overridden by OKW. "As a result," Admiral Ruge wrote later, "only the 21st Panzer Division was in the area where Rommel expected the blow to fall. He pleaded in vain"[88]

Finally, on March 29, Rommel and Geyr had a bitter (and no doubt inevitable) personal confrontation at La Roche-Guyon, and the Desert Fox made it clear that he would have fired him on the spot if he had had the authority. The snobbish aristocrat—cut to the core because a Swabian commoner had dared to reprimand him—said nothing; he simply saluted and walked out, resolving never again to speak to Rommel unless he simply had to. The deadlock continued."[89]

Perhaps to counter Rommel's growing influence, Field Marshal von Rundstedt created a new command, *Armee Gruppe* G under Colonel General Johannes Blaskowitz. It included the 1st and 19th Armies and was responsible for the defense of southern France. Table 1.2 shows the Order of Battle of OB West on May 1, 1944.

Table 1.2
Order of Battle, OB West
May 1, 1944

OB West: *Field Marshal Gerd von Rundstedt*

Army Group B: *Field Marshal Erwin Rommel*
Armed Forces Netherlands: *General of Fliers Friedrich Christiansen*
15th Army: *Colonel General Hans von Salmuth*
7th Army: *Colonel General Friedrich Dollmann*

Armee Gruppe G[1]: *Colonel General Johannes Blaskowitz*
19th Army: *General of Infantry Georg von Sodenstern*[2]
1st Army: *Colonel General Johannes Blaskowitz*[3]

Panzer Group West: *General of Panzer Troops Baron Leo Geyr von Schweppenburg*

1st Parachute Army: *Luftwaffe Colonel General Kurt Student*[4]

NOTES
1. An Armee Gruppe was not a regular Heeresgruppe (army group) but rather was an ad hoc headquarters, intermediate between an army and an army group. This one was formed on April 28, 1944, and was eventually upgraded to full army group status.
2. Succeeded by General of Infantry Friedrich Wiese on June 29, 1944.
3. Succeeded as commander of the 1st Army on May 3, 1944, by General of Panzer Troops Joachim Lemelsen and on June 4 by Kurt von der Chevallerie.
4. At this time, 1st Parachute Army was employed as a training command only.

Throughout the six months of his command of Army Group B before D-Day, Erwin Rommel bombarded Hitler and OKW with requests for aid, particularly in the Normandy sector, which he felt was far too weak. Rommel proposed that the Luftwaffe be used to lay mines along possible Allied approach routes, but his request was denied. He received somewhat better cooperation from Naval Group West, where Admiral Krancke disagreed with Rundstedt (who expected the invasion to come in the Somme River sector, in the zone of the 15th Army) and had come around to Rommel's view—that the invasion might come further west, in the Cotentin peninsula sector of Normandy. Krancke cooperated with Army Group B on coastal artillery measures, but Rommel and Ruge were unable to persuade him to mine the Bay of the Seine—through which the Allied invasion fleet later sailed unmolested.[90]

At the beginning of May, Rommel demanded that Luftwaffe Lieutenant General Wolfgang Pickert's III Flak Corps (which had 24 batteries grouped into four regiments) be concentrated in Normandy.[91] At that moment, it was scattered all over France. Goering, as usual, refused to cooperate, and so did Pickert; the III Flak remained present everywhere but with no strength anywhere. Rommel also begged Hitler for a panzer division to place near St.-Lô in Normandy. His request was turned down.[92]

On April 23, the former Afrika Korps commander wrote to his old enemy, Alfred Jodl, to try to convert him to his concept of coastal defense. Again he emphasized the vital importance of getting strong panzer and mobile forces to the endangered coastal sectors within hours of the Allied landings. Failing that, he declared, victory would be in serious doubt. Again, however, he gained no converts. Several days later Rommel demanded that the High Command send an entire antiaircraft corps, a *Nebelwerfer* (rocket launcher) brigade, the 12th SS Panzer Division, and the Panzer Lehr Division to Normandy. Again, OKW turned down his "request."[93]

In May, Rommel again tried to draw the remaining panzer and panzer grenadier divisions of Panzer Group West closer to the coast. Rundstedt protested immediately, informing OKW that this move would be tantamount to committing the reserves prior to the beginning of the battle.[94] Again Rommel's ideas were rejected. "He [Rommel] pleaded in vain to move Panzer Lehr [Division] and 3rd AA Corps up between the Orne and the Vire, the 12th SS Panzer to straddle the Vire, and to have a rocket-launching brigade stationed west of the Orne," the naval advisor to Army Group B recalled. "They would have been exactly in the right places to counter the invasion."[95]

All this was very frustrating to a professional of Rommel's caliber. Here he was, trying to save Germany from defeat but found himself blocked at every turn. One reason for all the opposition to Rommel's concept of operations was the fact that no one on the German side had anything but the vaguest idea of where the enemy would land. By this, the fifth year of the war, the German intelligence network in England—which was never very good—had been badly damaged. Many of its best agents had been picked up, killed, or forced to hurriedly leave the country. Allied security measures were most thorough. Their total domination in the air made long-range reconnaissance flights almost suicidal, and information from neutral countries was often contradictory. German intelligence estimates were based on logic rather than on real facts; they amounted to little more than educated guesses, and they had to rely far too heavily on signal intelligence: the kind most easily used by an enemy to deceive the recipient. The Allies were, of course, eager to oblige and, by early 1944, had the *Abwehr* (OKW's military intelligence bureau) convinced that the British 4th Army had 12 divisions concentrated around the Firth of Forth in Scotland, preparing to attack Norway. As a result, Hitler kept 30 coastal U-boats in the Bergen sector to help meet the threatened invasion. Another British army, "Force Anderson"—under Lieutenant General Kenneth Anderson, who had commanded the

British 1st Army in the Tunisian campaign—was believed to be in Essex and Suffolk, preparing to invade the Netherlands. Finally, by the spring of 1944, OKW had been deceived into believing that an entire U.S. 1st Army Group—led by the redoubtable U.S. Lieutenant General George S. Patton, Jr.—was assembling in Kent to launch the main cross-Channel invasion at the Pas de Calais.[96]

It should be noted here that German military intelligence work was generally poor to nonexistent throughout the war. "A weakness of the German Army was the lack of instinct and knowledge in practical intelligence work," especially among the senior generals, General von Geyr wrote later. "In the unwritten tradition of the Army, intelligence work had a slight odor of not being respectable—at any rate, not as important as the work of operational personnel who controlled the fighting."[97]

A good example of this phenomenon is Admiral Wilhelm Canasis, the chief of the Abwehr. Many of Canasis's intelligence estimates were wrong or at least very wide of the mark, such as in 1941, when he estimated that there were 10,000 British troops in Crete, that they would not put up serious resistance against a German airborne assault, and that the native Cretan population would support the Germans. In fact, there were almost 40,000 British troops in Crete. When the German parachute and gliderborne forces landed, the British put up a fierce resistance and—with the active aid of the indigenous population—inflicted disastrous casualties upon the German parachute corps and almost succeeded in destroying it altogether.

The final straw for Canasis came in January 1944 (shortly after Rommel assumed command of Army Group B), when he told the OB Southwest (Kesselring) that there was absolutely no danger of the Allies launching an amphibious assault behind his lines in Italy. As a direct result, Kesselring moved the bulk of his reserves to the front—less than three days before the Anglo-Saxons landed an entire corps in his rear at Anzio. Hitler, justifiably furious at this latest gross intelligence failure, sacked Canasis on February 11 and replaced him with Colonel Georg Hansen. Shortly thereafter, the entire Abwehr was absorbed by the SD (the SS intelligence agency) under SS General Walter Schellenberg.[98] (The myth that Canasis was sacked because of his part in the July 20, 1944, attempt on Hitler's life is not true—although he was later executed after the Gestapo discovered that he had conspired with and shielded members of the German resistance. In fact, after his anger abated, Hitler selected Canasis to head a minor naval transport special staff in the spring of 1944.) The change, however, came too late to help Rommel or effect the overall ineptitude of German military intelligence.

Most members of the High Command of the Armed Forces believed that the Allies would land on the English Channel near Cape Gris Nez. Rommel, however, did not believe that the Allies would attack the strongest point in the German defensive network just to have a short supply line. He also disagreed with those members of the High Command who believed that Eisenhower would attack at the mouth of the Scheldt on the coast of Belgium. Rommel believed that the Western Allies had one primary strategic objective: Paris. Therefore, they would have to come somewhere along the northern coast of France. This proved to be correct. He also felt that a secondary invasion force would land on the Mediterranean coast of France and push up the Rhone River Valley to take the Atlantic Wall in the rear.[99] Again his basic ideas were right, but again his views were largely ignored.

It would be impossible to expect even a top military power to be strong everywhere along the entire coast from the Spanish border to Norway. It was the common consensus that the sector of the 15th Army from the Scheldt to the Seine was most gravely threatened because of its short distance to England, and its nearness to the Ruhr, Germany's industrial heart. Rommel initially agreed with the consensus and concentrated his primary effort on the left flank of the 15th Army, but later he concluded that the invasion probably would come in Normandy and gave top consideration to the right flank of the 7th Army (i.e., the LXXXIV Corps sector), where the Allies actually landed. Adolf Hitler at various times picked the Gironde, Brittany, the Cotentin, the Pas-de-Calais, and Norway as the site of the invasion.[100] On March 20, for some unexplained reason, he changed his mind again. Normandy or Brittany, he declared, would be the target. Perhaps it was merely his intuition acting up again, but he nevertheless demanded that the Normandy sector be strengthened. "The Fuehrer sent his generals repeated warnings about the possibility of a landing between Caen and Cherbourg," B. H. Liddell Hart wrote. "Rommel," he continued, "came round to the same view as Hitler. In the last few months he made feverish efforts to hasten the construction of underwater obstacles, bomb proof bunkers and minefields" in the Normandy sector.[101]

Hitler's latest flash of inspiration had no effect on the views of OKW or on General Jodl, his most influential military advisor. The High Command still believed (as it did at the time of Operation "Sealion," the aborted invasion of Great Britain) that the cross-Channel invasion was little more than an extended river crossing; as a result, the Calais sector continued to receive the lion's share of concrete and military resources and equipment, as allocated by OKW. The densest fortifications and the heaviest massing of forces and coastal defense batteries continued to be along the narrowest part of the English Channel. Eisenhower, of course, knew this, and was not about to attack the strongest part of the

German defensive zone just so his supply lines would be a few miles shorter.

Colonel Albert Seaton, one of the world's foremost military historians, has a different version of this story. According to Seaton, Hitler believed that Normandy would be the *first* Allied target. This landing, the Fuehrer believed, would be a diversionary operation that would occur prior to the main landings in the Pas de Calais.[102] Although I am unable to confirm Colonel Seaton's explanation, it has the ring of truth to it, and it certainly makes a lot of sense; in fact, it is the most logical way to explain what transpired on D-Day and in the weeks after, as we shall see.

Rommel's reasons for picking Normandy as a likely landing site were more scientific than Hitler's. The Desert Fox noted that Allied airplanes were bombing all the bridges into Normandy, as if they were trying to isolate it. He also noted that the Bay of the Seine area off the Normandy coast was left unmined by the U.S. and Royal navies, but the English Channel waters were heavily mined. Also, Rommel discounted the Scheldt area—which at first seemed a good site for an invasion—because it was also heavily mined and its hinterland was completely ignored by the Allied air forces. All of this suggested that the Great Invasion would come between Le Havre and Cherbourg—that is, in the Bay of the Seine. "The longer Rommel worked on his assignment, the more he became convinced that the major thrust would occur in the Bay of the Seine," Admiral Ruge recalled.[103] On May 9 the Desert Fox wrote in his war diary: "Drive to Cotentin Peninsula, which seems to become the focal point of the invasion."[104] As a result, the Field Marshal began to shift whatever units he could muster into the Normandy zone and especially into the east coast of the Cotentin peninsula. In the month of May alone he dispatched the 91st Air Landing Division, the 6th Parachute Regiment, the 206th Panzer Battalion, the 7th Army *Sturm* (Assault) Battalion, the 101st Stellungswerfer (Rocket Launcher) Regiment, the 17th Machine Gun Battalion, and the 100th Panzer Replacement Battalion to Normandy. These units varied greatly in quality. The 6th Parachute Regiment under Lieutenant Colonel Baron Friedrich-August von der Heydte was an elite, veteran formation. It was placed under the operational control of Major General Wilhelm Falley's 91st Air Landing Division, which was also an experienced and reliable combat force. The 206th Panzer Battalion was of less value, because it was equipped with miscellaneous French, Russian, and obsolete German light tanks (PzKw Is, PzKw IIs, and probably a few old Czech tanks). The assault battalion was an irregular force of 1,100 infantrymen, designed for use as a shock unit. The Stellungswerfer regiment consisted of three mobile rocket-launcher battalions, armed with 210mm, 280mm, and 320mm launchers. The 100th Panzer Replacement Battalion was equipped with a few light French and Russian tanks and therefore was of very little value. Most of these units were initially assigned anti-para-trooper missions.[105]

Years after the war, the controversial historian David Irving wrote a slanted and largely derogatory biography of Erwin Rommel, entitled *Trail of the Fox*. In it (among other things), he tries to prove that Hitler alone foresaw where the Great Invasion would strike. Admiral Ruge, Rommel's close friend and senior naval advisor, wrote later that Irving "makes Rommel look to the narrow part of the Channel (coast north of the Somme River) all the time, which is simply not true. . . . Rommel first favored the beaches on both banks of the Somme (like Rundstedt) but soon saw the beaches in the Bay of the Seine were better protected against the prevailing westerly winds."

Irving puts the Seine Bay completely out of action by writing that the 'German naval experts' declared it unsuited for landing operations on account of submerged reefs. . . . Rommel never said anything like that. One look at the chart clearly showed that there were good landing beaches everywhere between Cherbourg and Le Havre. . . . I had already pointed out in my war diary [16 to 31 May 1942, in the military archives in Freiburg] that the Bay of the Seine was well suited for large landing operations. But Irving demotes me to Rommel's 'naval aide,' besides converting me into a Swabian, whereas I am a Saxon.[106]

Admiral Ruge conceded that David Irving is an excellent writer (who would not?) and

is indefatigable in unearthing new sources. The drawback is that he starts writing with preconceived ideas. In addition, his vivid imagination (and lack of realism?) causes him to describe people and events as they should be according to his ideas, and not as they really were. . . .

Irving sees Rommel as a rough and rather primitive warrior. Consequently, he refers to him 'yelling' and 'shouting himself hoarse' repeatedly. I never heard Rommel yell or shout. A few times he raised his voice a bit because somebody had been too lazy, but that was all. Irving also makes Rommel 'Stomp across the muddy fields around Fontainebleau . . . gunning down the rabbits, hares and wild boars. . . .' Pure invention! Around Fontainebleau, we hardly took any walks, but we took many from La Roche-Guyon. We were armed, of course (possibility of 'resistance'), but I cannot remember that Rommel fired a single shot. I certainly never did.[107]

Ruge (who went on walks with Rommel almost daily) was particularly upset about Irving's treatment of General Speidel.

Irving's picture of General Speidel . . . is completely warped. To go into all the details would fill a book. But I can vouch for it that Speidel did not have any 'gloomy influence' on Rommel or that 'Rommel stood in obvious awe' of Speidel. There was no 'abject defeatism' in our table discussions; neither did Speidel's whole conversation 'revolve only around that asshole at the Berghof, meaning Hitler'. It was typical for Irving that he did not ask any of the few officers who had their meals with Rommel and Speidel, but cites a major, who joined the 'outer' staff a month after Speidel for no more than two months, and never was at our table but in a kind of 'junior mess'. Now he declines to answer pertinent questions.[108]

Irving went on to suggest that Speidel deliberately deceived Rommel and hoodwinked him into withholding divisions from the Normandy front, especially the 116th Panzer Division, because Speidel wanted them available for employment against the Nazis in the anti-Hitler coup. "Speidel certainly did not hold back any divisions," Ruge declared.

Irving's assertion that Speidel then betrayed Rommel is typical for his way of writing 'history.' There does not exist any proof, and betrayal certainly was not in Speidel's nature. But quite apart from that, Speidel could only hope to survive if he denied all knowledge of the attempt on Hitler's life. There are good witnesses enough who were in a similar situation.
Irving can write and he is good at details, but he adjusts the facts to his preconceived ideas. With his vivid imagination it is particularly dangerous when he writes what he considered history.[109]

I have made it my policy throughout my career never to attack another author. Unfortunately, Irving's highly colored version of the events of 1944 has received such widespread acceptance that I feel I must articulate my opinion, which is this: David Irving is just as wrong in his interpretation of Erwin Rommel's character, personality, and military astuteness as he was in his later work, *Hitler's War*, when he suggested that Adolf Hitler knew nothing about the Holocaust until 1943 at the earliest.[110]
It is unfortunate that such a truly outstanding researcher marred his work with such fallacious opinions.

In the months prior to D-Day, several excellent combat divisions were withdrawn from OB West's control and sent to the Eastern Front because of the deteriorating military situation there. In February 1943, after an epic siege, the 6th Army surrendered at Stalingrad, and Germany lost 230,000 of her best soldiers. Field Marshal Erich von Manstein temporarily restored the situation in the following months. Despite odds of 5 to 1 he counterattacked, retook Kharkov on March 14, and brought the Russian winter offensive to a halt. Unfortunately, Hitler did not leave the direction of the Eastern Front to Manstein or any other commander. In July 1943 the Nazi dictator launched a major offensive at Kursk, despite the objections of Jodl, Manstein, Guderian, and others. lt was a disaster. Germany lost more panzers in this single battle than she was ever able to commit on the Western Front at any single time. Hitler had exhausted his capabilities and resources in the East, and the initiative passed forever to the Soviets. Defeat after defeat followed: Kharkov fell, the siege of Leningrad was broken, German armies were beaten on the Mius and at Bukrin, the Donetz industrial region was overrun, the Dnieper line was breached, and the Zaporozhye bridgehead was lost. At Cherkassy, two German corps were surrounded. They broke out, but their losses were ruinous just the same. Kiev was threatened, as was Minsk in Belorussia. The 17th German Army was cut off in the Crimea and eventually destroyed at Sevastopol. In Galicia, the 1st Panzer Army was encircled. In March 1944 Hitler dismissed two of his best "Eastern" marshals: Ewald von Kleist, who commanded Army Group A; and Manstein, then commander of Army Group South. He replaced them with two rabid Nazis who could be relied on to obey orders from the Fuehrer despite the costs. It did not take a mental giant to see that the situation on the Eastern Front would grow even darker in the near future, and Rommel was very upset and depressed when he heard the news—all the more so because he very much liked Erich von Manstein.

(Manstein and Rommel had met the summer before under very unusual circumstances. Manstein had been called to Rastenburg, Hitler's East Prussian headquarters, for a conference. For some reason the conference was delayed and—taking advantage of their isolated surroundings—Manstein and his aide, Captain Alexander Stahlberg, went swimming ["skinny dipping"] in a nearby lake. Rommel apparently saw the whole thing; in any case, he hid their uniforms. Stahlberg recalled a slight smile on Rommel's face when Generalfeldmarschall Fritz Erich von Lewinski gennant von Manstein—nephew of Hindenburg, conqueror of Sevastopol, originator of the plan that conquered France, military genius of the first order and Commander-in-Chief of Army Group Don—was forced to present himself to Erwin Rommel, in the nude. Despite the practical joke, Manstein and Rommel soon became fast friends. The Desert Fox even went so far as to suggest that he would support Manstein if he attempted to take control of the Third Reich's military situation away from Hitler and the Nazis. Field Marshal Guenther von Kluge was present when Rommel brought up the idea. Typically, Kluge [a neutralist and a born fence-sitter] promptly excused himself, and Manstein rejected the idea. Now he was gone, and Germany had lost its best military brain.)[111]

The political situation was equally bleak. At the Casablanca conference in January 1943 Roosevelt demanded an unconditional surrender. Gone forever was the chance of a negotiated peace. In September 1943

Italy defected, and Hitler's other allies (Hungary, Romania, Finland, and Bulgaria) grew exceedingly nervous as the Red Army neared their borders. They could no longer be counted on to remain loyal.[112] The only really dependable ally the Nazis had left were the Japanese. Both were in full retreat, each too weak to help the other.

On the Western Front, the Allies introduced a second subtheater in Italy with an amphibious landing at Anzio on January 22, 1944. Rundstedt transferred the motorized 715th Infantry Division to Kesselring in Italy to help contain the beachhead. Two months later the Russian spring offensive resulted in the collapse of large sections of the Eastern Front. The German Army could no longer contain the Russians, even in good campaigning weather. The Panzer Lehr Division, the 361st Infantry Division, and the 349th Infantry Division were all hurried east to help stem the tide. At the same time the 326th, 346th, and 348th Infantry divisions and 19th Luftwaffe Field Division were ordered to give up their assault gun battalions for use on the Russian Front. On March 26 the big blow fell, as far as OB West was concerned: The entire II SS Panzer Corps (9th and 10th SS Panzer Divisions) was withdrawn from Panzer Group West and sent to Galicia, with orders to help rescue the trapped 1st Panzer Army. This mission was accomplished, but its transfer and that of a number of other panzer divisions left OB West with only one fully mobile armored division (the 21st), and the Allied invasion was less than three months away. The OKW historian went so far as to suggest that had the Allies struck at this moment, Rundstedt could not have offered effective resistance.[113]

During the next six weeks the shuttling of units from the Western Front, plus the skill and courage of the German defenders in the East, temporarily stabilized the situation in Russia. Hitler was able to begin rebuilding the mobile reserves of OB West for the invasion he knew must come soon. Panzer Lehr Division, led by former Afrika Korps chief of staff Lieutenant General Fritz Bayerlein, returned from Hungary, and the old fighters of the 1st SS and 2nd SS Panzer divisions returned from Russia to rebuild their battered regiments in France. At the same time, the XXXXVII Panzer Corps Headquarters of General of Panzer Troops Baron Hans von Funck was transferred from Russia to OB West. Funck and his staff represented one of the most experienced armored leadership teams in all the Third Reich.[114] Even the II SS Panzer Corps would eventually return to the West, although not before the Allies had landed on the shores of France. Table 1.3 shows the Order of Battle of Army Group B on May 15, 1944.

Table 1.3
Order of Battle, Army Group B
May 15, 1944

ARMY GROUP B: Field Marshal Erwin Rommel

Armed Forces Netherlands: *General of Fliers Friedrich Christiansen*

> LXXXVIII Corps: *General of Infantry Hans Reinhard*
>> 347th Infantry Division: *Lieutenant General Wolf Trierenberg*
>> 16th Luftwaffe Field Division: *Major General Karl Sievers*
>> 719th Infantry Division: *Major General Carl Wahle*

15th Army: *Colonel General Hans von Salmuth*

> LXXXIX Corps: *General of Infantry Baron Werner von und zu Gilsa*
>> 165th Reserve Division: *Major General Wilhelm Daser*
>> 712th Infantry Division: *Lieutenant General Friedrich-Wilhelm Neumann*
>> 48th Infantry Division: *Lieutenant General Karl Casper*

> LXXXII Corps: *General of Artillery Johann Sinnhuber*
>> 18th Luftwaffe Field Division: *Lieutenant General Joachim von Treschow*
>> 47th Infantry Division: *Lieutenant General Otto Elfeldt*
>> 49th Infantry Division: *Lieutenant General Sigfrid Macholz*

> LXVII Corps: *General of Infantry Walther Fischer von Weikersthal*
>> 344th Infantry Division: *Lieutenant General Felix Schwalbe*
>> 348th Infantry Division: *Lieutenant General Paul Seyffardt*

> LXXXI Corps: *General of Panzer Troops Adolf Kuntzen*
>> 245th Infantry Division: *Lieutenant General Erwin Sander*
>> 17th Luftwaffe Field Division: *Lieutenant General Hans-Kurt Hoecker*
>> 711th Infantry Division: *Lieutenant General Josef Reichert*

> In Army Reserve:
>> 19th Luftwaffe Field Division: *Lieutenant General Erich Baessler*
>> 182nd Reserve Division: *Lieutenant General Richard Baltzer*
>> 326th Infantry Division: *Lieutenant General Viktor von Drabich-Waechter*
>> 346th Infantry Division: *Lieutenant General Erich Diestel*
>> 84th Infantry Division: *Lieutenant General Erwin Menny*
>> 85th Infantry Division: *Lieutenant General Kurt Chill*
>> 331st Infantry Division: *Major General Heinz Furbach*

7th Army: *Colonel General Friedrich Dollmann*

> LXXXIV Corps: *General of Artillery Erich Marcks*
>> 716th Infantry Division: *Lieutenant General Wilhelm Richter*
>> 352nd Infantry Division: *Lieutenant General Dietrich Kraiss*
>> 709th Infantry Division: *Lieutenant General Karl-Wilhelm von Schlieben*
>> 243rd Infantry Division: *Lieutenant General Heinz Hellmich*

>> 319th Infantry Division: *Lieutenant General Count Rudolf von Schmettow*
> LXXIV Corps: *General of Infantry Erich Straube*
>> 77th Infantry Division: *Major General Rudolf Stegmann*
>> 266th Infantry Division: *Lieutenant General Karl Sprang*

Table 1.3 (continued)

7th Army: *Colonel General Friedrich Dollmann* (continued)

    XXV Corps: *General of Artillery Wilhelm Fahrmbacher*
        343rd Infantry Division: *Lieutenant General Erwin Rauch*
        265th Infantry Division: *Lieutenant General Walther Duevert*
        275th Infantry Division: *Lieutenant General Hans Schmidt*
        353rd Infantry Division: *Major General Paul Mahlmann*

    In Army Reserve:
        II Parachute Corps: *General of Paratroopers Eugen Meindl*
            2nd Parachute Division: *Lieutenant General Hermann Bernard Ramcke*
            3rd Parachute Division: *Lieutenant General Richard Schimpf*
            5th Parachute Division: *Major General Gustav Wilke*

In Army Group B Reserve:

    LXIV Reserve Corps: *General of Engineers Karl Sachs*
    LXV Corps: *General of Artillery Erich Heinemann*
    2nd Panzer Division: *Lieutenant General Baron Heinrich von Luettwitz*
    21st Panzer Division: *Major General Edgar Feuchtinger*
    116th Panzer Division: *Lieutenant General Count Gerhard von Schwerin-Krosigk*

Sources: *Die Geheimen Tagesberichte der Deutschen Wehrmachtfuhrung im Zweiten Weltkrieg,* 1939– 1945, Volume 10, 1. Marz 1944–31. August 1944, p. 501; Tessin, *Verbaende und Truppen,* Volume 3, p. 51.

Despite the return of these and other panzer units, Rommel did not face D-Day with any degree of optimism. Of the three modes of warfare—land, sea, and air—Germany could compete only on the ground. At sea the German Navy was a broken reed, and what little power it had left was destroyed soon after the invasion. On June 14 a low-level air attack at Le Havre destroyed 38 surface vessels, including nearly all remaining torpedo and patrol boats. It was almost the final blow for Naval Group West. On June 29 Admiral Krancke had only one torpedo boat, a dozen patrol boats, and eight schnorkel-equipped U-boats left. The Navy was operationally bankrupt.[115] More importantly, the Luftwaffe had reached approximately the same straits.

To tell the story of the final decline of the Luftwaffe, we must regress a bit. On August 17, 1943, the Allies launched two major bombing raids. One target was the ball-bearing plants at Schweinfurt, and the other was the Messerschmitt aircraft factory at Regensburg, where the Me-109s were built. Both targets were located deep inside the Reich. Of the 474 aircraft involved, 60 were shot down, a very heavy loss for the British and American bomber commands, particularly in view of the fact that little damage was done to the targets. On October 14 the Americans tried again, this time only against Schweinfurt. The result was an unmitigated disaster. Casualties exceeded 25 percent, and again little damage was done. These aerial defeats demonstrated clearly that the Allied air forces possessed air superiority only over the fringe areas of German air space.[116]

Following the debacle at Schweinfurt, Allied planners reevaluated their strategic position and increased their numbers and use of long-range fighters. By February 1944 the U.S. 8th Air Force under Lieutenant General James H. Doolittle felt strong enough to plan bombing missions designed to deliberately provoke air battles with the Luftwaffe. Although the German fighter pilots, led by Lieutenant General Adolf Galland, put up quite a battle, they were unable to overcome the huge swarms of USAAF and RAF Spitfires, Hurricanes, Mustangs, and Mosquitoes that protected the Allied bombers. Despite heavier Allied casualties, the Luftwaffe was driven from the sky. The losses the German Air Force suffered in these battles could never be replaced. By June so many planes and pilots had been lost that Allied aircraft flew virtually unchallenged (except by AA guns) over the skies of Berlin, even in broad daylight. Experienced fighter pilots were in particularly short supply, because the Luftwaffe training establishment had collapsed. The pilot training program of the Luftwaffe was reduced from 260 hours of flight time per student in 1940 to as little as 50 in 1944, and even then it could not keep up with losses. The new, green German pilots were no match for the superbly trained British and American aviators; many of them could not even land properly. In May, for example, the Luftwaffe lost 712 aircraft to hostile action and 656 in flying accidents.[117] It was the loss of its veteran fliers, not the loss of aircraft, that finally broke the back of the misused German Luftwaffe.

In the West, Rommel had to deal with Luftwaffe Field Marshal Hugo Sperrle, once a man of dynamic energy who had "gone to seed" in the luxurious city of Paris, where he headquartered in a palace and ate, drank, and gambled to excess. Personally the two marshals got along well together, despite Sperrle's frequent outbursts of bitter sarcasm. Unfortunately for Rommel, Sperrle did not have the resources to help him, except on very rare occasions, and Sperrle did little or nothing to maintain the quality of his command, which had both bloated remarkably and deteriorated drastically from 1940 to 1944. It controlled, for example, nearly 340,000 of the 1,400,000 Wehrmacht personnel in the West in 1944,[118] yet, according to General Speidel, Sperrle had only 90 bombers and 70 fighter aircraft in his entire 3rd Air Fleet on June 1, 1944.[119] Even if flak troops (100,000 men) and the ground parachute divisions (30,000 men) are deducted, the size of the Luftwaffe ground and service establishments vis-à-vis the number of airplanes they put into the air is still enormous.[120] On D-Day, Eisenhower's pilots flew 14,674 sorties, against approximately 319 for the Germans.[121] Almost all of these were intercepted miles from the actual landing sites. It was a complete rout in the sky. Hitler, Goering, and their staffs played right into the Allies' hands by dissipating the remaining air power they had on strategically senseless raids on civilian targets in England. In January 1944 the England Attack Command ("Angriffsfuehrer England") launched the so-called "Baby Blitz." From January 21 until May 29, the United Kingdom was struck by 29 separate raids with an average strength of 200 aircraft per raid. Despite Rommel's pleas that the Allied embarkation ports (especially Portsmouth and Southampton) be bombed, the attacks centered on heavily defended London. When the Baby Blitz began, Attack Command England had 462 operational aircraft; by the end of May it could put only 107 planes into the air. Conditions were so bad that the Luftwaffe had to abandon its airfields on the French coast and retreat to the interior.[122]

Eisenhower finally gained control of the Allied strategic air forces in April, and he used them with devastating effect against two primary targets: the French rail network and the German fuel industry. Because it was common knowledge that OB West did not have enough motor transport or gasoline to make up for the loss of the railroads, the aerial offensive was a sure tip-off that D-Day was near. Goering's Luftwaffe was powerless to prevent the wholesale destruction of the French rail network. The scattered III Flak Corps was as ineffective as 3rd Air Fleet against these attacks. Six hundred locomotives were shot up by American and British fighters and fighter-bombers, and attacks against railroad bridges were even more successful. The destruction of the Brussels-Paris-Orléans line made it impossible to organize a railroad supply line, and by the middle of May the German supply network was in chaos. All the bridges on the Seine below Paris and all those on the Loire below Orléans were knocked out. By the end of April, 600 army supply trains were backlogged in France alone.

To meet this crisis, von Rundstedt canceled all military leaves. In April, 18,000 construction workers were taken off the Atlantic Wall and put to work on the railroads. Another 10,000 were transferred in May, but it was all in vain: Repairs simply could not keep pace with the destruction. Allied bomber experts selected 80 railroad depots as primary targets, and by D-Day more than 50 of these were either heavily damaged or virtually obliterated. The attacks against the locomotives also continued at an accelerated pace. On May 21 alone, U.S. and British aircraft destroyed 113 railroad engines, 50 of which were claimed in the 7th Army's sector. Before the antirail offensive began, the German transportation staff was running more than 100 supply trains a day in France. By the end of April this figure had been reduced to 48; by the end of May only 20 trains per day were operating throughout France.[123] After D-Day this figure would drop even lower. By the end of May, traffic over the Seine, Oise, and Meuse rivers was at a virtual standstill.[124]

Charles B. MacDonald and Martin Blumenson were right when they wrote: "Allied air attacks had weakened the railroad transportation system in France to the point of collapse."[125] Although not as hard-hit as the railroads, the French highway system was by no means neglected. By June 6 the French National Railway was operating at only 10 percent of its normal capacity, and Normandy was, for all practical purposes, a strategic island. German reinforcements to the invaded sector would now have to march there overland over damaged roads, which would increase their travel time by days when hours counted. For example, when Hitler finally released the 1st SS Panzer Division from OKW reserve to Rommel's Army Group B, it took the division seven days to cover the 186 miles (300 kilometers) from Louvain, Belgium, to Paris—a trip that normally took one day by train[126]—and the 1st SS was still 90 miles from the battle zone. It was also exposed to repeated aerial attacks from strong fighter-bomber squadrons reserved specifically for that purpose. Eisenhower had won a major, perhaps decisive victory on the very eve of the invasion; what is more, he knew it.

The Allied bomber offensive against German fuel installations was carried out by American pilots on pinpoint, daylight raids and was only slightly less successful than the offensive against the French rail network. The fuel industry was always one of Nazi Germany's critical weaknesses, and any decline in fuel production severely damaged the German war effort. By early May 1944, production had fallen from 5,850 to 4,820 metric tons per day, causing Munitions Minister Albert Speer to bluntly tell Hitler, "The enemy has struck us at one of our weakest points. If they persist this time, we will soon no longer have any fuel production worth mentioning. Our one hope is that the other side has an air force General Staff as scatterbrained as ours!"[127]

They did not.

As the bombing offensive heightened and the season for the invasion grew near, Rommel redoubled his efforts to meet it. Appendix IV shows his itinerary from March 23 to June 4, 1944. On April 29 he set out for the Bay of Biscay, Pyrenees, and Mediterranean zones, again trying to deceive Allied intelligence into thinking that his area of responsibility was greater than it actually was. Five days later he was back at La Roche-Guyon, but on May 9 he was off once more, back to LXXXIV Corps in Normandy. He found work in Marcks's zone proceeding to his satisfaction, although a great deal more needed to be done. Things were less satisfactory in the 21st Panzer Division area, where Nazi Major General Edgar Feuchtinger held command. Feuchtinger had organized the annual Nuremberg party rallies in the 1930s and held his command for political reasons. (He had commanded a horse-drawn artillery regiment on the Eastern Front in 1942 but had no experience in leading armored

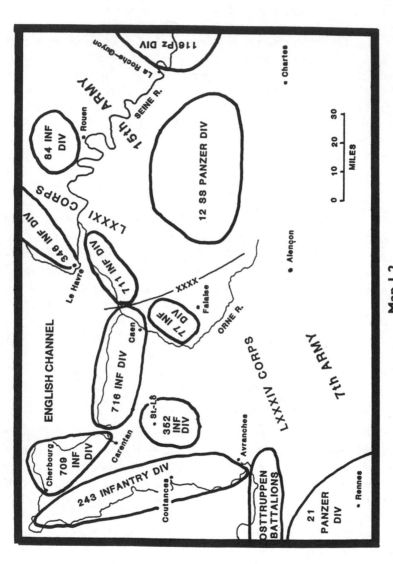

Map 1.2
NORMANDY: April 1944
(Adapted from Wilmot, p. 202)

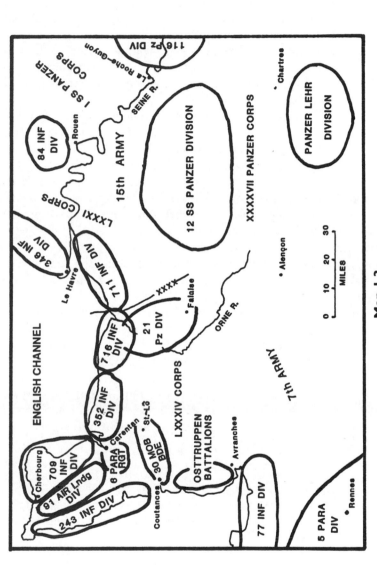

Map 1.3
NORMANDY: June 1944
(Adapted from Wilmot, p. 203)

units prior to assuming command of the 21st Panzer.) Rommel appeared at the division's 100th Panzer Regiment headquarters at Falaise at 8:00 A.M. one morning and found nobody of any rank there. Half an hour later the regimental commander, Colonel Hermann von Oppeln-Bronikowski, a well-known horseman and winner of an Olympic medal, showed up—drunk at 8:30 in the morning! Rommel asked him what would happen if the Allies landed before 8:30 A.M. "Catastrophe!" replied the inebriated colonel, who then fell backward into a chair. Remarkably enough, Rommel overlooked the incident and left von Oppeln-Bronikowski in command of the regiment.[128]

From mid-May, there was little Rommel could do but wait. "My inventions are coming into action," he wrote on May 6. "Thus I am looking forward to the battle with profoundest confidence."[129] Much remained to be done, but much had been accomplished, especially in the critical Normandy sector. Many mines had been laid, obstacles constructed, booby traps set, and reinforcements acquired. Map 1.2 and Map 1.3 illustrate the strengthening of the defense between April and June 1944 in terms of combat units and their density on the ground. Perhaps of almost equal importance, the German people and particularly the soldiers of the Western Front no longer feared the invasion, as secret Gestapo reports indicated. "People see it as our last chance to turn the tide," one of them read. "There is virtually no fear of the invasion discernible."[130]

"No fear of the invasion discernible." This is a tremendous tribute to Rommel, who had achieved all he could have been expected to achieve, given the enemy's resources, the lack of cooperation from his superiors, and his own staggering material deficiencies. However, on June 4 he threw much of this advantage away and made the greatest mistake of his military career: he decided to return to Germany and personally ask Adolf Hitler for more reinforcements. When the invasion finally came, the one man who might have repulsed it was away from his post.

NOTES

1. Erwin Rommel, *The Rommel Papers,* B. H. Liddell Hart, ed. (New York: Harcourt, Brace and Co., 1953), p. 426 (hereafter cited as "Rommel").

2. David Irving, *The Trail of the Fox* (New York: E. P. Dutton and Co., 1977), p. 314 (hereafter cited as "Irving").

3. Gordon A. Harrison, *Cross-Channel Attack*, U.S. Army in World War II, European Theater of Operations, Office of the Chief of Military History (Washington, D.C.: United States Government Printing Office, 1951), p. 149.

4. Cornelius Ryan, *The Longest Day* (New York: Simon and Schuster, Inc., 1959; reprint ed., New York: Popular Library, 1959) pp. 22–23. Karl Rudolf Gerd von Rundstedt was born at Aschersleben in the Harz on December 12, 1875, the son of a hussar officer. He attended cadet schools and graduated from Gross Lichterfelde, the German equivalent of West Point, and entered the army in 1892

at the age of 16. Commissioned second lieutenant in the 83rd Royal Prussian Infantry Regiment in 1893, he became a member of the General Staff in 1909. He spent most of World War I on the Eastern Front and emerged as a major. He was promoted rapidly after the war and became commander of the 2nd Cavalry Division in 1928. He served briefly as commander of the 3rd Infantry Division in 1932 and took charge of the prestigious Army Group 1 later that year. He retired for the first time in 1938 but was recalled to active duty in 1939 and led Army Group South in the Polish campaign. He later commanded Army Group B (later South) in the French campaign (1940) and Russia (1941). Hitler sacked him for the first time in December 1941 but recalled him in March 1942 to command OB West. For the best biography of Rundstedt, see Charles Messenger, *The Last Prussian: A Biography of Field Marshal Gerd von Rundstedt, 1875–1953* (London: Brassey's, 1991). Also see Guenther Blumentritt, *Von Rundstedt: The Soldier and the Man* (London: Odham's Press, 1952).

5. Wilhelm Meise was born in Munich in 1891. He joined the 3rd Bavarian Engineer Battalion as a Fahnenjunker (officer candidate) in 1910 and spent virtually his entire career in the engineers. Prior to joining Army Group B, he was chief engineer officer of the 12th Army (1939–41) and Army Group Center on the Eastern Front (1941–43). He ended the war as inspector of engineers and was living in retirement at Otterberg in 1958 (Wolf Keilig, *Die Generale des Heeres* [Friedberg: Podzun-Pallas-Verlag, 1983], p. 221 [hereafter cited as "Keilig"]).

6. Irving, p. 315.

7. Carl Hilpert was recalled to active duty on June 22, 1942, as acting commander of the LIX Corps. Promoted to general of infantry on September 1, 1942, he later led XXIII, LIV, and I Corps on the Eastern Front (1942–44) and was named commander of the 16th Army in September 1944. He became Commander-in-Chief of Army Group Courland (formerly North) in March 1945, and surrendered to the Russians on May 9—eight days after he was promoted to colonel general. Hilpert died in a Soviet prison in Moscow in 1946.

Kurt Zeitzler became chief of the General Staff of the Army on September 24, 1942, and was promoted to general of infantry the same day, skipping the rank of lieutenant general altogether. He was promoted to colonel general on January 30, 1944, but was relieved of his duties on July 21, 1944—the day after Colonel Count von Stauffenberg's attempt on Hitler's life narrowly misfired. Hitler suspected that Zeitzler knew of the plot against his life—apparently with considerable justification. Zeitzler was dismissed from his post without the right to wear the uniform and was eventually discharged from the army. He nevertheless survived the war and was living in Hamburg in the late 1950s.

8. Alan F. Wilt, *The Atlantic Wall: Hitler's Defense in the West, 1941–1945* (Ames, Iowa: Iowa State University Press, 1975), p. 46.

9. Ibid., pp. 58–59.

10. Ibid., p. 3.

11. Harrison, pp. 137 and 142. Also see United States Army Military Intelligence Service, "Order of Battle of the German Army" (Washington, D.C.: Military Intelligence Service, October 1942, April 1943, and January 1945) (hereafter cited as "OB"). The phrase "three regiment" in the three-regiment division referred to the line units (infantry, panzer, panzer grenadier, etc.). It excluded the artillery regiment.

12. Friedrich Ruge, "The Invasion of Normandy," in H. A. Jacobsen and J. Rohwer, eds., *Decisive Battles of World War II: The German View* (New York: G. P. Putnam's Sons, 1965), p. 321 (hereafter cited as "Ruge, 'Invasion' ").

13. Leo Geyr von Schweppenburg, "Panzer Tactics in Normandy," U.S. Army ETHINT 3, an interrogation conducted at Irschenhausen, Germany, 11 December 1947. On file, U.S. National Archives.

14. Leo Geyr von Schweppenburg, "Panzer Group West (mid-1943–15 July, 1944)," Foreign Military Studies *MS # 258*, Office of the Chief of Military History, U.S. Army (hereafter referred to as "Geyr *MS # B-258*." Another draft of the same manuscript will be referred to as "Geyr *MS # B-466*"). Guenther Blumentritt, who was promoted to general of infantry on April 1, 1944, had previously served as Rundstedt's operations' officer in the Polish and French campaigns (1939–40). He had also served as chief of staff of 4th Army (late 1940–early 1942) and chief of operations at OKH (January–September 1942). He was dismissed from this post when Hitler abruptly sacked Franz Halder as chief of the General Staff and replaced him with Zeitzler. Blumentritt had been chief of staff of OB West since September 24, 1942.

Later, Blumentritt was acting commander of the XII SS Corps (October 1944–January 1945), acting commander of the 25th Army (January–March 1945), and acting commander of the 1st Parachute Army (March–April 1945). He ended the war as commander of the *ad hoc* Army Blumentritt (Keilig, p. 38). After the war he wrote a laudatory biography of Rundstedt. He died in 1967.

15. Geyr *MS # B-466*.

16. Ryan, p. 23.

17. Ibid., p. 26.

18. Rommel, p. 461; Irving, p. 313.

19. Ruge, "Invasion," p. 323. Colonel General Alfred Jodl, the Chief of Operations at OKW, conducted his own tour of the Atlantic Wall in January 1944 and agreed with Rommel's conclusions wholeheartedly. Jodl was especially peeved at the Luftwaffe, which was not planning ahead for the invasion at all. See David Irving, *Hitler's War* (New York: The Viking Press, 1977), p. 603 (hereafter cited as "Irving, *Hitler's War*").

20. Rommel, p. 453.

21. Ibid., pp. 454–55.

22. Alfred Gause was born in Koenigsberg, East Prussia, in 1896. He entered the Imperial Army as a Fahnenjunker in the 18th Light Engineer Battalion in 1914 and was commissioned in 1915. A career staff officer, he had served as chief of staff of the X Corps (1939–40) and the XXXVIII Corps (1940–41), before becoming Rommel's chief of staff in early 1941.

Dr. Speidel had served as Ia (chief of operations) of the 33rd Infantry Division, Ia of the IX Corps, Ia of Army Group B, and chief of staff of the military commander of Paris before joining the staff of the military governor of France in 1940.

23. Gerry S. Graber, *Stauffenberg* (New York: Ballantine Books, 1973), p. 116.

24. For the story of the German resistance movement against Hitler, see Constantine FitzGibbon, *20 July* (New York: W. W. Norton and Co., Inc., 1956); James Forman, *Code Name Valkyrie: Count von Stauffenberg and the Plot to*

Kill Hitler (New York: S. G. Phillips, Inc., 1973; reprint ed., New York: Dell Publishing Co., Inc., 1975); Erich Zimmermann and Hans-Adolf Jacobsen, *Germans against Hitler, July 20, 1944* (Bonn: Federal German Government Press and Information Office, 1960); and Peter Hoffman, *The History of the German Resistance, 1933–1945* (Cambridge, Mass.: MIT Press, 1977).

25. Vice Admiral Friedrich Ruge was born in Leipzig on December 24, 1894, and entered the navy in 1914. Commissioned in 1916, he spent most of World War I in torpedo boats. He joined the minesweeper branch in 1928 and became chief of the branch in 1937. Later he became commander of Minesweepers, West (1939–41) and led a battle group in the invasion of Norway (1940). Ruge became commander of Naval Security Forces, West, in 1941, and in 1943 he headed a special naval staff in Tunisia. In May 1943 Ruge became commander of German Naval Forces, Italy. He was assigned to Headquarters, Army Group B in November 1943 (Hans H. Hildebrand and Ernst Henriot, *Deutschlands Admirale, 1849–1945* [Osnabrueck: Biblio Verlag, 1990], Volume 3, pp. 164–65).

26. Speidel, p. 39.

27. Rommel, pp. 462–64.

28. Irving, p. 316.

29. Harrison, pp. 150–51.

30. Friedrich Christiansen was born on December 12, 1879, and joined the Imperial Army near the end of the century. He became a fighter ace during World War I and was awarded the Pour le Merite (the "Blue Max"). He was Armed Forces Commander in the Netherlands from May 29, 1940, until April 7, 1945. From November 10, 1944, until January 28, 1945, he was simultaneously commander of the 25th Army, until he was succeeded in that post by Blumentritt. Christiansen died on December 3, 1972. Rudolf Absolon, comp., *Rangliste der Generale der deutschen Luftwaffe nach dem Stand vom 20. April 1945* (Friedberg: Podzun-Pallas-Verlag, 1984), p. 20 (hereafter cited as "Absolon").

31. *Kriegstagebuch des Oberkommando des Wehrmacht,* Book IV: *1 Januar 1944–22 Mai 1945* (Frankfurt-am-Main: Bernard and Graefe Verlag fuer Wehrwesen, 1961), p. 414 (hereafter cited as *"Kriegstagebuch des OKW"*); Hans Speidel, *Invasion, 1944* (Chicago: Henry Regnery Co., 1950; reprint ed., New York: Paperback Library, Inc. 1950), p. 41; Joseph Goebbels, *The Goebbels Diaries*, Louis P. Lochner, ed. (Garden City, N.Y.: Doubleday and Co., Inc. 1948; reprint ed., New York: Universal-Award House, 1971), pp. 391–92.

32. *Kriegstagebuch des OKW*, IV, Part 1 (1944), pp. 279–80; Speidel, p. 41.

33. Hans von Salmuth was born in Metz (then part of Germany) in 1888. He entered the service as a Fahnenjunker in the 3rd Grenadier Guards Regiment in 1907. After 31 years in the army, Salmuth was promoted to major general on August 1, 1939, one month before World War II broke out. He served as chief of staff of Army Group North (later B) from 1939 to May 1941, when he assumed command of XXX Corps, which he led on the Eastern Front. During this period, he actively assisted the SS *Einsatzgruppen* (murder squads) in their efforts to exterminate Russian Jews. He served briefly as acting commander of the 17th and 4th Armies (also on the Eastern Front) in 1942, before assuming command of the 2nd Army on July 15, 1942. He was sacked on

February 4, 1943, after his army had been smashed during the Soviet winter offensive of 1942–43. Salmuth returned to active duty as acting commander of the 4th Army in Russia in June 1943. He assumed command of the 15th Army on August 1 of that same year.

Salmuth developed a hatred for National Socialism after he had been unjustly relieved of his command in February 1943. Due to his anti-Nazi attitude and the fact that he had been in contact with the German resistance in 1944, Salmuth was again relieved of his command on August 25, 1944, and was never reemployed. After the war, he was sentenced to 20 years imprisonment by the U. S. Military Tribunal at Nuremberg; however, he secured an early release in 1953. He then retired to Wiesbaden and died in Heidelberg on January 1, 1962.

34. Speidel, pp. 41–42.

35. Friedrich Dollmann was a large and physically impressive officer who showed great political adaptability throughout his career. A Bavarian Catholic, he was one of the first officers to jump on the Nazi bandwagon—even to the point of dressing down his Catholic chaplains for not having a sufficiently positive attitude toward National Socialism. Largely as a result of his pro-Nazi sympathies, he had been promoted to commander of Wehrkreis IX (IX Military District) in Kassel in 1935 and to the command of the 7th Army on August 25, 1939. As of the beginning of 1944, his only action in World War II had been a mopping-up assignment at the end of the French campaign of 1940. To his credit, however, Dollmann withdrew his support of the Nazi regime after he came to understand the true nature of National Socialism, and he felt guilty and ashamed of his previous support of Nazism. He was also deeply concerned about the future of both his country and his command.

36. Speidel, p. 43. The 17th SS Panzer Grenadier Division and the remnants of the 352nd Infantry Division were later assigned to the II Parachute Corps (*Kriegstagebuch des OKW*, IV, Part 1 [1944], pp. 279–80.

37. Georg Tessin, *Verbaende und Truppen der deutschen Wehrmacht und Waffen-SS im Zweiten Weltkrieg, 1939–1945* (Osnabrueck: Biblio Verlag, 1973–81), Volume 15, p. 250.

38. Baron Leo Geyr von Schweppenburg (commonly called "Geyr" or "von Geyr") was born in Potsdam on February 2, 1886. He joined the army as a Fahnenjunker in 1904 and was commissioned second lieutenant in the 26th Light Dragoon Regiment in 1905. By 1931 he was commander of the 14th Cavalry Regiment. Bright, articulate, and well-educated, he served as military attaché to London, Brussels, and The Hague (1933–37). Seeing that the future belonged to the armored branch, he befriended Heinz Guderian, transferred to the panzer arm in 1937, and commanded the 3rd Panzer Division (1937–40), the XXIV Panzer Corps (1940–42), XXXX Panzer Corps (1942), and LVIII Panzer Corps (late 1942–1943) before being assigned to OB West in October 1943. He later became Inspector General of Panzer Troops (1944–45). Despite his strong anti-Nazi sympathies, Geyr refused to join the anti-Hitler conspirators, who approached him as early as 1938.

39. Speidel, p. 42.

40. Wilt, p. 128; Harrison, p. 238.

41. Harrison, p. 238.

42. Rommel, p. 481; Harrison, p. 146.

43. Rommel, p. 481; Harrison, p. 144; also see John Toland, *Adolf Hitler* (New York: Random House, 1976; reprint ed., New York: Ballantine Books, 1977), p. 1072 (hereafter cited as "Toland").

44. Harrison, p. 242.

45. Ibid., p. 241.

46. Bryan Perrett, *Knights of the Black Cross* (New York: St. Martin's Press, 1986), p. 196.

47. Friedrich Ruge, *Rommel in Normandy*, Ursula R. Moessner, trans. (San Rafael, Calif.: Presidio Press, 1979), p. 60 (hereafter cited as "Ruge, *Rommel*").

48. Paul Carell, *Invasion: They're Coming!* (Boston: Little, Brown and Co., 1965; reprint ed., New York: Bantam Books, 1966), p. 14 (hereafter cited as "Carell"); Ryan, p. 15.

49. Harrison, p. 247.

50. Irving, pp. 317–18, 324.

51. Ruge, *Rommel*, pp. 122–23.

52. Speidel, pp. 50–51.

53. Harrison, p. 141.

54. Ruge, "Invasion," p. 326.

55. Rommel, p. 455.

56. Charles B. MacDonald and Martin Blumenson, "Recovery of France," in Vincent J. Esposito, ed., *A Concise History of World War II* (New York: Frederick A. Praeger, Publishers, 1964), p. 84 (hereafter cited as "MacDonald and Blumenson, 'Recovery' "); Irving, p. 323; Rommel, p. 457.

57. Irving, p. 323.

58. Rommel, pp. 458–59.

59. Ibid., p. 460.

60. Ruge, "Invasion," p. 328.

61. Harrison, pp. 250–52.

62. Ryan, p. 29.

63. Carell, p. 9.

64. Ryan, p. 22.

65. Desmond Young, *Rommel: The Desert Fox* (New York: Harper and Row, 1950; reprint ed., New York: Perennial Library, 1965), pp. 192–93.

66. Ruge, *Rommel*, p. 51.

67. Speidel, p. 40.

68. Ruge, *Rommel*, p. 31.

69. Irving, pp. 320–25.

70. *Kriegstagebuch des OKW*, Volume IV, Part 1 (1944), p. 312. The 155th Reserve Panzer Division was absorbed by the 9th Panzer Division in May 1944. At the same time, the 179th Reserve Panzer Division was combined with the 16th Panzer Grenadier Division to form the 116th Panzer Division, and the 273rd Reserve Panzer Division was absorbed by the 11th Panzer Division.

71. Geyr *MS # B-466.*

72. Tony Foster, *Meeting of the Generals* (Toronto: Methuen, 1986), p. 294.

73. Speidel, pp. 23, 40.

74. Theodor Krancke was born in Magdeburg in 1893 and entered the Imperial Army in 1912. From October 1940 to April 1941 he sank 113,233 tons of Allied shipping as captain of the surface raider ("pocket battleship") *Admiral Scheer*. In June 1941 he became chief of the Quartermaster Division of the naval staff, and in June 1942 he was named naval representative to Fuehrer Headquarters. In April 1943 he assumed command of Naval Group West, which included all naval surface vessels in France and Belgian ports. These included torpedo boats, S-boats (*Schnellboote*, called E-boats by the Allies), minesweepers, patrol boats, and others.

Krancke remained in command of Naval Group West until April 1945 and played a major role in suppressing the anti-Hitler conspiracy in Paris on July 20, 1944. He ended the war as commander of Naval Group Norway. Released from Allied captivity in 1947, he retired to Wentorf (near Hamburg), where he died in 1973. See Theodor Krancke, "Invasionabwehrmassnahmen der Kriegsmarine im Kanalgebiet, 1944," *Marine-Rundschau*, Volume 66 (1969), pp. 170–87; and Juergen Rohwer, "Theodor Krancke," in David G. Chandler and James L. Collins, Jr., eds., *The D-Day Encyclopedia* (New York: Simon and Schuster, 1993), pp. 334–35.

75. General of Infantry Carl-Heinrich von Stuelpnagel was born in Berlin on January 2, 1886, and entered the Imperial Army as a Fahnenjunker in the 115th Infantry Regiment in 1904. He was promoted to major general in 1935 and was a general of infantry when the war broke out. Stuelpnagel was named chief of operations at OKH shortly after the Polish campaign and was looked upon as a "rising star" in the Wehrmacht. Despite the fact that his performance as commander of the II Corps during the Battle of France left much to be desired, he was nevertheless given command of the 17th Army during Operation "Barbarossa," the invasion of Russia. Here, on November 25, 1941, Field Marshal Walter von Brauchitsch, who was then Commander-in-Chief of the Army, judged his performance to be so poor that he relieved him of his command. Brauchitsch himself was sacked by Hitler three weeks later, and Stuelpnagel was recalled from professional disgrace by his friends in the High Command who secured his appointment as military governor of France in February 1942. Stuelpnagel was, however, given no further commands and no more promotions.

Carl-Heinrich von Stuelpnagel was anti-Semitic and cooperated with the SS murder squads in Russia in 1941.

76. Alexander von Falkenhausen attended various cadet schools and entered the Imperial Army as a second lieutenant in 1897. He retired as a lieutenant general in 1930 and was military adviser to Nationalist China from 1934 to 1939. He was recalled to active duty when the war broke out and served as commander of Wehrkreis IV (Silesia). He was named military governor of Northern France and Belgium on May 20, 1940, and was promoted to general of infantry shortly thereafter.

An anti-Hitler conspirator, Falkenhausen was sacked by Hitler a few days before the July 20, 1944, attempt on the Fuehrer's life; as a result, he survived the ensuing purges and was living in retirement at Gross Gruesselbach in 1957 at the age of 79 (Keilig, p. 85).

77. Speidel, pp. 57–59.

78. Heinz Guderian, *Panzer Leader* (New York: E. P. Dutton, 1957; reprint ed., New York: Ballantine Books, 1967), pp. 262–63 (hereafter cited as "Guderian").

79. General of Infantry Georg von Sodenstern was born in Kassel in 1889 and entered the service in 1909. He served as chief of staff of Army Group A (later South) until August 13, 1943, when he was named commander of the 19th Army. He was relieved of his command a few days before D-Day and was never reemployed. Although he had been privy to the anti-Hitler conspiracy as early as 1939, Sodenstern's anti-Nazi activities were never discovered by the Gestapo and he survived the war. Sodenstern died in Frankfurt/Main in 1955.

80. Harrison, p. 253. Sodenstern had been chief of staff of Army Group A in Poland and France (1939–40) and chief of staff of Army Group South (under various designations) on the Russian Front (1941–early 1944).

81. Rommel, p. 467.

82. Harrison, p. 258.

83. Rommel, p. 466.

84. Irving, pp. 336–37.

85. Rommel, p. 466, and Harrison, p. 248.

86. Johannes Blaskowitz commanded the 8th Army (1939), 2nd Army (1939–40), and 1st Army (1940–41). He led Army Group G until September 21, 1944, when he was placed in Fuehrer Reserve. Later recalled, he commanded Army Group G again (December 24, 1944–January 28, 1945) and Army Group H (January 28–April 7, 1945). He was Commander-in-Chief of OB Netherlands when Germany surrendered. A gentleman of the old school, he was never promoted to field marshal because Adolf Hitler despised him. Broken in spirit after the war, Blaskowitz committed suicide in his cell at Nuremberg on February 5, 1948 (Keilig, p. 36).

87. Wilt, p. 110.

88. Ruge, "Invasion," p. 330.

89. Speidel, p. 52; Irving, *Trail*, p. 404.

90. Rohwer, "Theodor Krancke," p. 335; Speidel, p. 52; Irving, *Trail*, p. 404.

91. Wolfgang Pickert (born 1897) had commanded the 9th Flak Division on the Eastern Front, until it was destroyed at Stalingrad. Pickert flew out of the pocket prior to the collapse of the 6th Army. He was promoted to general of flak artillery on March 1, 1945, and ended the war as general of the flak arm at OKL (Absolon, p. 30).

The III Flak Corps was formed from Headquarters, 11th Motorized Flak Division. It included the 431st, 653rd, 37th, and 79th Flak regiments (Tessin, Volume 2, p. 161).

92. B. H. Liddell Hart, *History of the Second World War* (New York: G. P. Putnam's Sons, 1972), Volume II, p. 549 (hereafter cited as "Hart"); Speidel, p. 33.

93. Rommel, pp. 468–69.

94. Harrison, p. 257.

95. Ruge, "Invasion," p. 330.

96. Albert Seaton, *The Fall of Fortress Europe 1943–1945*. (New York: Holmes and Meier Publishers, Inc., 1981), p. 105 (hereafter cited as "Seaton, *Fortress*").

97. Geyr *MS # B-466*.

98. See Heinz Hoehne, *Canasis,* J. Maxwell Brownjohn, trans. (Garden City, N.Y.: Doubleday and Co., Inc., 1979) for the best account of Canasis's life and career.

99. Speidel, pp. 33–34.

100. Harrison, p. 138.

101. Hart, II, pp. 548–49.

102. Seaton, *Fortress*, p. 106.

103. Ruge, *Rommel*, p. 27.

104. Ibid., p. 153.

105. Ruge, "Invasion," p. 322; Harrison, pp. 138, 259–60.

106. Friedrich Ruge, "The Trail of the Fox: A Comment," *Military Affairs*, Volume XLIII, No. 3 (October 1979: p. 158. *Military Affairs* is the professional journal of the American Military Institute.

107. Ibid.

108. Ibid.

109. Ibid.

110. See Irving, *Hitler's War*. Also see Gerald Fleming, *Hitler and the Final Solution* (Berkeley: University of California Press, 1984).

111. Alexander Stahlberg, *Bounden Duty: The Memoirs of a German Officer, 1932–1945*. Patricia Crampton, trans. (London: Brassey's, 1990).

112. Rumania in particular was bitterly resentful of the 18 divisions she lost between the Don and the Volga in late 1942 and early 1943.

113. Harrison, p. 234.

114. Hans von Funck was born on his family's estate on December 23, 1891, and volunteered for active duty when World War I broke out. He spent most of the war on the Eastern Front and was commissioned second lieutenant in 1915.

Baron von Funck was one of the pioneers in the movement to mechanize the German Army and commanded a motorized machine gun squadron as early as 1919. He worked closely with Oswald Lutz, the first general of panzer troops, and Heinz Guderian, the "father" of the Blitzkrieg, in the 1920s and 1930s. Funck was military attaché to Portugal when the war broke out. Later he led the 5th Panzer Regiment in France (1940) and the 7th Panzer Division on the Russian Front (1941–43). He was named acting commander of the XXIII Corps on December 7, 1943, and commander of the XXXXVII Panzer Corps on March 5, 1944.

Funck's corps was sent to Normandy on May 12, 1944, where it was initially used as an intermediate headquarters for several rebuilding panzer divisions.

115. Speidel, pp. 44–45.

116. Harrison, pp. 210–11; also see Glenn Infield, *The Big Week* (Los Angeles: Pinnacle Books, 1974), pp. 45–48.

117. Harrison, p. 266.

118. Seaton, *Fortress*, p. 107.

119. Speidel, pp. 46–47.

120. Seaton, *Fortress,* p. 107. Naval Group West, by way of contrast, had fewer than 100,000 men, including the naval-manned coastal artillery units.

121. John Terraine, "Allied Expeditionary Air Force," in David G. Chandler and James L. Collins, Jr., eds., *The D-Day Encyclopedia* (New York: Simon and Schuster, 1994), p. 25.

Sperrle, who first achieved fame as the original commander of the Condor Legion during the Spanish Civil War, was sacked by Hitler in August 1944 and was never reemployed. He was tried for war crimes at Nuremberg but was acquitted, and died in obscurity in Munich in 1953.

122. Speidel, pp. 46–47.

123. See Harrison, pp. 225, 267; Ruge, "Invasion," pp. 323–29; MacDonald and Blumenson, "Recovery," p. 80; and Speidel, pp. 46–47.

124. J.F.C. Fuller, *The Second World War, 1939–45: A Strategical and Tactical History* (New York: Duell, Sloan and Pearce, 1949), p. 294 (hereafter cited as "Fuller, 1949"); Harrison, pp. 228–30.

125. MacDonald and Blumenson, "Recovery," p. 80.

126. Alfred C. Mierzejewski, "Railroads," in David G. Chandler and James L. Collins, Jr., eds., *The D-Day Encyclopedia* (New York: Simon and Schuster, 1994), p. 448.

127. Toland, p. 1071.

128. Irving, pp. 346–47; Ruge, *Rommel,* p. 158. Hermann von Oppeln-Bronikowski was born in Berlin on January 2, 1899. He attended various cadet schools and entered the service as a senior officer-cadet in 1917. Commissioned in the 10th Ulan Regiment later that year, he remained in the Reichsheer and was squadron commander of the II/10th Cavalry Regiment in 1937. This unit became the reconnaissance battalion of the 24th Infantry Regiment when the war broke out. After Poland, von Oppeln was on the staff of the General of Mobile Troops at OKH and assumed command of an ad hoc panzer brigade on the Eastern Front in the fall of 1941. Here he survived the destruction of his tank by enemy fire on three occasions. In the meantime, he commanded the 35th, 204th, and 11th Panzer Regiments (1941–autumn 1943), but was not given command of his own division, possibly because of a drinking problem. He assumed command of the 100th Panzer Regiment in late 1943. In October 1944 he was given command of the 20th Panzer Division on the Eastern Front, and was decorated with the Knight's Cross with Oak Leaves, Swords, and Diamonds. He survived the war and was living in Hanover in 1958 (Keilig, p. 247).

129. Irving, *Hitler's War,* p. 625.

130. Irving, p. 351.

CHAPTER 2

D-DAY

On the eve of its greatest battle, OB West was weaker than German planners had hoped it would be, but nevertheless it represented a formidable military force. Field Marshal von Rundstedt had 58 combat divisions, of which 33 were either static or reserve, suitable only for defensive missions. Of the 24 divisions classified as fit for duty in the East, 13 were mobile infantry, two were parachute, four were panzer, four were SS panzer, and one (the 17th) was an SS panzer grenadier division. One Army panzer division (the 21st) was classified as unfit for duty on the Russian Front, because it was largely equipped with inferior, captured material. The U.S. Army's official history assessed OB West's condition this way: "The steady drain of the Eastern Front left to Rundstedt on the eve of his great battle two kinds of units: old divisions which had lost much of their best personnel and equipment, and new divisions, some of excellent combat value, some only partially equipped and partially trained."[1] Map 2.1 shows German dispositions on the Western Front on June 5, 1944.

The panzer divisions varied as greatly in numbers and strengths as did the infantry divisions. They ranged from 12,768 men in the 9th Panzer to 21,386 in the recently rebuilt 1st SS Panzer. All the panzer divisions were larger than their American and British counterparts, with the 1st SS Panzer (Leibstandarte Adolf Hitler) being twice as large. On the other hand, they all had fewer tanks than the Allied armored divisions. All the SS panzer divisions had six panzer grenadier (i.e., motorized or mechanized infantry) battalions, as opposed to four in the Wehrmacht's armored divisions. Therefore, all SS panzer divisions were larger than their Army counterparts, at least in terms of their tables of organization.

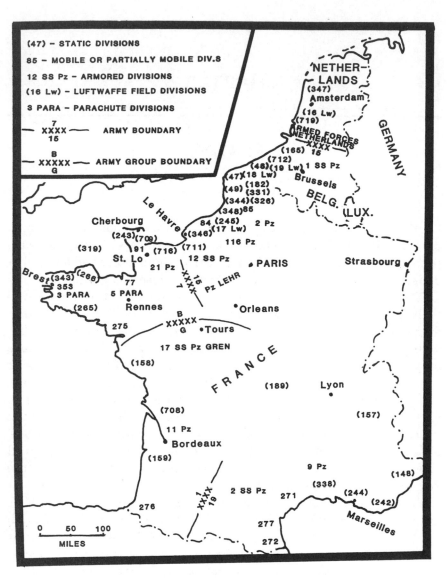

Map 2.1
DISPOSITIONS, OB WEST: June 5, 1944

If authorized strength and equipment varied somewhat, actual differences within divisions fluctuated remarkably. Although both Army and SS divisions each were to have a panzer regiment with one battalion of PzKw IVs and one battalion of PzKw Vs, their actual equipment figures differed in almost every case. The 1st SS Panzer, for example, was authorized 101 PzKw IV and 81 PzKw V Panther tanks but had only 88 tanks in all (50 PzKw IVs and 38 PzKw Vs), which means it had only 48 percent of its authorized armored strength at the time of the invasion. Like so many other German divisions, this unit was well below its assigned strength because of losses suffered on the Russian Front. Every German panzer division was understrength in terms of tanks except Panzer Lehr, which had 183. Second Panzer Division was close to full strength, having 161 panzers (94 PzKw IVs and 67 PzKw Vs); however, five of the panzer divisions in the West had fewer than 100 tanks. The figures for the 2nd SS "Das Reich" Division shown in Table 2.1, are typical. Note that this unit was particularly deficient in heavy tanks (i.e., PzKw Vs and PzKw VIs, or Tigers).[2]

Table 2.1
Actual versus Authorized Strength
2nd SS Panzer Division
June 6, 1944

Item of Equipment	Number Authorized	Number on Hand
Assault Guns	75	33
PzKw IIIs	7	0
PzKw IVs	57	44
PzKw Vs (Panthers)	99	25
PzKw VIs (Tigers)	0	0
TOTAL NUMBER OF PANZERS	163	69

Percent of authorized tank and assault gun strength on hand: 42.3%

Source: Harrison, p. 240.

The Allied armies suffered from few of the difficulties and deficiencies under which Rommel and von Rundstedt labored, and certainly not to the same degree. Rommel's chief of staff estimated that the Western Allies had about 75 divisions on June 6, of which 65 were at full strength and fully trained. Actually, they had 2,876,000 men in 45 full-strength divisions.[3] All were either armored, mechanized, airborne, or motorized, and all were fully mobile. They were supported by 17,000 aircraft, which opposed 160 in the entire 3rd Air Fleet, and the Allies had an overwhelming naval superiority, an excellent intelligence network, and a chain of command that functioned much better than that of Nazi Germany. Table 2.2 shows their basic organization on D-Day.

Table 2.2
Allied Organization
June 6, 1944

Supreme Headquarters, Allied Expeditionary Force (SHAEF): *General Dwight D. Eisenhower*

British 21st Army Group: *General Sir Bernard L. Montgomery*

British 2nd Army: *Lieutenant General Sir Miles Dempsey*
British XXX Corps: *Lieutenant General G. C. Bucknall*
British I Corps: *Lieutenant General J. T. Crocker*

U.S. 1st Army: *Lieutenant General Omar Bradley*
U.S. VII Corps: *Major General J. Lawton Collins*
U.S. V Corps: *Major General Leonard T. Gerow*

Allied Expeditionary Air Force: *Air Chief Marshal Trafford Leigh-Mallory*

Allied Naval Expeditionary Force: *Admiral Sir Bertram Ramsay*

The actual landings took place in the zone of the LXXXIV Corps of the 7th Army. Rommel (in his capacity as Commander-in-Chief of Army Group B) first inspected this corps sector in February 1944 and was not satisfied with what he saw; specifically, he felt that the 352nd Division at St.-Lô was positioned too far inland. As a result of his objections, Colonel General Dollmann ordered this unit forward to the coast, where it took over the left flank of the 716th Infantry Division in March. This move was routinely reported to Allied intelligence by the French underground via the usual method: carrier pigeon. The procedure was to dispatch each message twice, just in case German soldiers armed with shotguns killed one of the birds. This time, however, the specially assigned pigeon hunters got lucky and shot down both birds. As a result, the Americans did not learn of the strengthening of the sector until the men of the 352nd started firing on them. It provided General Omar Bradley with a nasty shock on D-Day, as we shall see, and it almost cost the Americans one of their beachheads.

Rommel's comments also led to the stationing of two "Eastern" battalions (the 795th Georgian and the 642nd Ost of the 709th and 716th Infantry divisions, respectively) closer to the coast. One reinforced regiment of the 352nd Division was held in corps reserve at Bayeux. Marcks periodically rotated his reserve forces to give the soldiers in all three of the 352nd's regiments occasional rest periods from mine laying, obstacle building, and the like. On D-Day, the 915th Infantry Regiment held Bayeux. As elsewhere in his army group's area, Rommel's construction program had greatly improved the defenses, but work was far from complete. LXXXIV Corps suffered from shortages of transport and cement, a problem that became especially critical in late May, after the cement plant at Cherbourg was shut down due to a lack of coal. On May

25 General Marcks estimated that the construction program in his area was only half finished. Between the Orne and Vire rivers, where the British and Americans landed, strong points and machine-gun nests were still an average of 875 yards apart.[4] Rommel's overall antiseaborne landing system, with its four belts of obstacles, had shown significant progress only in belts 1 and 2 (see Chapter 1). As a result, the obstacles would be deadly if the Allies came at high tide as Rommel expected, but would be left high and dry, and therefore useless, if they struck at low tide. If the Allies did come at low tide, however, they would have to cross a greatly enlarged strip of beach—about 300 yards wide—and this would drastically increase the effectiveness of any German machine gunners who survived the naval bombardment.

In other aspects of the defense, Rommel was not satisfied with the progress of his antiairborne obstacles, although he complimented Marcks for doing all that he could do. As a result of the inexcusable slowness of response from OKW, he received the major shipment of captured French mines only in early June. It was with these mines that he intended to arm his antiglider obstacles in the rear of LXXXIV Corps. Now it would be too late.[5]

Rommel inspected the 21st Panzer Division again in late May and seems to have been satisfied with the antitank hedgehogs at Cairon, halfway between Caen and the sea, which later held up the Canadian 3rd Infantry Division for eight days. This was all he was happy with, however. He found a divisional transport composed mainly of captured French vehicles, minefields still surrounded by barbed wire and labeled as such, and, worst of all, French civilians still wandering freely about the area, despite orders he had given to the contrary. Erwin Rommel was quite angry about this state of affairs and, as usual, made no secret of the fact. Unfortunately for the German Army, however, he stopped short of relieving General Feuchtinger of his command. This decision would have serious consequences for the Third Reich in the very near future.

One final factor must again be mentioned before the picture of the LXXXIV Corps on the eve of D-Day can be considered complete, and this is the intangible factor of morale. As the German soldiers faced their greatest test, this vital element was very high indeed. Since Rommel's arrival, the West Wall soldiers had gained a new sense of self-value. Germany's greatest general had been chosen to command them! No longer was duty in France looked upon as a soft job for used-up men who were not fit for duty on the Eastern Front; now they counted for something! Feverishly they prepared to meet the challenge, and their self-confidence rose accordingly. The American President Franklin D. Roosevelt had unwittingly aided Hitler and his propaganda minister in their efforts to stir the private soldier into a white heat on January 24,

1943, at the end of the Casablanca Conference, when he announced: "Prime Minister Churchill and I have determined that we will accept nothing less than the unconditional surrender of Germany, Italy and Japan." He went on to suggest that the entire conference might be labeled the Unconditional Surrender Conference.

As his less astute colleague rattled on, Churchill sat there stunned. Roosevelt had not bothered to inform him that he was going to make this announcement. Did the American president have any idea what the implications of his remarks would be?

Apparently not. Charles Wilmot later wrote:

To those whose minds ran along these lines, 'Unconditional Surrender' seemed to be an appropriate demand to make of an enemy who waged 'Total War.' This point of view was not unreasonable in the light of past experience, but it was one thing to form this resolve in secret for ultimate enforcement; it was quite another to proclaim it to the enemy in advance.

By doing this, the Anglo-Saxon powers denied themselves any freedom of diplomatic maneuver and denied the German people any avenue of escape from Hitler. Ten months before Casablanca Goebbels had written . . . 'The more the English prophesy a disgraceful peace for Germany, the easier it is for me to toughen and harden German resistance.' After Casablanca Goebbels had delivered into his hand a propaganda weapon of incalculable power.[6]

U.S. General Alfred C. Wedemeyer, the chief of the War Plans Office and perhaps America's greatest strategic thinker at the time, agreed. "Our demand for unconditional surrender naturally increased the enemy's will to resist and forced even Hitler's worst enemies to continue fighting to save their country," he wrote later. "The courage of despair imbued the German armed forces with a heroic spirit until the very end," he added.[7]

Paul Joseph Goebbels, of course, took full advantage of Roosevelt's blunder. "Since the enemies of Germany are determined to enslave the German nation, the war has become an urgent struggle for national preservation in which no sacrifice is too great!" he roared to an audience in Berlin.[8] The ensuing applause was so enthusiastic and prolonged that it satisfied even his monstrous ego.

The Roosevelt pronouncement undoubtedly cut the ground out from under the German resistance, which was even now plotting to assassinate the Fuehrer and overthrow the Nazi regime. General of Infantry Georg Thomas, the chief of the economic branch of OKW, for example, had been an active conspirator since 1938; after Casablanca, however, he refused to play any further role in the German resistance, on the grounds that to do so no longer made any sense. The Unconditional Surrender declaration also proved that the German people and the Nazis were viewed as one and the same by people like Roosevelt.

It also had its effect on the *Landser*, the ordinary German soldier. "Unless those terms are softened," General Sir Alan Brooke, the chief of the Imperial General Staff, told Churchill, "the German Army will fight with the ferocity of cornered rats."[9]

Prophetic words indeed, as the U.S. forces at Kasserine Pass soon found out. Others would soon find it out on Omaha Beach as well.

The Unconditional Surrender declaration was, in my view, a criminal piece of stupidity on the part of the American leadership. It weakened the hand of Colonel Count Claus von Stauffenberg and his coconspirators (including Rommel), for its harsh terms allowed Germany no reward for an early capitulation. Even many of the anti-Nazi or non-Nazi officers and men in the Wehrmacht now felt that they had to resist to the utmost, not for Hitler and his regime but in defense of the Fatherland and generations to come. A typical comment on Allied propaganda broadcasts at this time was an ominous "They're coming." To this, the German soldiers frequently replied, "Let them come." The entire "Unconditional Surrender" policy materially strengthened German resistance on the mainland and unnecessarily inflated the Anglo-American casualty lists.

For months Erwin Rommel had been laboring against incredible odds. As Harrison wrote: "To stake everything on a battle whose place and timing would be entirely of the enemy's choosing was to put an all but impossible burden on the defense, demanding of it a mobility it did not have and a sure knowledge of enemy intentions it had no means of acquiring."[10] The strain of labor and uncertainty took its toll on the Desert Fox. In early June he needed a rest. He also wanted to see Adolf Hitler again—to ask for more reinforcements—so he planned a trip to Berchtesgaden, where he intended to again ask that two additional panzer divisions and a mortar brigade be sent to Normandy.[11] He decided to take June 4–7 off. June 6 was his wife's 50th birthday, and he wanted to spend it with her at Herrlingen before continuing on to Hitler's Bavarian residence in the Alpine region. He even took time off to buy her a new pair of shoes—a rare and valuable commodity in Nazi Germany in the fifth year of the war. Before departing, Rommel checked the weather reports, which were encouraging. Colonel Professor Walter Stoebe, the chief Luftwaffe weather forecaster in Paris, and his deputy, Major Ludwig Lettau, predicted increasing cloudiness, high winds (Force 7 winds at Cherbourg and Force 6 winds at Pas de Calais), and rain. It was already drizzling in some locations, and Channel winds were 20–30 miles per hour at 6:00 A.M. on June 4. So certain were Stroebe and Lettau that an Allied landing in this weather was impossible that they gave part of their staff the day off to enjoy the delights of Paris. What they did not know (due to the absence of German weather observers in the Atlantic) was that sandwiched between the low pressure systems approaching the continent from the west was an intermediate area of high pressure, which promised to bring an improvement in the weather for about 36 hours on June 6 and 7. Eisenhower had his "window of opportunity," and he was not slow to take advantage of it.

From the German perspective, the weather forecasts from Poland were equally encouraging. The Allies were not expected to invade until the Red Army launched its summer offensive, and the late thaw of 1944 would not dry up until the latter part of June. Thus reassured, the Desert Fox left his headquarters at La Roche-Guyon at 6:00 A.M., convinced that the British and Americans would not land in the immediate future. Field Marshal von Rundstedt also labored (if that is the proper word) under a false sense of security. On June 5 he had a long, enjoyable luncheon with his son, a lieutenant, at a well-appointed restaurant outside Paris. He then returned to his luxurious chateau at Saint-Germain. He signaled OKW that there was "no immediate prospect" of the Great Invasion and retired early. He planned to spend the next day—June 6—showing his son the Atlantic Wall.[12] Little did he realize that the next day and hundreds of miles away Dwight D. Eisenhower would make the decision he was born to make. Despite the bad weather, he unleashed his forces for the long-awaited invasion. With tears in his eyes he watched the airplanes take off, loaded with paratroopers. This courageous decision marked the beginning of the end for the Third Reich.[13] It also meant that Erwin Rommel would not be on hand for what many consider the most important battle of his career.

Colonel General Dollmann, the 7th Army commander, was also convinced that the invasion would not be launched in such miserable weather. To keep his subordinates on their toes, he ordered a map exercise to be conducted at Rennes. All divisional commanders plus two regimental commanders per division were ordered to attend. He left his headquarters at Le Mans to observe the war game in person. As a result, the 7th Army would be without many of its important leaders on June 6. Major General Max Pemsel, Dollmann's chief of staff, would act as de facto commander of the 7th Army for much of D-Day, just as Dr. Speidel did at Army Group B Headquarters.[14]

Eisenhower's decision also took Admiral Krancke by surprise. He canceled the sea patrols scheduled for the night of June 5/6, because he was sure that the enemy would not attempt any significant naval operations in such foul weather. The huge Allied naval armada had the English Channel to itself: It approached the European mainland undetected. In fact, the Allied naval commander, British Admiral Bertram H. Ramsay, reported that the Allied passage had an "air of unreality" because of the complete absence of any kind of German reaction.[15]

The Luftwaffe was also unlucky. As a result of the bad weather, it chose this moment to rotate its fighter units. For reasons known only to Reichsmarschall Hermann Goering, the 26th Fighter Wing (which contained 124 of the 3rd Air Fleet's 160 operational aircraft) was sent from Lille (within range of Normandy) to Metz in eastern France. No replacements were available, because Goering had moved the other fighter squadrons from France to Germany a few days before on the grounds that he needed them for the defense of the Reich. Colonel Josef Priller, the outspoken commander of the 26th Fighter who had personally shot down 96 enemy aircraft, denounced the order as "crazy."[16] On June 6 Priller could bring only two airplanes to bear against the huge Allied air armada; these had been left behind as a sort of rear guard when the rest of the wing moved to the French-German border. The Luftwaffe was debilitated before the battle began.

Shortly after nightfall on June 5, bombs began to fall all over northwestern France, with particular concentration in and behind the 7th Army's sector. Although this was not unusual in itself, the aerial attacks continued well into the night and soon reached an unprecedented level of fury. The French Resistance was also out in full force on the night of June 5/6. Since France had surrendered in 1940, this heterogeneous force had grown to a strength of 200,000 men, women, and children, but prior to May 1944 it had caused no major security problems for OB West or Army Group B, except in Brittany. Most of its attacks had been directed against French collaborators rather than against German military targets. Under the nominal command of General Joseph P. Koenig, it was informed of the imminence of the invasion only 48 hours beforehand. The Allied planners felt that it would be of highly dubious value in this battle and were worried that the messages to the underground would alert the Germans. The Resistance (known as the FFI, or Free Forces of the Interior) proved to be surprisingly effective. During June it cut German rail lines a total of 486 times. By June 7 twenty-six trunk lines were unusable, including the vital arteries to Normandy. The Avranches–St.-Lô, St.-Lô–Cherbourg, and St.-Lô–Caen rail lines were all sabotaged by multiple cuts. These and other critical rail lines were useless for some time, significantly slowing the speed with which reinforcements arrived in Normandy. At the same time, telephone systems were sabotaged, telegraph wires were cut, road bridges were blown up, and communications were generally disrupted throughout the rear of Army Group B.

The alerting of the FFI should have tipped off the Germans that the invasion was imminent, but it did not. On June 1–2, Gestapo agents who had penetrated the Resistance picked up at least 28 coded messages signaling the underground to stand by for orders to begin executing their sabotage missions. The SS intelligence agency quickly reported this development to Admiral Karl Doenitz, the Commander-in-Chief of the Navy, with the comment that the invasion could be expected within two weeks. Undoubtedly they also informed Reichsfuehrer-SS Heinrich Himmler, but neither he nor Doenitz took the warning seriously. Thinking that an exercise was in progress, the Grand Admiral did not see fit to inform Rommel's headquarters of the Gestapo's message.[17]

Fifteenth Army's Intelligence Officer, Lieutenant Colonel Helmut Meyer, also intercepted a signal (at 9:15 P.M. on June 5), telling the FFI that the invasion would come within 48 hours. He relayed the news to von Salmuth, but the general was not much interested. "I'm too old a bunny to get too excited about this," he said, and resumed his bridge game.[18] When Meyer took the intercepted message to Lieutenant General Rudolf Hofmann, Salmuth's chief of staff, however, he immediately put the entire army on alert. Colonel Meyer telephoned Army Group B and OB West and sent a teletyped message to OKW. Colonel General Jodl, however, did not order an alert, assuming that von Rundstedt would do so. Rundstedt did not give the order either, assuming that Army Group B would do so. Army Group B, whose commander had already left for Germany, did nothing; apparently General Speidel dismissed the message as just another rumor. As a result, 7th Army was not put on alert, and the invasion was only hours away. General Dollmann's HQ actually canceled an alert planned for that night! No information at all was passed down to LXXXIV Corps, which was about to be struck by the greatest amphibious assault in history.[19]

At midnight several officers entered General Marcks's command post at St.-Lô for a modest party. This day, June 6, was the general's birthday. A surprised Marcks rose and shook hands with his guests, and each man had a glass of Chablis. Then, after a short celebration, Marcks and his operations staff returned to work, because the LXXXIV Corps commander realized that something serious was afoot.[20]

General Marcks proved to be both more accurate and quicker of decision than any of his superiors. On May 30, during Rommel's last preinvasion visit to LXXXIV Corps, Marcks said; "From my knowledge of the British, they will go to church again on Sunday, June 4, and will come on the Monday."[21] Now, on the night of June 5/6, he was both alert and suspicious. Scattered and fragmentary reports came in to his headquarters with disturbing frequency. At 12:40 A.M. on June 6, elements of the 919th Grenadier Regiment (of the 242nd Infantry Division) clashed with enemy paratroopers east of Montebourg. The enemy units were identified as part of the elite U.S. 82nd Airborne Division. A few minutes later, British parachute units seized the Caen Canal crossing at Benouville and blew up the Dives bridge on the Varaville-Grangues road. More importantly, glider forces blew up the Dives River bridge at Troarn. This explosion cut the road that connected Caen with the Seine

River cities of Rouen, Le Havre, and Paris and did much to isolate LXXXIV Corps from the rest of OB West. Meanwhile, at 711th Infantry Division headquarters on the far left flank of 15th Army (near the LXXXIV Corps boundary), Major General Josef Reichert was playing cards with members of his staff when two British paratroopers landed on his lawn and were taken prisoner by his intelligence officer.[22] Reichert informed von Salmuth's headquarters immediately. The message was relayed to General Marcks about 1:45 A.M. At the same time, Marcks received a report from Colonel Hamann, the acting commander of the 709th Infantry Division (whose leader was en route to the famous map exercise at Rennes). The dispatch stated that his men had captured prisoners from the U.S. 101st Airborne Division. Twenty-one minutes later Major General Wilhelm Richter, who commanded the 716th Infantry Division on the LXXXIV Corps' right flank, reported to Marcks that enemy paratroopers had landed east of the Orne. This news convinced Marcks, who put his corps and the nearby 21st Panzer Division on immediate top alert. Then he telephoned General Pemsel and told him that the invasion was definitely in progress. It was a little after 2:00 A.M.

In the absence of his commander, Pemsel put 7th Army on the highest state of alert and telephoned General Speidel at La Roche-Guyon at 2:15 A.M., but Speidel did not believe that the invasion had come in such miserable weather. Besides, Speidel was convinced that the real invasion would come at Pas de Calais. He told Pemsel that it was merely a diversion and that he should sit tight. Then he hung up. About the same time, von Salmuth phoned for Rommel and was put through to Speidel. The 15th Army commander had just talked to General Reichert. Over the wires, the sound of machine-gun fire had been clearly audible; the men of the 711th Infantry were clashing with enemy paratroopers very near divisional HQ. Speidel listened, but still refused to believe—even now—that the invasion might really have come.[23] Miles away, in Germany, Erwin Rommel, the one man who might have saved the situation, was sound asleep.

Although his was a fine staff officer, General Speidel's performance as *de facto* army group commander on D-Day left very much to be desired. While he did nothing, the American 82nd and 101st Airborne divisions landed in the left rear of the 352nd Division and the British 6th Airborne dropped down on both sides of the Orne River. Their objectives were obvious from the very beginning: cut off the flow of supplies to LXXXIV Corps and seal off the coastal areas from any possible reinforcements. Meanwhile, a huge Allied air force destroyed airfields, supply depots, and bridges far into the French interior. The rear echelons of LXXXIV Corps were pulverized. Meanwhile, all the railroad bridges over the Seine between Paris and the ocean were knocked out by fighter-bombers. Thirteen highway bridges between the

French capital and the coast were destroyed, as were the five main highway bridges between Orléans and Nantes. The LXXXIV Corps sector was virtually a strategic island on the morning of June 6.

Field Marshal von Rundstedt, General Blumentritt, and Lieutenant General Speidel all felt that the airborne attack was a diversion designed to attract attention away from the 15th Army's sector. Field Marshal Sperrle, the Commander-in-Chief of the 3rd Air Fleet, suspected the truth, but he had long since lost any influence he may have had with OB West. To pacify Marcks, who was hotly insisting that the invasion was imminent and would come in his sector, they took the 91st Air Landing Division and the mobile elements of the 709th Infantry Division out of reserve and gave them to him. These units, located in the western Cotentin, were ordered to counterattack the American paratroopers. Little else could be done to directly assist the LXXXIV Corps at this stage of the operation.

On the enemy's side, the plan was this: Both U.S. airborne divisions (a total of more than 13,000 men in 822 planes) were to drop in the eastern half of the Cotentin Peninsula between Ste.-Mère-Eglise and Carentan, establish a bridgehead, and wait for the U.S. VII Corps, which would form the right flank of the Allied landing forces. It was to link up with the paratroopers, build up forces and supplies for a few days, and then cut the peninsula at its neck and divide the German army in the Cotentin. Eventually, VII Corps would have the goal of taking the port city of Cherbourg, the strategic objective of the landings (Map 2.2).

Immediately to the left of the VII Corps, U.S. V Corps would land. Its job was to link up with the VII Corps 15 miles to its right and the British XXX Corps to its left. The British Army landed with two corps on three beaches. On the British right flank (i.e., the Allied center), the XXX Corps had the objectives of linking up with the Americans and capturing the important town of Bayeux on the Caen-Cherbourg highway. To the left of the XXX, British I Corps formed the Allies' left flank. It was to land on two beaches and was thus the only corps on D-Day to be responsible for more than one beach. Its objectives were to join up with the British 6th Airborne Division on the Orne and to capture Caen, the only really strategic objective in the British sector. South of this university city was country fit for armored operations. North of it, the Germans would have the advantage of excellent defensive terrain. It was therefore critical that Caen fall on the first day of the invasion, before Rommel could build up a defensive front and place the entire invasion in a stalemate.

Each of the corps had a code-named landing site assigned to it. U.S. VII Corps landed at Utah Beach; U.S. V Corps went ashore at Omaha

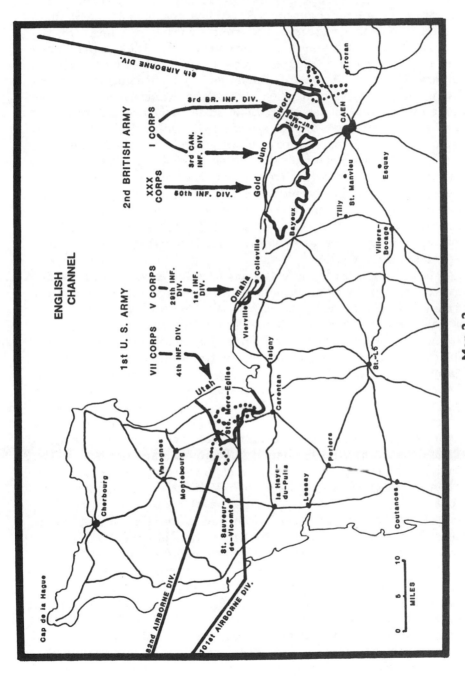

Map 2.2
D-DAY: THE ALLIED ASSAULT

Beach. The British XXX Corps landed at Gold Beach; the British I Corps entered the continent at Juno and Sword beaches. Map 2.2 shows these landings, as well as the divisions that spearheaded them and the airborne drops that screened and supported them. Although the British 6th Airborne Division "dropped precisely on its objectives along the estuary of the Orne" and secured Montgomery's left flank,[24] the American paratroopers were unlucky as a whole. Their formations were broken up by low clouds and sporadic antiaircraft fire, and the 101st Airborne was scattered over an area 28 by 17 miles. The 101st lost 30 percent of its men and 70 percent of its equipment in the landing, and nearly 1,500 of its 6,600 men were killed, wounded, seriously injured, captured, or drowned within two hours of the start of operations.[25] By the end of the day, the division could account for only 2,500 of the 6,600 men it dropped more than 22 hours before. It also failed to effectively link up with the 82nd Airborne to its west. The "Screaming Eagles" did, however, secure the southern exits to Utah Beach, thus covering it from German counterattack.[26]

The U.S. 82nd Airborne was even less successful than its sister division, for most of its units jumped into the wrong target areas. Most of the 82nd's men landed on the edges of the 91st Air Landing Division's assembly areas and were immediately heavily engaged by aggressive German junior officers and their battalions, companies, and platoons. The drop of the 82nd was even more scattered than that of the 101st. Many of its men landed in swamps, or in areas recently flooded on Rommel's orders, and were drowned before they could shed their heavy equipment. Brigadier General James Gavin, the assistant division commander, tried to establish a bridgehead over the small Merderet River with the men he could find but was soon defeated. Other elements of the division took the crossing at la Fiere but could not hold it. The 82nd, in fact, accomplished only one of its divisional missions, but it was the most important: Elements of the 505th Parachute Infantry Regiment seized and held the vital crossroads town of Ste.-Mère-Eglise. This victory very effectively screened Utah Beach from German counterattacks. The tough paratroopers flocked to the town in small groups, formed a perimeter defense under whatever officers and NCOs were present, and dug in. They would have to be ousted before any attempt could be made to overrun Omaha Beach while it was still vulnerable. Considering the high level of spirit and training of the paratroopers, coupled with the tremendous blows it was absorbing elsewhere, this would be a tall order indeed for the understrength LXXXIV Corps.

An isolated and anonymous band of lost American paratroopers also scored a major victory in the early morning hours of June 6, although they did not know it at the time. Major General Wilhelm Falley, the commander of the 91st Air Landing Division, was on his way to the map exercise at Rennes when the air raids began. He soon became alarmed about their intensity and decided that they might well be the start of the invasion. He ordered his driver to return to base. Near the chateau that served as his headquarters, Falley heard the rattle of automatic weapons fire. He drew his pistol and went to investigate. A few minutes later he lay dead, the victim of an enemy paratrooper. The Battle of Normandy had claimed its first general.[27] The 91st Air Landing Division would be without a leader on the most important day of its existence.

Elsewhere, the British and American navies and air forces were paving the way for the actual troop landings. They had at their disposal 3,467 heavy bombers and 1,645 medium bombers, light bombers, and torpedo planes, protected by 5,409 fighters and fighter-bombers. The Luftwaffe was utterly incapable of penetrating the Allied fighter screen, except for one isolated case. Two German fighters, flown by extremely brave pilots (one of whom was Colonel Priller), broke through the wall, did whatever damage they could do by strafing one of the beaches, and then miraculously escaped to tell the tale. All other German aircraft were either shot down or forced to turn back. Isolated flak batteries provided all the antiaircraft protection 7th Army had on D-Day, and it was not much. These batteries shot down the bulk of the 113 aircraft the Allies lost that day, but there simply were not enough guns available to reduce the enemy's aerial effectiveness. If Rommel's pleas to concentrate the entire III Flak Corps in Normandy had been heeded, the story might have been much different. As it was, Allied aircraft bombed, strafed, and generally shot up German positions almost at will. The heavy battery at St. Marcouf was a prime target, because its four 210mm long-barreled guns and single 150mm gun represented a major threat to Allied shipping. The enemy airmen attacked it with more than 100 aircraft, and the battery's six 75mm antiaircraft guns were quickly knocked out. More than 600 tons of bombs struck in and around the battery. All its guns were destroyed.

Two and a half miles further inland, the battery at Azeville was overrun by American paratroopers, and its four 122mm guns were captured. Two of the largest coastal batteries in Normandy had been neutralized before they could fire on a single Allied ship. The Royal and U.S. air forces flew thousands of sorties on D-Day, and dropped 11,912 tons of bombs. Within a few hours more bombs were dropped on Normandy than on Hamburg, the most heavily bombed city of 1943.[28] Many of these Allied bombs were designed to blast sideways, to wipe out German positions without making deep craters that might delay the Allied tanks when they advanced. In towns and villages this side-blast effect increased casualties and collapsed houses. The rubble thus created clogged Nazi supply lines, particularly those that passed through

St.-Lô and Caen. Between obliterated roads and the ever-present fighter-bombers, German supply vehicles were unable to reach the coast, and the frontline soldiers could not be resupplied. Many were soon running short of ammunition.

The Allies did make one critical mistake, and it involved the 329 heavy bombers they sent to destroy German positions dominating Omaha Beach. General Doolittle, the 8th U.S. Air Force commander, informed General Eisenhower that, owing to poor weather conditions, the B-17s would have to drop their bombs by instruments. Doolittle wanted to delay the bomb release for several seconds, to be sure that the bombs did not fall on the naval and amphibious forces gathering off the beach. It was a tough decision, for delay might mean missing the target. An early drop, however, would mean a catastrophe, because it would land on the assault vessels, which were now full of troops. The delayed release was approved. As a result, the bombs fell as much as three miles inland, missing the 352nd Infantry Division's coastal positions entirely.[29] The defenses would be very much intact when the American infantry landed.

On Utah Beach the story was considerably different. Here, the 9th U.S. Air Force employed 226 medium bombers at lower altitudes. They dropped 4,400 tons of bombs in the sector and obliterated some, but by no means all, of the German positions. Still, Utah Beach would prove to be a much safer place for the average American soldier than Omaha Beach on June 6.

Eisenhower came with 7,000 ships and more than 190,000 men.[30] He had achieved three elements of surprise: he was expected at Pas de Calais, not Normandy; he was coming at low tide, not high tide as predicted by Rommel; and he was expected to come in calm weather, not in near-gale conditions.

At 5:30 A.M., the Allied fleet attacked the surviving German shore batteries with a devastating bombardment from six battleships, 23 cruisers, and 104 destroyers. Meanwhile, Allied special service teams began to demolish the beach obstacles, left exposed by the low tide. If Rommel had been allowed time to complete his preparations, this would have been impossible. German riflemen and machine gunners made it difficult enough as it was.

On Utah Beach, the Americans faced a 709th Division strong point named W-5. Erwin Rommel had personally inspected this position on May 11, just 26 days before. That day he had been in a foul mood, which was quite usual for him when he was dissatisfied with the performances or preparations of his underlings. This day he was in a particularly ill temper, and he "sent rockets" after Lieutenant General von Schlieben and his regimental and company commanders. Only Second Lieutenant Jahnke, the strong-point commander, refused to be intimidated. This young officer was no new hand, as his rank might imply. He had won the Knight's Cross on the Russian Front and was even courageous enough to face the wrath of Field Marshal Rommel. He informed his Commander-in-Chief that, at this particular point, the tide washed up the Czech hedgehogs, mined stakes, and other obstacles as quickly as they were planted. Rommel listened, unconvinced. Suddenly he demanded to see Jahnke's hands. The surprised lieutenant presented a pair of hands covered with scratches and calluses, proving that he had personally helped his men lay the obstacles in question.

The Desert Fox nodded with satisfaction, his anger melting. He complimented Jahnke on his efforts and declared that an officer's blood shed in constructing obstacles was every bit as valuable as that shed in combat. Thus appeased, and convinced that sufficient effort was being made, the field marshal had his driver, Corporal Daniel, present Jahnke with an accordion (as he often did to troops with whom he was pleased) and departed.

Now, covered by naval gunfire and at low tide, the enemy came. Most of the light guns and automatic weapons of strong point W-5 were already knocked out before the first landing craft unloaded. Rommel's cunning obstacles were left high and dry. Lieutenant Jahnke vainly called for artillery support from the 901st Artillery Regiment, but the guns assigned to support him were already scrap iron. The young officer sent a messenger to a nearby battery of Colonel Triepel's 1261st Army Coastal Artillery Regiment, desperately calling for help. The messenger never made it, however; he was shot to death by a fighter-bomber. No help was forthcoming.[31]

Meanwhile, the efforts of the 7th Army to send reinforcements to the coast were just beginning. Colonel General Dollmann ordered Lieutenant General Schlieben to break through to the ocean.[32] This meant that Ste.-Mère-Eglise would have to be taken. To do the job, von Schlieben was given the 1057th and 1058th regiments (of the 91st Air Landing Division), the 6th Parachute Regiment, and the 100th Panzer Replacement Battalion. Later, Dollmann also sent up the 7th Army Assault Battalion.

Schlieben's counterattack never really got off the ground for a number of reasons. First, the 91st Air Landing Division had no real leadership since the death of General Falley. Second, von Schlieben himself was absent much of the morning—he was still on his way to his headquarters from the 7th Army map exercise at Rennes. Third, all the units were delayed and harassed by scattered bands of lost American paratroopers, who were quite good at setting up ambushes. Fourth, the Allied air forces continually disrupted all German efforts to establish order out of the confusion. Finally, the 6th Parachute Regiment was in the vicinity of

Carentan, too far away to take part in the Battle of Ste.-Mère-Eglise, at least on June 6.

Schlieben finally reached his HQ at noon, almost the exact time the 101st Airborne Division and the U.S. VII Corps linked up south of Utah Beach. The lieutenant general recognized what was happening, but he did not have the forces to do much about it. He did launch an evening attack on Ste.-Mère-Eglise, using his heavy artillery batteries and a few obsolete tanks, but they were beaten back by the paratroopers. Meanwhile, at strong point W-5, time had run out.

The U.S. 4th Infantry Division under Major General Raymond O. Barton spearheaded the U.S. VII Corps landings on Utah Beach. They quickly overwhelmed W-5, captured Jahnke, and killed or captured almost all of his men. Personally led by the assistant division commander, Brigadier General Theodore Roosevelt (the son of the former U.S. President of the same name), the men of this division surged forward in an attack reminiscent of San Juan Hill. Roosevelt won the Congressional Medal of Honor for his courage on this day. Ironically, he would die in his sleep before the Battle of Normandy was over; nevertheless, June 6 was his day. Utah Beach was secure, and the Allies had their first toehold in "Fortress Europe."

Fifteen miles east of Utah Beach lay the defensive positions of Lieutenant General Dietrich Kraiss's 352nd Infantry Division.[33] It occupied a thinly held coastal line from the Vire Estuary to Port-en-Bessin. Unlike most static divisions at the time, it had four infantry regiments: the 726th Grenadier (under Colonel Korfes, attached from the 716th Infantry Division), the 916th Grenadier (under Colonel Ernst Goth), and Lieutenant Colonel Ernst Heyna's 914th Grenadier Regiment were forward, while Lieutenant Colonel Karl Meyer's 915th Grenadier Regiment (with the 352nd Fusilier Battalion attached) was in divisional reserve. Lieutenant Colonel Karl-Wilhelm Ocker's 352nd Artillery Regiment deployed further inland to provide indirect fire support. Unlike the defenders of Utah Beach, the men of the 916th Grenadier Regiment (which defended Omaha Beach) had been missed by the bombings; even their intraregimental telephone systems were operative. Rather than smashing the defenders as planned, Doolittle's bombers had only killed a few dozen cattle and alerted the German soldiers that something serious was afoot. When the first assault wave came, they were ready. Two very distinguished military historians later referred to the 352nd as "an elite German infantry division."[34] It was not. It had been created only seven months before, when the remnants of the 268th and 321st Infantry divisions had been withdrawn from Army Group Center on the Russian Front and consolidated.[35] Although not elite, the 352nd was a tough, skilled, and disciplined collection of veterans. They were entrenched in eight well-constructed concrete bunkers with guns of 75mm or higher; 35 pillboxes with various types of artillery and/or automatic weapons; six mortar pits; 35 rocket-launching sites; and 85 machine-gun nests.[36] Survivors of the first wave of American infantry later reported that they could hear the bullets striking against their amphibious vessels even before they were grounded and their ramps dropped. The U.S. 16th Infantry Regiment, spearhead of the 1st Division, was slaughtered.

The U.S. 1st Infantry Division, nicknamed "The Big Red One" from its emblem, led the U.S. V Corps onto Omaha Beach and came in at two points: "Fox Green" (16th Regiment) in the vicinity of Colleville, and "Dog Green" (116th Regiment) in the Vierville area, west of Colleville. They committed 32 amphibious Sherman tanks for "Dog Green" but released them too far offshore, and almost all of them sank. Those that did reach the beach were immediately knocked out by German antitank gunners. At "Dog Green" the American naval gunfire overshot the mark, and their rocket fire fell short. Unaware that their support fire had been a complete fiasco, the first six American landing craft approached the beach. They met a hail of antitank gunfire, and two of them went down in the ocean. The remaining four reached the first sandbar and dropped their ramps. The American infantrymen ran into a hail of bullets. Within 10 minutes, every officer and NCO in the leading company had been killed or wounded. Most of the men were also casualties, and the rest were pinned down on the edge of the beach, unable to advance or retreat.[37] Other assault waves rushed ashore with similar results. The 1st Infantry Division bogged down on "Bloody Omaha." By midmorning, U.S. casualties were tremendous, particularly among their artillery units. All but one of the 111th Field Artillery Battalion's howitzers were sunk or destroyed. The 58th Armored Field Artillery Battalion suffered a similar fate: All their amphibious tanks were gone, their crews killed, drowned, or pinned down with the infantry on the far edge of the beach. On the right flank of Omaha Beach, 16 more Shermans were brought in but not launched. The naval officer in charge obviously felt that the sea was too rough, so he courageously disregarded both his original orders and German shellfire and carried the tanks right on to the beach. Half of these tanks were soon knocked out by German antitank gunners.[38] This left a total of eight Allied tanks intact on Omaha Beach.

On the far right flank of the U.S. 1st Division, American Rangers tried to capture the heavy gun emplacements at Pointe du Hoc, on the west end of Omaha. They fired ropes with grappling hooks attached and used ladders borrowed from the London Fire Department in attempts to scale the cliffs. The German defenders tipped over the ladders and rolled boulders on top of the exposed Rangers. More conventionally, they fired machine guns and threw hand grenades at them. The Rangers, who had almost no cover, were checked and decimated.

At 8:00 A.M., the battle for Omaha Beach had been in progress for less than three hours. The first assault was over, and there were 3,000 casualties on the sand, or a body for every six feet of beach. U.S. Intelligence reported to General Bradley aboard his flagship *Augusta* that the 352nd Division, as well as the 716th, was defending the heights above the beaches. Bradley was shocked by this report, for it represented a gross intelligence failure. An entire division had been moved from St.-Lô to the forward area without being detected: an entire division! Unlike most German divisions in France, this one had three grenadier regiments, which made things even worse. Bradley must have wondered what other unpleasant surprises would be in store for him that day. Already German resistance was twice as strong as expected.

At approximately 8:20 A.M., Colonel Talley, the deputy chief of staff of the U.S. V Corps, signaled General Bradley that the German guns had to be silenced at all costs, or no further advance could be expected.[39] This dispatch made up Bradley's mind: he ordered the fleet to bombard the seashore, regardless of the casualties it caused to his own men. The U.S. Navy trained their huge 15-inch and 16-inch guns on the coastline and began to blast the strong points of the 352nd and 716th divisions. Some of the destroyers came in so close that their bottoms drug sand. Individual courage and leadership by the American infantrymen kept hope alive on Omaha Beach when it looked as if the beachhead would have to be written off. German pressure finally weakened in the face of Bradley's persistence and because the 352nd Artillery Regiment was running out of ammunition. The Allied aircraft prevented any resupply of the gunners. Any attempt to drive an ammunition truck to the forward gun positions would be pure suicide.

The combination of naval gunfire and desperate courage of the isolated Americans led to the fall of WN-62, the first strong point on Omaha to be taken by the Allies. The defenders fought furiously but were finally overwhelmed. Lieutenant Grass, the strong point commander, was killed, along with most of his men. The Americans now had a tenuous foothold on "Bloody Omaha."

The 916th Grenadier Regiment, which held the center of the 352nd Division's line, called desperately for reinforcements. They were not forthcoming, however, because the few German reserves were even more urgently needed elsewhere. After three hours of violent combat, the German front began to waver, even on Omaha Beach.

On the right flank of the beachhead, the Ranger companies also made a penetration. They finally scaled the cliffs and began to move inland, across ground pockmarked with craters dug by the Navy's superheavy guns. They found the German 155mm battery, which had caused so much trouble on Omaha, lying deserted. Apparently the gunners had abandoned the guns during the naval bombardment, or else they had run out of ammunition. The Rangers quickly destroyed the 155s and continued to move inland, until they were stopped by a counterattack from elements of the 914th Grenadier Regiment. The specially trained American shock troops held on but lost most of their men in a battle that lasted, off and on, for two days. When it ended, only 90 Rangers were left standing, but they won the battle just the same.[40]

Omaha Beach was established at a tremendous cost. However, German resistance still continued in three zones near the beach: at Vierville, at St. Laurent, and at Colleville. At 11:00 A.M. the U.S. 116th Infantry Regiment and the 5th Ranger Battalion cleared Vierville. A whole series of confused firefights broke out in and around the other two villages, but the Germans continued to hold out. Omaha Beach was still far from secure when D-Day ended, and the survivors of the 352nd were still putting up a fierce resistance. As a result of the time lost in making the initial breakouts, the obstacles off the coast were not cleared by the American engineers when the tide came in. About half of the engineers sent to do this job were killed or badly wounded, and most of their equipment was wrecked. The initial losses to the armor and artillery could not be made good for some time. As D-Day ended, the Americans on Omaha still had almost no heavy weapons. The confusion incurred in the first assault waves was compounded by each succeeding wave, and organization ceased to exist in many units. Although hundreds of individual soldiers continued to wage their private wars against Nazi Germany, the situation on Omaha Beach was still a fine mess as the sun set. Of the five beaches the Allies attacked on June 6, it was the only one still in serious jeopardy the next day.

Meanwhile, the German High Command was making one of those decisions (or, more precisely, nondecisions) that cost the Third Reich the war. At 5:00 A.M. on D-Day, (i.e., more than two hours before the British landings began), Field Marshal von Rundstedt ordered the 12th SS Panzer Division to move up behind the 711th Infantry Division and alerted the Panzer Lehr Division to be ready for immediate movement.[41] He took this step even though he was not convinced that the main blow had come and even though he had formerly advocated fighting the decisive battle in the interior of France, not on the water's edge. This order, more than anything else, indicates how much von Rundstedt had come under Rommel's dynamic influence, for these units were not supposed to be committed without Hitler's personal approval. Nevertheless, realizing not a moment could be wasted if the invasion had come, the old Prussian issued the orders anyway; he put in a formal request for approval to OKW some 20 minutes later.

About 7:00 A.M. Jodl's deputy, General Walter Warlimont, telephoned his chief at his temporary headquarters near Obersalzberg in the mountains of southern Germany, near Hitler's own temporary HQ.

When Warlimont informed the OKW Operations Officer of von Rundstedt's request, Jodl replied: "According to the reports I have received it could be a diversionary attack. . . . OB West has sufficient reserves. . . . OB West should endeavor to clean up the attack with the forces at their disposal. . . . I do not think that this is the time to release the OKW reserves."[42]

Jodl was being influenced by his own preconceived opinion that the invasion would be at Pas de Calais and (like Speidel) by the fact that the Allies had dropped dummy paratroopers in some sectors in order to confuse the Germans. (It worked.) In any case, the question of committing the panzers should have been referred to Hitler immediately; however, he was in a drugged sleep and everybody at Fuehrer Headquarters was afraid to wake him! Warlimont was shocked by Jodl's refusal to release the panzers but knew better than to argue with his boss; instead, he telephoned von Rundstedt's chief of staff, General Blumentritt, and told him of Jodl's decision.

By 7:30 A.M. "shock and incredulity" reigned at OB West. Lieutenant Colonel Bodo Zimmermann, von Rundstedt's chief of operations, remembers that the old man "was fuming with rage, red in the face, and his anger made his speech unintelligible." Zimmermann himself tried to have the decision reversed and got himself chewed out for his troubles. "These divisions are under the direct control of OKW," Major General Baron Horst von Buttlar-Brandenfels of the Army's operations staff yelled at him. "You had no right to alert them without our prior approval. You are to halt the panzers immediately—nothing is to be done before the Fuehrer makes his decision!" Zimmermann tried to argue but was cut off. "Do as you are told!" von Buttlar-Brandenfels snapped.[43]

It was at this point that von Rundstedt should have phoned Hitler himself and insisted on being put through—as a field marshal he had that right; however, the proud and aristocratic Commander-in-Chief refused to plead with the man he habitually referred to as "that Bohemian corporal." Sir Basil H. Liddell Hart speculates that had Rommel been at his post, he might well have telephoned Hitler personally and secured the release of the panzer divisions. Rommel "still had more influence with him than any other general," Hart writes.[44] The accuracy of this last comment is subject to debate, for Rommel had lost much of his influence by mid-1944. It is almost certain, however, that the Desert Fox would have made the attempt, for he never hesitated to personally contact Hitler when he wanted something or did not like something. Such speculation is academic, however, for Rommel was not at his post and did not even learn that the invasion was in progress until 3 hours and 45 minutes after the landings began.

Command paralysis had reigned at La Roche-Guyon for over eight critical hours when General Speidel finally telephoned Erwin Rommel at his home in Herrlingen at 10:15 A.M. Rommel listened to his chief of staff calmly and then muttered quietly, as if to himself, "How stupid of me. How stupid of me." "The call had changed him," his wife recalled. "There was a terrible tension."[45]

Within the next 45 minutes, the Field Marshal twice telephoned his aide, Captain Hellmuth Lang, at his home in Strasbourg. Rommel kept changing the time for their departure to what was now truly the Western Front. The captain was worried: It was not like Rommel to be so indecisive. "He sounded terribly depressed on the phone," Lang remembered, "and that was not like him either."[46]

Meanwhile, at Berchtesgaden, Adolf Hitler was also being told of the landings. OB West had notified Fuehrer Headquarters of major Allied parachute and glider attacks in Normandy as early as 3:00 A.M. Nevertheless, Hitler's entourage refused to believe that the invasion might have come, until 9:33 A.M. when Eisenhower's press aide announced to the world that the Allies had landed in France. At 10:00 A.M. Hitler's naval aide, Admiral Karl Jesko von Puttkamer, phoned Jodl and was told that there were "definite indications" that a landing had taken place. Immediately after the call Lieutenant General Rudolf Schmundt—Army Personnel Officer and Rommel's only friend at Fuehrer Headquarters—woke Hitler up.[47] The dictator took the news calmly at first and ordered Schmundt to have Keitel and Jodl report to him at once. The calm had evaporated by the time they arrived. "Well, is it or isn't it the invasion?!?" Hitler shouted as they entered.[48] Nevertheless, it would be more than five hours before he gave the vitally important Panzer Lehr and 12th SS Panzer divisions to Army Group B.

While Erwin Rommel's car sped across southwestern Germany and eastern France, and Hitler, Speidel, Jodl, and the others vacillated or did nothing, elements of the LXXXIV Corps were being cut to ribbons by the British 2nd Army.

The paratroopers of the British 6th Airborne Division had several prelanding objectives, including seizing and holding the Orne River and Caen Canal bridges at Benouville, eliminating the coastal battery at Merville, destroying the Dives River bridges at Troarn, and covering the left flank of the entire Allied invasion front. Unlike the American paratroopers, the 6th Airborne accomplished most of its objectives, despite a scattered jump and heavy casualties. Many of the British troops landed in one of the areas Rommel had flooded, and a large number of the British 5th Parachute Brigade's soldiers were drowned. Brigadier Hill, the brigade commander, was wounded by an RAF fighter-bomber that mistook him for a German. Nevertheless, the brigade managed to take the Benouville bridge by glider assault and attacked the battery at Merville, while other elements of the division, led by

Major John Howard, seized Pegasus Bridge in perhaps the most perfectly executed airborne operation of the war, and effectively screened
the British beachheads from an attack from the east.[49]

Taking the battery was a critical mission, for it was in a position to
shell Sword Beach if it could not be neutralized. It fell prior to 5:00 A.M.,
with severe losses on both sides. The bridges on the Dives were both
destroyed by 5:20 A.M.; now the Germans would not be able to threaten
the beachheads from the west. The 21st Panzer Division to the south,
however, was still in a position to attack and overrun the lightly armed
paratroopers.

At 6:40 A.M. more than 1,000 heavy and medium bombers (Flying
Fortresses and Liberators) dropped nearly 3,000 tons of bombs on
German positions in and around Gold, Juno, and Sword beaches.[50] The
main British assault forces began "hitting the beach" at 7:15 A.M. The
overall plan for their amphibious landings was as follows: The British
2nd Army under General Dempsey was to land on the western part of
the Calvados coast, north of Caen, on a 19-mile strip of beach. His three
beachheads, running west to east, were code-named Gold, Juno, and
Sword. The script called for a rapid armored breakthrough of the
German front, the seizing of the vital road junctions at Bayeux and
Caen, a quick linkup with the paratroopers east of the Orne River, and
a rapid joining of the individual beachheads. Monty planned to be 32
miles inland by nightfall.[51]

The naval bombardment began 40 minutes before dawn. At half-light
the airplanes appeared to cover the infantrymen. Then came the amphibious assault forces. The British landings at Gold Beach, immediately east of Omaha, posed the greatest threat to the LXXXIV Corps on
D-Day. Here, as on all his beaches, Montgomery had much more tank
and heavy artillery support than did the Americans. When Montgomery
heard that Rommel would be in command at Normandy, he decided to
weight his initial waves with armor, because he knew from experience
what type of defense to expect. The American generals did not listen to
his advice and suffered heavier casualties as a result.

The British faced Lieutenant General Richter's badly overextended
716th Infantry Division, which held a front 21 miles long with four
battalions, plus a few attached elements of the 352nd Infantry Division.[52] They never had a chance. At Juno Beach, for example, three
companies of second-rate troops—about 400 men—were facing 2,400
well-trained and superbly equipped Canadians, who were supported by
76 amphibious tanks. In this sector, Richter had organized four resistance nets (*Widerstandsnestern*), each manned by a platoon, each spaced
about 2,000 yards apart. Most of the Canadian losses—in terms of
equipment at least—were caused by Rommel asparagus, which ripped
the bottoms out of the LCIs. Brigadier Harry Foster, the commander of

the 7th Canadian Infantry Brigade, looked through his binoculars and commented that the shoreline was "beginning to look like a Nova Scotian junkyard."[53]

Due to the obstacles, the rising tide, and the delays caused by the poor weather and heavy seas, the Canadians (who touched down at 7:45 A.M.) did not secure the exits from their beachhead until almost 10:00 A.M. Then, because of stiffer-than-expected German resistance, they had to fight their way through the village of Courselles-sur-Mer (the most heavily fortified position in the Juno sector) house by house, and the beachhead was not considered secure until noon. After that, however, German resistance slackened somewhat.

At Gold Beach, the British 8th Armored Brigade ripped through Richter's thin line—which had already been smashed by fighter-bombers and naval gunfire—and reached dry ground by 8:00 A.M. Bayeux was threatened almost at once. On the center and left flanks of the British landings the story was the same, except it was the British 27th Armoured and Canadian 2nd brigades breaking through. The Germans were simply not able to halt the British, and the 726th and 736th Grenadier regiments were cut to pieces.

The major gap in the 716th Division's line was in the sector of the 441st Ost Battalion, or at least where that unit was supposed to be. These former Russian POWs simply ran away, confirming the validity of a remark General von Schlieben had made some time earlier: "We are asking rather a lot if we expect Russians to fight in France for Germany against Americans."[54]

On Gold Beach the British 50th Infantry Division quickly overcame the initial resistance and pushed inland five miles. On Juno Beach, the Canadian 3rd Division met stiff resistance on the coast, but after the thin outer shell was broken, the Canadians advanced rapidly inland and cut the Caen-Bayeux highway by nightfall. On the British left the British 3rd Infantry Division also met initial resistance but was soon moving rapidly inland and linked up with the 6th Airborne.

In the morning it looked as if Montgomery might get his 32-mile penetration. However, he had not counted on the stubbornness of the individual German infantryman. Far too many of these men did not surrender but hid, let the tanks roll by, rallied, and attacked the flanks and rear of succeeding British assault waves. This maneuver, a common tactic on the Eastern Front from whence many of Richter's men had come, surprised more than a few of the Allied commanders. Major Lehman of the II Battalion, 726th Grenadier Regiment, made a determined stand against the Canadian 3rd Division at the hill of St. Croix, near Juno Beach. The Canadians had to recall their armor to take the position. At 3:48 P.M. the II Battalion radioed in its final message: "Hand to hand fighting inside command post." Then there was silence. Major

Lehman was dead, his battalion smashed. However, they had bought important time. The II Battalion of the 736th Grenadier held Tailleville with the same determination as the II/726th had shown at St. Croix. They were still fighting at 4:00 P.M. The III Battalion of the 736th Grenadier, supported by a surviving battery of 150mm guns from the decimated 1716th Artillery Regiment, also allowed the first Allied assault wave to pass; then they counterattacked in the rear of the British 3rd Infantry Division and retook the village of Lion-sur-Mer, on the very edge of Sword Beach. They were finally cut off and crushed, but all this took irreplaceable time. A number of strong Allied units that had surged inland had to be recalled to deal with the stubborn, bypassed members of the 716th Division, which they had written off too quickly. Montgomery did not get his 32-mile penetration.[55] He could not even cover the 10 miles to Caen. These delays gave Rommel, Marcks, and Dollmann 24 hours to establish a loose front. This was not much time, but it was enough: Monty would still be fighting for Caen six weeks later. Many small German units ambushed and fought the British and Canadians in the coastal sector all day long. When darkness fell, they faded away and escaped to the south, alone or in small groups, and helped form the new front that was already beginning to solidify.

Despite the gallant stands of its various units, most of the 716th Division was destroyed by nightfall. One by one the strong points signed off. That evening Colonel Krug, the commander of the 736th Grenadier Regiment, rang his division headquarters and informed General Richter that the enemy was on top of his bunker, demanding his surrender, and that he had lost contact with most of his men. "What am I to do?" he asked.

Richter informed the colonel that he could no longer give him any orders. "You must act upon your own judgment," he said. Then he added "Auf Wiedersehen," and slowly replaced the receiver.

Present in Richter's HQ at the time were General Feuchtinger of the 21st Panzer and SS Colonel Kurt Meyer of the 25th SS Panzer Grenadier Regiment, 12th SS Panzer Division. No one said a word. The silence was oppressive.[56]

Colonel Krug continued fighting until 6:45 the following morning. In doing so, he tied down important Allied forces. When he finally surrendered, he had only 3 officers and 70 men left alive. The 716th Infantry Division had been smashed. Of its six infantry battalions, five had been destroyed, and the sixth had been decimated. Eighty percent of the division's artillery had been destroyed.

As night fell on D-Day, the British bridgehead had a length of 20 miles but a depth of only 3–6 miles. They had reached the outskirts of Bayeux, which was defended by Colonel Meyer's 915th Grenadier Regiment, but were miles short of Caen. Bayeux fell the next day, but Caen (a city of

42,000) had to be placed under siege. The German front had contained, but not repulsed, the Great Invasion.

And what had happened in the 21st Panzer Division's zone while all of this was going on? The surprising answer is very little, because the command paralysis that seemed to dominate the Western Front on June 6 was particularly severe at General Feuchtinger's headquarters.

Rommel had recognized the possibility of an Allied invasion at this very point, so he had positioned the 21st Panzer to counterattack against it. This division included a large number of veterans of the Afrika Korps who had escaped the disaster in Tunisia. Many of them had been in Europe at the time, recovering from wounds or illness. Other members of the 21st were veterans of the Eastern Front. All too many of the others, however, were *Volksdeutsche*—Germanic peoples from the Eastern territories—some of whom did not even speak the German language. The unit's principle weakness, however, lay not in its men but in its equipment. The division's panzers bore little resemblance to the old 21st that General von Ravenstein had commanded so successfully in Libya three years before. Its panzer regiment (the 100th) under Colonel Hermann von Oppeln-Bronikowski had only two tank battalions: the I, under Captain Wilhelm von Gottberg; and the II, under Major Vierzig. Gottberg had 80 tanks, but none was of German manufacture. Vierzig's battalion was outfitted with 40 PzKw IVs, but they were older models and were fitted with obsolete, short-barrel guns, so their range was far too short. Certainly they were no match for the up-to-date Shermans and other weapons of the invaders.

The division's two panzer grenadier regiments, the 125th and the 192nd, had the same poor-quality equipment as the 100th Panzer Regiment, except that they did have the new German-made antitank weapon, the *Panzerfaust*. This single-shot, disposable, shoulder-fired weapon could destroy any Allied tank that advanced too close and would cause Eisenhower severe armored losses in the bitter days ahead. The grenadier regiments had another advantage: Unlike the division, their commanders—Baron Hans von Luck of the 125th and Colonel Josef Rauch of the 192nd—were highly competent. (von Oppeln-Bronikowski was also competent—when he was sober.)

On D-Day, General Feuchtinger was headquartered at St. Pierre-sur-Dives, too far from the coast to be of immediate help to the infantry. Colonel von Oppeln-Bronikowski was camped at Falaise, but his regiment was widely scattered along a line from Tours to Le Mans, so it would take him some time to assemble it. The first step in committing the division, however, was to find the general. This proved to be no easy task, as he was in Paris with his Ia, taking a spot of unauthorized leave. "He was fond of all the good things of life, for which Paris was a natural attraction," Baron von Luck recalled.[57] Eventually he was fetched out of a sleazy nightclub. When he returned to his command cannot be determined exactly, but it was after 1:00 A.M.

The 21st Panzer Division was mishandled all day long on June 6. Its activities were somewhat confusing and absolutely uncoordinated, owing partially to the divided command system established under Adolf Hitler and his cronies but mainly to the hesitancy and ineffectiveness of its division commander.

Lieutenant General Richter had the authority to issue orders to the panzer grenadier regiments but not to the 100th Panzer Regiment. Initially he felt that the main threat to his sector was from the British paratroopers, who landed east of the Orne River. Shortly after 2:00 A.M. on June 6, he committed the II Battalion of the 192nd Panzer Grenadier Regiment to the fighting at Benouville, along with reserve elements of his own 716th Division. This force, named Combat Group Zippe after its commander, Major Zippe, retook Benouville and its bridge by 3:30 A.M. The isolation of the 716th was now somewhat mitigated. General Richter ordered Zippe to stay put and hold the bridge, no matter what. Richter also tried to get Feuchtinger to commit the rest of his division against the British 6th Airborne. At 1:20 A.M. he phoned the panzer commander, but Feuchtinger did not feel that he had the authority to employ his unit without approval from OKW.

At 2:00 A.M. Richter—who outranked Feuchtinger—gave him a direct order to attack the vulnerable paratroopers, but Feuchtinger again refused. Several angry conversations took place in the next 4 1/2 hours, but the panzer leader refused to budge. More time was lost. At the command post (CP) of the 125th Panzer Grenadier Regiment, Baron von Luck recalled, "I paced up and down and clenched my fists at the indecision of the Supreme Command in the face of the obvious facts. If Rommel had been with us instead of in Germany, he would have disregarded all orders and taken action—of that we were all convinced."[58] Feuchtinger finally decided to move against the parachutists at 6:30 A.M. If he had attacked the 6th Airborne at 2:00 A.M. as Richter had ordered, he might have done the Allies a great deal of damage. Now, however, his attack was to Montgomery's advantage, for it tied down vital German reserves east of the Orne against relatively insignificant British forces. It was 8:00 A.M. before the 100th Panzer Regiment was assembled and could start its advance. By this time, it should have been growing clear to Feuchtinger that the airborne troops did not constitute the main threat. Even so, he continued on against the paratroopers. It was a little after noon before Feuchtinger received orders from General Marcks, who did not bother appealing to him but went directly over his head. The one-legged corps commander informed him that 21st Panzer Division was now part of LXXXIV Corps. Marcks ordered Feuchtinger to leave Combat Group von Luck (the 125th Panzer Grenadier Regiment, Major Becker's 200th Assault Gun Battalion, the 21st Panzer Reconnaissance Battalion, and a company from the 100th Panzer Regiment) to deal with the airborne bridgehead and send the rest toward Caen (i.e., west of the Orne), on which the British and Canadians were now advancing.

Finally, early in the afternoon, the 100th Panzer Regiment was moving in the right direction. Unfortunately for them, movement was not as easy as it would have been earlier, for it was now full daylight, the cloud cover had lifted somewhat, and swarming Allied aircraft took a heavy toll of the panzer troops. The 100th finally reached Caen but found the city in ruins, and Colonel von Oppeln-Bronikowski had to order a long detour, during which it was repeatedly attacked by "Jabos," as the Germans called the Anglo-Saxons' fighter-bombers. No one saw the Luftwaffe. "Hardly any of these thousands of Allied aircraft saw any sign that the German air force still existed," the British Official History recorded. Only 36 German aircraft were seen in the British sector all day, and almost all of these were miles from the battlefield. Of these, only 12 fought—of which 7 were shot down and 3 were damaged. On D-Day, 31 aircraft of the 3rd Air Fleet were destroyed and 7 damaged by Allied fire. Another 5 were destroyed and 11 damaged "not by enemy action": an indication of the lack of experience from which the Luftwaffe pilots suffered.[59] In fact, a grim joke made the rounds among the German ground troops: "If the airplane above you is camouflaged, it's British; if it's silver, it's American; and if it isn't there at all, it's Luftwaffe!"

On June 6, 3rd Air Fleet was ordered to reconnoiter the invasion area, destroy all enemy landing forces, bomb the airborne landing zones, protect the bombers, and provide cover and close air support for the ground forces. It did not accomplish a single one of these missions.[60]

It was 2:30 P.M. before Colonel von Oppeln got his unit—which was accompanied by Colonel Rauch's 192nd Panzer Grenadier Regiment—into position south of the British I Corps. He had already lost more than 50 of his 124 tanks on the approach march. He sent 35 tanks under Captain von Gottberg to take Periers Ridge, 4 miles from the coast. Von Oppeln decided to assume personal command of the remaining 25 tanks and attack the British on the ridge at Bieville. As he prepared to move out, he was joined by Generals Marcks and Feuchtinger. "Oppeln, the future of Germany may very well rest on your shoulders," the corps commander told him. "If you don't push the British back into the sea, we shall have lost the war."[61]

Von Oppeln must have been shocked. The future of Germany depended on a single motorized infantry regiment and a motley collection of 60 foreign-made tanks that had been obsolete for years?! Nevertheless he saluted and promised to attack at once. As he deployed, von Oppeln was hailed by another German general. This one was Wilhelm Richter, the commander of the 716th Infantry Division. He "was almost demented with grief," the colonel remembered. "My troops are lost," Richter said, with tears in his eyes. "My whole division is finished."[62]

Von Oppeln and von Gottberg struck as quickly as was humanly possible, but they never had a prayer. Their inferior tanks were simply outgunned by the superbly equipped defenders on Periers and Bieville Ridges. Oppeln's own tank was knocked out before it could get close enough to fire a shot, so he called off the attack. He had lost six tanks in 15 minutes. Gottberg did no better, losing ten tanks in a matter of minutes; he was repulsed before he could even get within range of the British positions. The 100th Panzer Regiment was shattered. The defeat also broke its spirit: Its morale was gone, never to be recovered.[63]

Meanwhile, General Marcks personally led the 192nd Panzer Grenadier Regiment into the attack. Its I Battalion was lucky enough to strike exactly between Sword and Juno Beaches and penetrated to the coast, which it reached at 8:00 P.M. However, its position was isolated at best. Marcks wanted the battalion reinforced, but at 11:00 P.M. a misdirected glider lift for the British 6th Airborne Division was mistaken for a British attempt to cut it off via glider assault, and General Feuchtinger ordered the unit to abandon its position and withdraw immediately. The chance to keep the British 2nd Army split was thus forfeited. Lieutenant Colonel Zimmermann of the OB West staff accused Feuchtinger of taking to his heels,[64] which seems to be fairly accurate.

Meanwhile, von Oppeln and von Gottberg dug in to await the British attack on Caen which, incredibly, did not come that day. "Caen and the whole area could be taken within a few hours," the colonel said later. He watched "German officers with 20 to 30 men apiece, marching back from the front, retreating toward Caen." The remnants of Richter's infantry division were coming home. "The war is lost," von Oppeln said aloud.[65]

Lost it was. Map 2.2 shows the situation at the end of June 6. The next day the Canadian 3rd Division from Juno Beach and the British 3rd from Sword Beach linked up to form a solid British front, but the Battle of Normandy was far from over. Erwin Rommel would see to that.

While Colonel von Oppeln was working his way around Caen, Rommel met Captain Lang at Freudenstadt and raced across France toward La Roche-Guyon and Normandy. It was 1:00 P.M. when Lang got into the car. Rommel spoke hardly a word the whole trip, except to urge his driver, Corporal Daniel, to drive faster. Captain Lang had never seen his chief so depressed as he was then. Once, about 3:00 P.M., the Field Marshal looked at Lang and said: "I was right all along . . . all along." This thought did not seem to comfort him very much, however.

About 6:00 P.M. Rommel's automobile reached Rheims. He phoned Speidel at La Roche-Guyon and talked for more than 15 minutes; then he silently climbed back into the car. Obviously the news had been bad. Sometime later he struck his palm with his fist and said bitterly: "My friendly enemy, Montgomery." Still later he added, "My God! If the 21st Panzer can make it, we might just be able to drive them back in three days!" After night fell, Germany's youngest marshal became more realistic. "Do you know, Lang," he muttered thoughtfully, "if I was commander of the Allied forces right now, I could finish the war in 14 days."[66]

He reached headquarters at 10:00 P.M. and immediately requested that all regimental combat teams from 15th Army be sent to Normandy, to be followed by all divisions of the second line at Pas de Calais. OKW turned down all his requests, except one: It gave him Lieutenant General Erich Diestel's 346th Infantry Division.[67] Rommel ordered it to anchor his far right flank, which was now held only by Group von Luck and a few stragglers from the 716th Infantry Division.

Meanwhile, Captain Lang had also become very depressed. He approached his commander in the hall of the Chateau of the Dukes de la Rochefoucauld. "Sir," he asked, "do you think we can drive them back?"

"Lang, I hope we can," came the answer. "I've nearly always succeeded up to now." Then, patting his aide on the shoulder, he said, "You look tired. Why don't you go to bed? It's been a long day." Rommel turned away, headed for his office, and shut the door.[68]

As a result of Eisenhower's gamble on the weather, Rommel had literally missed one of the most important battles, if not the most important battle, of his career. By day's end, the Anglo-Saxons had lost more than 10,000 men but had pushed their way inland an average depth of 4–6 miles along a 24-mile front, had put more than 156,000 men on shore, and were threatening to shatter the thin German defense and burst into the interior of France.[69] The Allied beachhead was established. Somehow it had to be wiped out, or the Third Reich was doomed. The burden of destroying it fell onto the shoulders of Erwin Rommel. Before he could even consider this task, however, he had to somehow gain control of the battle that was already in progress.

NOTES

1. Harrison, pp. 236, 248.
2. Ibid.
3. Speidel, p. 29; MacDonald and Blumenson, p. 85.
4. Harrison, pp. 257, 263; Ruge, "Invasion," p. 329.
5. Rommel, p. 460.
6. Chester Wilmot, *The Struggle for Europe* (New York: Harper & Row, Publishers, 1981), p. 123.

7. Albert C. Wedemeyer, *Wedemeyer Reports!* (New York: Henry Holt and Co., 1958), p. 95.

8. William B. Breuer, *Drop Zone Sicily* (Novato, Calif.: Presidio Press, 1983), p. xiv.

9. Ibid, p. xi.

10. Harrison, p. 231.

11. Carell, p. 14; Toland, p. 1073.

12. Breuer, *Cherbourg*, p. 77.

13. For the full story of Eisenhower's decision from a meteorologist's point of view, see Charles C. Bates and John F. Fuller, *America's Weather Warriors, 1814–1985* (College Station: Texas A & M Press, 1986), pp. 88–95.

14. Max Pemsel was born in Regensburg on January 15, 1897, and entered the army as a *Fahnenjunker* (officer-cadet) in the 11th Bavarian Infantry Regiment in 1916. A member of the mountain branch, he was Ia of the 1st Mountain Division when the war broke out. He was named chief of staff of the XVIII Mountain Corps in late 1940, a post he held until May 1943, when he became chief of staff of the 7th Army.

Pemsel was sacked by Field Marshal von Kluge in late July 1944, because the marshal was not satisfied with 7th Army's operations and he could not (or was afraid to) sack the army commander, SS General Hausser; in addition, Kluge needed a scapegoat following the American breakthrough in Operation "Cobra." Pemsel was nevertheless named commander of the 6th Mountain Division in Norway at the end of August. He was promoted to lieutenant general in November 1944 and was earmarked to be commandant of Berlin in the last days of the war. He was flown back to the capital of the Reich but due to weather-imposed delays did not reach the city before another officer was named in his place—much to the relief of General Pemsel. He was then sent to Italy and was named chief of staff of the Ligurian Army. Here he narrowly avoided being killed by partisans. Pemsel surrendered to the Americans at the end of the war. As of 1958, he was *Generalleutnant*, commanding the II Corps of the West German Army and was living in Ulm (Keilig, p. 253).

15. Bernard Law Montgomery, The Viscount of Alamein, *Normandy to the Baltic* (London: Hutchinson and Co., Publishers, Ltd., 1958), p. 43 (hereafter cited as "Montgomery").

16. Carell, p. 22.

17. Harrison, pp. 206, 283–89.

18. Richard D. Law and Craig W. H. Luther, *Rommel* (San Jose, Calif.: R. James Bender Publishing, 1980), p. 282 (hereafter cited as "Law and Luther").

19. Ryan, pp. 113, 145–49; Carell, pp. 31–32.

20. Friedrich Hayn, *Die Invasion von Cotentin bis Falaise* (Heidelberg: Kurt Vowinckel Verlag, 1954), p. 20 (hereafter cited as "Hayn").

21. Hans von Luck, *Panzer Commander* (New York: Praeger Publishers, 1989), p. 150 (hereafter cited as "Luck"). Erich Marcks was born in Schoeneberg (now Berlin-Schoeneberg) on June 6, 1891, the son of a prominent history professor and Bismarck scholar at the University of Berlin. Erich studied law and philosophy at Freiberg before joining the 9th Field Artillery Regiment as a second lieutenant in 1911. He was severely wounded in the face in the war and was then transferred to staff work, becoming a member of the General Staff in

1917. Later he was active in forming Freikorps (Free Corps) units, to protect the Weimar Republic from unrest—especially against leftists and Communists. He became press chief in the Armed Forces Ministry in 1929 and left the service in 1932 to become press chief for Chancellor Franz von Papen. He rejoined the service in 1933 as a battalion commander in Muenster and became chief of staff of Wehrkreis VIII (later VIII Corps), a post he held when the war broke out in 1939.

22. Major General Josef Reichert was born in Burgfeld, Bavaria, in 1891, the son of a customs official. He joined the Royal Bavarian Army in 1918 and rose to battalion commander. A colonel at the start of World War II, he successively commanded the 6th Infantry Regiment (1939–41), the 177th Division z.b.V. ("for special purposes") (1941–43), and the 714th Infantry Division (1943). He assumed command of the 711th Infantry Division on March 15, 1943, and led it until he was seriously injured in an automobile accident on April 14, 1945. In the meantime, he was promoted to lieutenant general on September 1, 1944.

Reichert was captured by the Americans in May 1945 and was released in 1947. He died in Gauting on March 15, 1970. See Keilig, p. 270; Georg Meyer, "Josef Reichert," *D-Day Encyclopedia*, p. 454.

23. Ryan, pp. 113, 145–49; Carell, pp. 31–32.

24. Fuller, p. 295.

25. Breuer, *Cherbourg*, p. 77.

26. Carell, pp. 50–51; Harrison, pp. 300–301.

27. Carell, pp. 50–51. Major General Wilhelm Falley was born in Metz, the capital of Lorraine (then part of Germany) in 1897. He was educated in various cadet schools and entered the Imperial Army as a Fahnenjunker in 1915. He was commanding I Battalion/433rd Infantry Regiment in the Koenigsbrueck Maneuver Area when the war broke out.

Although he did not see action in either the Polish or French campaigns, Falley was promoted to colonel in 1941 and was given command of the 4th (Prussian) Infantry Regiment, which he led with distinction during the Battle of the Demyansk Pocket on the Eastern Front. Wounded in action in 1942, he served on the staff of various army schools until October 5, 1943, when he assumed command of the 243rd Infantry Division on the Eastern Front. He was transferred to France and assumed command of the 91st Air Landing Division on April 25, 1944. He was promoted to major general six days later.

28. Ibid., p. 55.

29. Harrison, pp. 300–301; Carell, pp. 55–56.

30. The 190,000 men included air and naval personnel.

31. Carell, pp. 33–34, 56. The 1261st Army Coastal Artillery Regiment was formed in December 1943 and was a 7th Army GHQ unit. It included 10 batteries in three battalions. Its second and third battalions (II/1261 and III/1261) were composed largely of Osttruppen. It was destroyed by July 1944 (Tessin, Volume 13, p. 345).

32. Lieutenant General Karl-Wilhelm von Schlieben was born in Eisenach in 1894 and entered the service as a Fahnenjunker when World War I broke out in 1914. He was commissioned second lieutenant in the elite 3rd Foot Grenadier Regiment. He remained in the Reichsheer during the Weimar era

and was adjutant of Wehrkreis XIII (XIII Military District) when the war broke out. Later he commanded the 108th Rifle Regiment (1940–42), the 4th Rifle Brigade (1942), and the 18th Panzer Division (April 1–September 7, 1943). Apparently he was wounded on the Eastern Front, for he did not return to duty until December 1943, when he assumed command of the 709th Infantry Division. He was promoted to lieutenant general on May 1, 1944 (Keilig, p. 302).

33. Lieutenant General Dietrich Kraiss was born in Stuttgart in 1889, was educated in various cadet schools, and joined the army as a second lieutenant in the 126th Infantry Regiment in 1909. He remained in the Reichsheer (the 100,000 man army) after World War I and was commanding the 90th Infantry Regiment when the war broke out. He led the 168th and 355th Infantry Divisions on the Eastern Front prior to assuming command of the 352nd in November 1943.

A holder of the Knight's Cross with Oak Leaves, General Kraiss was mortally wounded near St.-Lô on August 2 and died on August 6, 1944 (Keilig, p. 183).

34. MacDonald and Blumenson, "Recovery," p. 87.

35. OB 1945, p. 238.

36. Ryan, p. 199.

37. Carell, p. 82; Harrison, pp. 311–13.

38. Harrison, p. 313.

39. Carell, p. 86.

40. Harrison, p. 320.

41. Lionel F. Ellis, *Victory in the West*, Volume I, *The Battle of Normandy* (London: Her Majesty's Stationery Office, 1968), p. 223.

42. Ryan, p. 256. General of Artillery Walter Warlimont had served as Jodl's deputy at OKW since 1938. Their relationship was strained by 1944, and Warlimont was involuntarily retired in September and was never reemployed. He was later convicted at Nuremberg as a minor war criminal and spent several years in prison.

43. Ryan, pp. 256–57. Major General Horst von Buttlar-Brandenfels took command of the 9th Panzer Division on the Western Front in March 1945 and led it for the rest of the war.

44. Hart, II, p. 550.

45. Ryan, pp. 284–85.

46. Ibid, p. 285.

47. In army circles, Lieutenant General Rudolf Schmundt was considered a hard working man of integrity (despite his unquestioning loyalty to Hitler) but was considered to be not very bright. He had been Hitler's armed forces adjutant since early 1938 and was named chief of the Army Personnel Office (HPA) in October 1942.

Schmundt was blinded during the July 20, 1944, attempt on Hitler's life and for weeks hung between life and death. He finally succumbed in the Rastenburg hospital on October 1, 1944. Hitler had promoted him to general of infantry the month before.

48. Toland, p. 1075.

49. For the full story of the Battle of Pegasus Bridge, see Stephen Ambrose, *Pegasus Bridge, June 6, 1944* (New York: Simon and Schuster, Inc., 1988).

50. Ellis, I, p. 199.

51. Alexander McKee, *Last Round against Rommel* (New York: Signet Books, 1966), p. 34.

52. Wilhelm Richter was born in Hirschberg in 1892 and entered the Imperial Army as a Fahnenjunker in 1913. Commissioned in the artillery in 1913, he fought in World War I and then served in the Reichsheer. In 1939 he was a colonel, commanding the 30th Artillery Regiment, when World War II started. He was named commander of the 35th Artillery Command in 1941 and in early 1943 was deputy commander of a Luftwaffe Field division. He was named commander of the 716th Infantry Division in April 1943, a month after he had been promoted to major general. He was promoted to lieutenant general on April 1, 1944 (Keilig, p. 276).

53. Foster, pp. 298–302.

54. Carell, p. 91.

55. Ibid., pp. 91–92. Hart (II, p. 546) blames the British failure on the "excessive caution of the commanders on the spot."

56. Ibid., p. 92.

57. Luck, p. 150. Despite his failures on D-Day, Feuchtinger was promoted to lieutenant general effective August 1, 1944. Later, an investigation was launched to examine Feuchtinger's conduct during the Battle of Normandy. When the investigating officer arrived at the headquarters of the 21st Panzer Division on Christmas Eve, he learned that Feuchtinger was at home, spending the holidays with his family—away without leave while his division was fighting against vastly superior Allied forces on the West Wall! Feuchtinger was relieved of his command in January 1945 and court-martialed and condemned in March. Due to his Nazi Party connections, however, he was not executed. He worked for the Americans after the war and died in Krefeld about 1958.

58. Ellis, I, p. 212.

59. Ibid., p. 223.

60. Ibid., p. 212.

61. Ryan, p. 296; Carell, p. 101.

62. Ryan, p. 297. The 716th Infantry Division lost more than 6,000 men on June 6 and, on or about June 11, was withdrawn to Perpignan on the Mediterranean coast to rebuild. Here it was caught up in the Allied invasion of southern France. It was sent to Alsace to rebuild that fall. Despite the fact that he was largely responsible for preventing Montgomery from capturing Caen on D-Day, Richter's performance as a divisional commander was obviously judged as inadequate by OKW. He was relieved of his command in September and was unemployed until November, when he was named deputy commander of an infantry division—a definite demotion! He gave up this post on December 25 and was unemployed until February 1, 1945, when he assumed command of the 14th Luftwaffe Field Division, a static coastal defense unit in north-central Norway. He was still there when the war ended. After two years in prisoner-of-war camps, he retired to Rendsburg, the former home base of his regiment, where he died on February 4, 1971.

63. McKee, pp. 58–59; Carell, pp. 102–4.

64. Irving, p. 374.

65. Ryan, pp. 298–99.

66. Ryan, pp. 285, 294.
67. Ruge, "Invasion," p. 336.
68. Ryan, p. 301.
69. Irving, p. 374.

CHAPTER 3

HOLDING FAST

By nightfall on June 6 the German situation was quite precarious. The left flank of the LXXXIV Corps (i.e., Utah Beach/Ste.-Mère-Eglise sector) had collapsed; indeed, the Americans had lost fewer than 200 men on Utah Beach, which was the smallest number of casualties suffered on any of the beaches. The Americans at Omaha Beach had gained two to three miles, primarily because of Bradley's ruthless determination to succeed. He had sent in wave after wave of infantry and had shelled his own beaches until the 352nd Division could no longer hold. The American losses had been enormous. Of the 6,603 U.S. casualties reported on D-Day (1,465 killed, 3,184 wounded, and 1,954 captured or missing), the airborne divisions had lost 2,499. Almost all the remainder had been lost by the U.S. 1st and 29th Infantry divisions on Omaha Beach. As June 6 ended, Omaha Beach was the only landing point not secure. Of the 2,400 tons of supplies the U.S. planners had scheduled to put on the beach on D-Day, only 100 tons actually reached shore. Omaha was short about 45 percent of its men, 50 percent of its vehicles, and more than 70 percent of its materiel and heavy equipment. On both American beaches, Bradley had planned to land 107,000 men, 14,000 vehicles, and 14,500 tons of supplies by the evening of June 7; when the second day of the invasion ended, he had landed 87,000 men, 7,000 vehicles, and less than 4,000 tons of supplies.[1] This shortage of 20 percent of his manpower, half his vehicles, and 75 percent of his materiel in the opening round of the invasion was a direct result of Rommel's defensive methods and introduces the question of what would have happened had the Field Marshal been given a free hand in his conduct of the defense. This question, of course, can never be answered, but the U.S. position on Utah Beach might well have been untenable had Rommel been allowed to position the panzer reserves where he wanted them; there is little doubt that

Omaha Beach could have been wiped out under those circumstances. In addition, more than half of the 291 American landing craft lost or damaged on June 6 was due to Rommel's offshore obstacles.[2]

Conditions were better in the British zone, where only 3,500–4,000 casualties had been suffered (1,000 of which were Canadian). Second British Army had four divisions and three armored brigades (about 75,000 men and 900 tanks) on shore by the dawn of June 7. However, the British Official History also concludes that Rommel's obstacles were successful: 258 of their landing craft had been destroyed, many of them by obstacles.[3]

In the center of Marcks's line, Bayeux, defended by the small 915th Grenadier Regiment under Lieutenant Colonel Meyer, was about to fall. The right flank, which defended the approaches to Caen, was also on the verge of collapse but still held on, thanks primarily to the commitment of the 21st Panzer Division.

The commander of the LXXXIV Corps was ordinarily an easygoing man. A brilliant officer of the old school, General Marcks had always been disliked by the Nazis because of his connections with the former chancellor, General Kurt von Schleicher, whom Hitler had had murdered in 1934. (Marcks had been Schleicher's press officer during his 57-day chancellorship and prior to that had held the same position in the brief reign of Chancellor Franz von Papen.) On the other hand, they recognized his abilities, for he had been one of the architects of the 1941 invasion of the Soviet Union. Marcks was also quite popular with his men. He wore an artificial limb in place of the leg he had lost while commanding a division on the Russian Front in 1941. On June 6 Erich Marcks's customary calm was gone, not because of the invasion but because he could not get anyone to believe it had arrived. Since early morning he had been in almost constant contact with 7th Army, Army Group B, and Fuehrer HQ. "I need every available armored unit for a counterattack!" he exclaimed, but the panzer reserves remained uncommitted. Field Marshal von Rundstedt, even though he tried to help, still believed the landings were a diversion; Erwin Rommel was in a car, speeding back to the front, so no one could reach him; finally, Adolf Hitler was asleep, and his subordinates were afraid to awaken him. "It's a disgrace!" Marcks snapped in disgust.[4]

Major Friedrich Hayn, the corps intelligence officer, reported to the 7th Army that he had identified three Allied airborne divisions, which represented three-quarters of the paratroopers known to be in the United Kingdom. Other important units had also been spotted: elements of the U.S. 1st and 4th Armored Divisions, the British 3rd and 50th Infantry Divisions, and the Canadian 3rd Infantry Division, as well as the British 7th Armoured Division. That left only the 51st Highlander and the 1st British Armoured Division unaccounted for from the British elements of the 8th Army in North Africa. Clearly the Allies would not commit the bulk of their veterans of North Africa and Sicily to a diversionary operation. Major Hayn's report concluded: "If this isn't the invasion—then what units are they going to use for it?"[5]

Lieutenant Colonel Vorwerk, the 7th Army's Intelligence Officer, endorsed this report and immediately forwarded it to Paris, where Lieutenant Colonel Meyer-Detring, the Intelligence Officer for OB West, signaled, "I agree with you entirely."[6] However his boss, von Rundstedt, remained skeptical—as did Adolf Hitler.

One of the strangest aspects of the invasion was the metamorphosis that went on in Adolf Hitler's mind on June 6. The Fuehrer, who had correctly guessed the location and strategic objective of the invasion months in advance, now decided that the landings were in fact a diversion. Like Jodl, his chief military advisor, he became obsessed with the notion that Eisenhower's real thrust would come east of the Seine, in the Pas-de-Calais area. He clung to this idea for weeks and steadfastly refused to weaken the 15th Army.[7] As a result of the wishful thinking in Berlin and Berchtesgaden, few reinforcements were dispatched to Normandy in the first, decisive weeks of the invasion. The units OKW did send were armored, although the terrain was ideally suited for nonmotorized infantry. Rommel's front was and would remain extremely short of ground troops throughout his active tenure as commander of Army Group B. Conversely, when the front finally did break, the Germans were forced to wage mobile warfare at a time when most of their panzer divisions were burnt out. Unable to wage a war of maneuver, they had no alternative but to retreat to the frontiers of the Reich. The Battle of France was thus lost with the Battle of Normandy.

It was 3:40 P.M. on D-Day when General Blumentritt, chief of staff of OB West, telephoned General Speidel and informed him that SS Lieutenant General Fritz Witt's 12th SS Panzer Division and Lieutenant General Fritz Bayerlein's Panzer Lehr Division finally had been released to 7th Army.[8] Eleven hours had been wasted, but the waste would not end here. While his division assembled, Bayerlein drove to 7th Army headquarters, where Colonel General Dollmann ordered him to move out for Caen at 5:00 P.M.—in broad daylight! Bayerlein had shared Rommel's experiences against Allied fighter-bombers in North Africa and had been pinned down beside the Desert Fox on more than one occasion, so he understood the danger posed by enemy domination of the air. A night move was dangerous enough, but a daylight move positively invited disaster. Panzer Lehr, assembling at Nogent le Rotrou, 75 miles southwest of Paris, would have to travel 90 miles to reach Caen. Bayerlein objected strongly, saying that it would be better to advance cautiously and arrive on June 8, but Dollmann refused to budge. He even proposed a change in preselected approach routes, but Bayerlein held firm on this issue—any modifications at this stage would surely result in chaos, as Dollmann should have known. To make matters worse, Dollmann imposed radio silence on the division. "As if radio silence could have stopped the fighter-bombers and reconnaissance planes from spotting us!" an angry and bitter Bayerlein recalled.[9]

As Bayerlein foresaw, the Anglo-Saxons quickly detected the move. Panzer Lehr's approach march was a nightmare. The fighter-bombers were soon everywhere, shooting up the march columns and blasting bridges, crossroads, and towns along the division's five routes of advance. Night brought no relief, because the Allies now knew the location of the division's columns and illuminated the countryside with flares, enabling the pilots to attack new targets. All the while the columns became more and more scattered, disorganized, and fragmented. The panzers were relatively safe from the nighttime air attacks (only five were knocked out), but the rest of the division was mauled. During the night of June 6/7, Panzer Lehr lost 40 loaded fuel trucks; 84 half-tracks, prime movers, and self-propelled guns; and dozens of other vehicles.

The next day, June 7, Bayerlein met with SS General Josef "Sepp" Dietrich, the commander of the I SS Panzer Corps, at his headquarters north of Harcourt.[10] Dietrich informed him that Panzer Lehr and 12th SS Panzer would launch a counterattack on the morning of June 8 to push the Allies back into the sea. After receiving his orders from Hitler's former bodyguard, Bayerlein returned to his unit. On the way back, Allied fighter-bombers attacked his car. Bayerlein and his aide escaped with a few minor shrapnel wounds, but his driver was killed. Incidents of this nature would occur with alarming frequency for the rest of the campaign.

Panzer Lehr would not be able to counterattack on June 8. Its battered and disorganized formations continued arriving in their assembly areas in dribs and drabs; the division would not be able to function as a unit for another critical 24 hours.

The 12th SS "Hitler Jugend" Division also had problems reaching the area of operations. At 7:00 A.M. on D-Day, I SS Panzer Corps (Dietrich) placed it under LXXXI Corps Headquarters at Rouen and ordered it to move to Lisieux. The division was on the road by midmorning. Then, at midafternoon, Army Group B (i.e., General Speidel) changed its destination from Lisieux to a point west of Caen—meaning that it had been moving in the wrong direction. Its vanguard was now 44 miles from its assembly area, whereas it would have been only 22 miles from it had it not moved at all. The division changed directions at 4:00 P.M., by which time the cloud cover that had initially hampered Allied air activities had lifted. Promptly jumped by fighter-bombers (which the German soldiers called "Jabos"), the young SS men suffered heavy casualties and soon went to ground. SS Captain Rudolf von Ribbentrop—the commander of the 3rd Company, 12th SS Panzer Regiment, and the son of Hitler's foreign minister—was among the wounded. Further attempts to use the road network were suspended until after dark, and the division would not reach the Caen area in strength until June 8.

The III Flak Corps also accomplished very little on D-Day. The corps commander, Lieutenant General Wolfgang Pickert, left his headquarters south of Amiens for a tour of inspection early that morning and did not learn of the landings until after noon. Although he started his four regiments to the threatened sector immediately, the vital antiaircraft guns did not reach the front until June 8–9.[11]

Meanwhile, during the night of June 6/7, Field Marshal Erwin Rommel finally took charge of the German combat effort. It was already too late to repulse the invasion on the beaches, but the determined Swabian began to reestablish some degree of control over the battlefield. He found that the British under General Dempsey had secured a beachhead 20 miles long and up to 6 miles deep, while the Americans under General Bradley had a second beachhead 9 to 2 miles deep, although the Americans at Utah and Omaha Beaches had not yet linked up. All along the front the 716th and 352nd divisions were resisting stubbornly but were gradually being crushed by elements of nine enemy divisions. Early in the morning of June 7, Rommel (in agreement with Rundstedt) ordered two divisions to move to the western part of the Cotentin at once: the 77th Infantry (from near St.-Lô) and—with Hitler's permission—the 17th SS Panzer Grenadier (from OKW reserve, south of the Loire). Later that day, OKW also gave Rommel permission to use the 3rd Parachute Division and Headquarters, II Parachute Corps. The Fox ordered all of these units to the western Cotentin at once. Initially, all three divisions were placed under HQ, II Parachute Corps, which was temporarily subordinated to LXXXIV Corps.[12] The field marshal also called up the 2nd Panzer Division (then in Army Group B reserve near Amiens).

In the meantime, Rundstedt became convinced that Cherbourg was the target of the Allied invasion. He ordered up two more panzer divisions (the 1st SS and 2nd SS), as well as the 8th Mortar (*Werfer*) Brigade and the artillery forces from the three artillery schools in France. He also put in an urgent request to OKW for more reinforcements. The 2nd SS started for Normandy from southern France (it had been part of Army Group G's reserve), but the High Command would not release the 1st SS, which remained in Belgium as part of OKW reserve.

Meanwhile, the Desert Fox tried to throw the Allies back into the sea. He ordered a counterattack by the 21st and 12th SS Panzer divisions for June 7, but Feuchtinger had only about 70 "runners" (operational tanks) left, and the 12th SS—as we have seen—was badly delayed by the Allied air forces. Also, Dietrich's I SS Panzer Corps HQ, which had just come up to direct the counterattack, was having a hard time getting itself organized, because fighting the Western Allies turned out to be much more difficult than fighting Russians. Despite a personal visit from Rommel, Dietrich's staff could not get control of its sector, and the counterattack never materialized.

"It was also [now] clear to the last man that the invasion had succeeded, that it could now be only a matter of days or weeks before the Allies would have landed sufficient forces to be able to mount an attack on Paris, and finally the German Reich," Baron Hans von Luck wrote later.

If it were not for that damned air superiority!

Even by night 'Christmas trees' hung in the sky bathing the whole area in bright light. The air attacks never stopped; the navy laid a barrage of fire on our positions and bombarded the city of Caen, which was a focal point in our lateral communications.

By day it was even worse: at any movement on the battlefield, even of an individual vehicle, the enemy reacted with concentrated fire from the navy or attacks by fighter-bombers. Either our radio communications were being intercepted or the navy had divided up the area into grid squares and had only to pass on the square number to launch a sudden concentration of fire.[13]

On June 7 the American and British forces continued their unrelenting attacks, and Rommel desperately called for reinforcements. Lieutenant Colonel Baron von Aufsess's 30th Mobile Infantry Brigade was sent to the aid of General Kraiss's 352nd Infantry Division, but its inexperienced soldiers, equipped mainly with bicycles, were subjected to constant aerial attacks. It was smashed to bits and badly demoralized by nightfall and was never of much combat value after that.[14]

The mobile infantry brigade was supposed to have reinforced Lieutenant Colonel Karl Meyer at Bayeux, in the center of the German line. It was so badly scattered, however, that those who did arrive were too disorganized to be of effective help; thus, early on June 7 Meyer faced the bulk of the powerful British 50th Infantry Division with two understrength battalions of his 915th Grenadier Regiment. By noon the battle was lost. The Caen–St.-Lô road was cut and Bayeux was soon cleared, while the remnants of Combat Group Meyer was being pushed back toward Caen. By nightfall the 915th Grenadier no longer existed. Colonel Meyer was among the dead.[15] Meanwhile, the British 47th Commando successfully infiltrated German lines and took Port-en-Bessin, setting the stage for the linkup of the British beachheads with the American forces from Omaha Beach. (This took place the next day, June 8.)

On the German left flank, the U.S. 82nd Airborne Division linked up with the U.S. VII Corps, advancing inland from Utah Beach. The 795th Georgian Battalion collapsed, and Turqueville fell. Lieutenant General von Schlieben realized that the situation was deteriorating rapidly and that only a determined counterattack could restore it. His 709th Infantry Division, supported by three artillery battalions and the Sturm Battalion, attacked again. They pushed the paratroopers back to the outskirts of Ste.-Mère-Eglise, but at that moment the U.S. 4th Infantry Division arrived, along with about 60 Sherman tanks. They quickly overran the 1058th Grenadier Regiment, which broke up and ceased to exist as an organized combat force. The 709th Infantry Division was crippled. After this defeat, von Schlieben gave up all thought of offensive action and concentrated on blocking the American drive on Cherbourg, which he knew would begin soon.

The most important battles of June 7 occurred north of Caen, on the right flank of the German battle line. This old university city was the most vital position in Normandy. Fifty miles from the Seine and only 120 miles from Paris, Caen was a departmental capital and the hub of the highway and railroad network in the Cotentin area; more important, it dominated the surrounding region. North of the city lay terrain well-suited for the defense, but south of it the ground was much flatter. Here lay ideal tank country. If the Allies reached this area, they could not be stopped. For this reason Rommel sent most of his best units to this part of the front. Montgomery's failure to capture Caen on D-Day would have bitter repercussions for him and his men. They would have the thankless job of holding off Rommel and pinning down his panzer reserves, while the Americans extended Rommel's left flank and tried to stretch it to the breaking point.

Montgomery was never the type to give up easily. He tried to take Caen by frontal assault on June 7. The British 3rd and Canadian 3rd Infantry divisions surged forward against the survivors of the 21st Panzer Division. Each Allied division was accompanied by an armored brigade. The British 3rd was halted by the panzer soldiers, but the Canadians continued forward, ignoring the fact that their left flank was now exposed. Their leading brigade, the 27th Armoured, drove to the Carpiquet Airfield, only two miles north of Caen, completely unaware that SS Colonel Kurt "Panzer" Meyer's 25th SS Panzer Grenadier Regiment, the vanguard of the 12th SS Panzer Division, had arrived at the airfield shortly before. Meyer, the veteran of a dozen campaigns, including three years on the Russian Front, lay a skillful ambush for the inexperienced Canadians.[16] His young SS men maintained complete fire discipline until the tanks were within 200 yards of their positions;

then they opened up on the sides of the steel monsters, where the armor was much thinner than in the front. Twenty-eight Shermans were quickly knocked out, while machine-gun fire riddled the ranks of the advancing infantrymen, who had needlessly exposed themselves. The Canadians suffered heavy casualties and retreated in disorder. Sensing victory, Meyer launched a frontal attack, but the Canadians rallied quickly and turned them back with severe losses.[17]

After the battle, the SS men—who had heard rumors that the Canadians were shooting prisoners—began executing their own POWs. One survivor recalled seeing German troops shooting or bayoneting several wounded prisoners, while another was deliberately run over by a tank. Another group of Germans came upon a medic tending a wounded tanker. They shot them both.[18]

At the Abbaye Ardenne, "Panzer" Meyer's command post, members of the SS reconnaissance company tried to turn over seven prisoners of war to the regimental staff company. "What should we do with these prisoners? They only eat up rations," Meyer declared. Then, in a quieter voice, he ordered, "In the future no more prisoners are to be taken."[19]

When he heard that atrocities were being committed, Fritz Witt, the commander of the 12th SS Panzer Division, ordered an investigation and demanded a written report from Meyer; however, he never received it, as we shall see.

Fighting all along the Normandy front was fierce in June 1944, but between the Canadians and the SS it was particularly savage. The Canadians and SS quickly developed a special hatred for each other, and neither took the other prisoner very often. SS Major Bernard Siebken, the commander of the II/26th SS Panzer Regiment, for example, murdered several prisoners of war at Le Mesnil-Patry. He was tried by a British court in Hamburg after the war and, despite the protests of B. H. Liddell Hart, was executed on January 20, 1949. His regimental commander, SS Colonel Wilhelm Mohnke, was reportedly involved in more than one atrocity. A quick-tempered and harsh man—even toward other SS—he was generally disliked, even by his comrades. On June 11 he interrogated three Canadian prisoners and, after shouting at them and gesturing in anger, had them taken to the edge of a deep bomb crater and shot. The Allies discovered their bodies several days later. Mohnke was also accused of being involved in other atrocities and would probably have suffered the same fate as Siebken, had he not been captured by the Russians in 1945. He is one of the few people who can consider himself lucky to have been captured by the Soviets. He was released in October 1955; by then passions had died down, and the West German government had been established. He became a prosperous businessman and at last report (1992) was living in retirement in a suburb of Hamburg at the age of 82.

Like Siebken, "Panzer" Meyer was also tried after the war for shooting 30 Canadian prisoners at the Abbey, Authie, and Buron. He was found guilty of the Abbaye Ardenne atrocity, but not of the other two, and was sentenced to death on December 28, 1945. Two weeks later, however, Major General Chris Vokes, the commander of the Canadian Occupation Forces in Germany, commuted his sentence to life imprisonment. Dr. Konrad Adenauer, the chancellor of West Germany, engineered his release in 1954.

Atrocities in war are never confined to one nationality. When the 12th SS pushed back the Canadians on June 7, they found the bodies of several German soldiers, apparently murdered by the Canadians, but the war crimes of the winning side are seldom investigated. General Vokes freely admitted that his men shot German prisoners, both in Italy and in northwest Europe, which may explain why he commuted Panzer Meyer's sentence so quickly. Major General Harry W. Foster, who commanded the Canadian 7th Infantry Brigade and later the 4th Armoured Division in Normandy, was president of the court-martial that condemned Meyer. His son Tony, who grew up to be a writer, asked him if there had ever been any doubt in his mind about Meyer's guilt. Tony recalled:

'Not in the slightest,' he replied. 'He was just as guilty of murder as I was at the time . . . or any other senior officer in the field during a battle. The difference between us was that I was on the winning side. That makes a big difference.'

Had the court-martial been a sham then? Vindictiveness by the victor over the vanquished? My father sighed and sipped his port reflectively. 'I don't believe Meyer pulled the trigger on his captives or gave the orders to execute any of them. But I'm sure he knew what happened. SS discipline was such that he couldn't help but know. But does that make him guilty of murder any more than I'm guilty for knowing about the German prisoners my troops killed?'

'Then why did you convict him?'

'Because I had no choice according to the rules of warfare dreamt up by a bunch of bloody barrackroom lawyers who never heard a shot fired in anger. In wartime a commanding officer is responsible for the actions of his men.'

'But that's absurd!'

'It's also military justice.'

'Then where is the truth?'

'Ah!' He nodded as if the question had troubled him too. 'I suppose in the final analysis it lies in the conscience of the victor.'[20]

Although their hatred was probably the most intense, the shooting and abusing of prisoners was not limited to the SS and Canadians. One incident particularly infuriated the Germans. On June 8 a group of soldiers from the 130th Panzer Artillery Regiment of the Panzer Lehr Division was conducting a reconnaissance on a small hill (probably Hill 102), just south of Cristot, when they were surprised by a British patrol, which was operating behind German lines. Captured were Colonel Luxemburger, the regimental commander who had lost an arm in World War I; Major Zeissler, one of his battalion commanders; Captain Count Clary-Aldringen, the regimental adjutant; and six others. Two British officers beat Luxemburger into unconsciousness and bound him to the front of a scout car. All of the other Germans were shot. When the Allied patrol attempted to make its way back through German lines—using the one-armed man as a human shield—a German antitank round destroyed it. The critically wounded colonel was rescued, but died several days later in a field hospital.

Of the other eight Germans, only Captain Clary survived, and he was badly wounded. Feigning death until after the British left, he managed to crawl away and was found by some soldiers from the II/26th SS Panzer Grenadier Regiment. He was the only German to survive the atrocity.

Fortunately, such incidents were the exception, rather than the rule, on the Western Front in World War II. After they were captured, both Germans and Anglo-Americans stood a reasonably good chance of surviving the journey to the POW camps. This was not true on the Eastern Front, nor was it always true to SS men on the Western Front. Perhaps that is one reason they fought so hard.

Nor are Americans totally without guilt. During my conversations with U.S. veterans of World War II, including some of my relatives, I sometimes learned more than I really wanted to. But, to use the vernacular of my native South, "I ain't tellin'."

Like Hitler, OKW, OB West, and Army Group B, the High Command of the Luftwaffe (OKL) was paralyzed with indecision on D-Day. On its own initiative, I Fighter Corps of Air Fleet Reich dispatched 400 fighters to preselected bases in France on D-Day and D + 1 (i.e., June 7). Thus reinforced, 3rd Air Fleet was able to send 350–400 fighters against the Allies on June 8. Swarms of Allied fighters (perhaps as many as 4,000) intercepted them before they could even reach the invasion area. After several such futile efforts, the squadrons of I Fighter Corps returned to Germany in remnants on June 18.[21]

The organic elements of the 3rd Air Fleet (shown in Table 3.1) fared no better. On D-Day, Lieutenant General Alfred Buelowius's II Air Corps had only 67 FW-190F fighter-bombers, 42 reconnaissance aircraft, and 52 nearly useless Ju-88 long-range fighters designed to protect U-boats. Despite the odds against it, the corps nevertheless tried to perform its missions of providing reconnaissance information and close-air support for the ground forces. It was quickly decimated by Allied Spitfires, Mustangs, and Thunderbolts. Almost all of the fighter-bombers had to jettison their bombs before they even came near the beaches. About 150 fighter-bombers were sent from the Reich to reinforce II Air Corps, but they were also mauled within a day or so. On June 12 Sperrle admitted defeat and ordered all fighter-bomber operations to cease immediately. Second Air Corps was placed under the operational control of II Fighter Corps and was absorbed by it shortly thereafter.[22]

Table 3.1
Order of Battle, 3rd Air Fleet
June 6, 1944

3rd Air Fleet: *Field Marshal Hugo Sperrle*

    X Air Corps: *Lieutenant General Alexander Holle*
    Anti-Shipping Aircraft and Missile-Carrying Bombers

    IX Air Corps: *Major General Dietrich Peltz*
    Conventional Bombers

    II Fighter Corps: *Major General Werner Junck*
    Single-engine Day Fighters

    II Air Corps: *Lieutenant General Alfred Buelowius*
    Tactical Reconnaissance and Close-Air Support Aircraft

Major General Werner Junck's II Fighter Corps was reinforced to a strength of 350 aircraft (Me-109 and FW-190 fighters) by June 8, and it received another 100 on June 10. Operating out of damaged bases, without adequate fuel supplies and with inexperienced and under-trained pilots, however, it had little chance against the Anglo-Saxons. It was never able to relieve the hard-pressed ground forces, disrupt the Allied landings, or even protect its own bases. Junck was held responsible and was sacked on July 1. He was replaced by Lieutenant General Alfred Buelowius, but the change made no difference.[23]

Lieutenant General Alexander Holle's X Air Corps—a specialized, antishipping force—included 136 bombers (mostly Do-217s and FW-200s) modified to carry radio-controlled guided bombs and glider bombs, as well as the 136 Ju-88 torpedo bombers of the 2nd Air Division. Its attacks, however, were unsuccessful, and, during the first two weeks of the invasion, its guided and glider bombs sank only two Allied ships and damaged seven others. The torpedo bombers sank only three vessels and damaged two. General Peltz's IX Air Corps (the former Attack Command England) was somewhat more successful. By operating at night, some of its 261 twin-engine conventional bombers (Ju-88s, Ju-188s, and Do-217s) were able to reach the invasion area, drop naval mines near the Allied shipping lanes, and inflict some damage on the Anglo-American naval forces. Although its operations did cause delays and hindered the massive Allied buildup in Normandy, it never constituted a serious threat to the success of the invasion.[24]

At the same time the Anglo-Saxons and Germans were slaughtering each other in indecisive fighting at the front, events of even greater significance were taking place behind the lines. The British 49th Infantry, 51st Infantry, and 7th Armoured divisions were disembarking onto the mainland, almost totally unhampered by the German Navy and Luftwaffe. In the American sector the U.S. 1st Army had a strength of 5 divisions by nightfall of June 7. The Allies' foothold in Europe was growing stronger by the hour. By June 12 they had 15 divisions ashore, and 5 more landed from June 13 to 19, along with several separate armored brigades and battalions. The U.S. XIX and VIII Corps and British VIII Corps were all activated by June 16. Table 3.2 shows the arrival of the Allied divisions in the first 10 days of the campaign. The Allies had won the Battle of the Normandy Beachhead. The great buildup had begun, and the Battle of the Hedgerows was about to begin. The fall of Bayeux placed the British in a position to wheel southward on Caen. However, by June 8 Rommel's reinforcements had at last reached the area in significant numbers. His right flank was now held by the I SS Panzer Corps under Sepp Dietrich and included the 12th SS and Panzer Lehr divisions, as well as the 21st Panzer and 716th Infantry divisions, although the latter was a broken unit, with only a little more than an infantry battalion left and only a dozen artillery pieces. The Allied landings had ground it to bits. Marcks's LXXXIV Corps retained control of the left flank, with the remnants of the 352nd and 709th Infantry divisions, the disorganized 91st Air Landing Division (now under Colonel Bernhard Klosterkemper), and the newly arrived 6th Parachute Regiment, all operating against the Americans.

Rommel, who personally liked Sepp Dietrich, apparently did not think much of the idea of entrusting him with responsibility for directing the great counterattack, especially because his staff was in such chaos. Dietrich, a butcher's son and World War I sergeant major, was a longtime Nazi. His personal friendship with Adolf Hitler was his chief qualification for high command. Rundstedt later referred to him as "decent, but stupid." Rommel probably shared this opinion, for he used his remaining influence in the High Command to get General Geyr von Schweppenburg appointed commander of the entire sector east of Dives as far as Tilly, thus placing all three panzer divisions under his personal supervision. Although Rommel and Geyr had serious disagreements on strategic questions, Rommel recognized his tactical abilities and so chose him to attempt to throw the Allies into the sea. Initially, Rundstedt placed the Headquarters, Panzer Group West, directly under HQ, 7th

Table 3.2
The Allied Buildup
June 6–15, 1944

Division	Date of Arrival*
U.S. 82nd Airborne	June 6
U.S. 101st Airborne	June 6
British 6th Airborne	June 6
U.S. 4th Infantry	June 6
U.S. 1st Infantry	June 6
U.S. 29th Infantry	June 6
British 50th Infantry	June 6
Canadian 3rd Infantry	June 6
British 3rd Infantry	June 6
U.S. 2nd Infantry	June 8
British 7th Armoured	June 9
U.S. 2nd Armoured	June 13
British 49th Infantry	June 13
U.S. 30th Infantry	June 14
U.S. 90th Infantry	June 15
British 11th Armoured	June 15

*Refers to the date the division completed disembarkation; several of these divisions began arriving days earlier. This table excludes several British and Canadian independent armoured brigades.

Source: Montgomery, pp. 51–60.

Army, apparently so that his friend Geyr would not have to serve directly under Rommel. This arrangement proved to be cumbersome at first and then nominal; besides, now that the battle had been joined, Geyr and the Desert Fox were united in purpose and actually worked well together. Finally, on June 29, the panzer group was directly subordinated to Army Group B.

Geyr had excellent human material with which to work. The 12th SS Panzer, nicknamed the "Baby Division" by the propagandists, consisted almost entirely of highly trained volunteers, most of them teenagers recruited from the Hitler Youth. It had three regiments: the 12th SS Panzer (two battalions) and the 25th and 26th SS Panzer Grenadier regiments. Panzer Lehr was much larger and, according to one source, was the only panzer division in the German Army at 100 percent strength. Although it was short a number of wheeled vehicles, it had 183 tanks and 800 tracked vehicles in three regiments: the Panzer Lehr Regiment and the 901st and 902nd Panzer Grenadier regiments. This unit was specially designed to oppose the invasion, and its ranks were dominated by young veterans of North Africa and the Russian Front. The average age of its enlisted men was only 21 1/2 years. Colonel General Heinz Guderian, the Inspector-General of Panzer Troops, told Bayerlein in April 1944 that, with this single division, he (Bayerlein) would throw the Allies back into the sea."[25] However, like most of his contemporaries, Guderian was an "Eastern General" and did not reckon with Allied air power when he made his prediction.

The units were ready on June 8, but Geyr was not. It takes time to move a major headquarters and set up communications, and without the headquarters of Panzer Group West the attack would surely fail, so the counteroffensive was postponed until June 9. Meanwhile, thousands of additional American, British, and Canadian soldiers poured onto the European mainland.

It was necessary to commit the bulk of the 12th SS and Panzer Lehr divisions in a defensive role on June 8, just to hold the line. Most of the 12th SS engaged the Canadians and immediately began launching local counterattacks. They retook the villages of Bretteville and Putot-en-Bessin, although Putot changed hands again the next day. Panzer Lehr was also heavily engaged. By nightfall the lines in the Caen sector were solidifying.

Rommel himself turned up at Bayerlein's headquarters at the village of Le Mesnil-Patry on the evening of June 8. He angrily informed his former chief of staff that the British 50th Division had taken Bayeux and ordered Bayerlein to deploy Panzer Lehr in two combat groups from the Norrey-Brouay area to Tilly so that he would be in a position to attack Bayeux on the morning of June 9. Before leaving, however, Rommel told his old friend what he really thought—they would eventually be pushed back across the Rhine, and they would escape with virtually nothing.[26]

On the German left flank, the Americans were trying to consolidate their hard-won gains and link up their beachheads. The U.S. V Corps at Omaha Beach and the U.S. VII Corps at Utah were prevented from joining hands by elements of the 352nd Division at Isigny (near the coast) and the 6th Parachute Regiment at Carentan. On the afternoon of June 8 General Bradley sent the U.S. 29th Division against Isigny and the 101st Airborne Division against Carentan, while the U.S. 1st Infantry Division attacked eastward from Omaha Beach, with the objective of linking up the American and British sectors.[27]

The 29th Division met little organized resistance in its drive on Isigny. Kraiss's 352nd Division had already been shattered by two days of battle against five American divisions, the U.S. Navy, and huge numbers of aircraft. The rapid thrust of the U.S. 29th brushed aside the remnants of the 914th Grenadier Regiment and captured all the remaining guns of the 352nd Artillery Regiment. Isigny fell that night, and the American beachheads were effectively joined, although the junction lacked depth.

The U.S. 101st Airborne Division had a much harder time against the 6th Parachute Regiment. Here the American paratroopers met men of the same skill and toughness as themselves—a bitter fight ensued. Baron Friedrich-August von der Heydte's regiment had already lost all its vehicles at Ste.-Mère-Eglise, and one of its battalions had been cut off and was still missing. (Later, it was discovered that the Americans had trapped it against the swamp near the village of Ste.-Mère-du-Mont and destroyed it. Of its 700 men, more than 200 were killed and 25 escaped. The rest were captured.)[28] Despite being shorthanded, the battle-hardened survivors of the 6th Parachute still had a lot of fight left; they also had excellent defensive positions, for this was hedgerow country.

The hedgerows of the French *bocage* country are not the simple bushes the normal American associates with the term "hedge." These are earthen dikes, averaging about four feet in height but frequently higher, constructed to box in fields and orchards of a few acres. None is large, but all are potential earthworks. Bushes, tangled vegetation, and even trees grow all over the dikes. In 1944 they provided the Germans with excellent concealment and cover. (There are not nearly as many hedgerows in Normandy today as there were in 1944.) No sooner was one hedgerow taken than another faced the Allies. Each field became a separate battleground. The hedgerow country was ideal for the static defense and very difficult for either side to launch even local attacks. Under these conditions, the U.S. 101st Airborne was unable to take Carentan on June 8. Bradley realized that this town must fall before the U.S. beachhead was completely out of danger. Against this background, the Battle of Carentan began in earnest. It would continue for six days.

While Geyr organized his counterattack on the right flank and von der Heydte held the center, Rommel turned his attention to the left, where General von Schlieben had organized a makeshift defensive line along the Montebourg–Ste.-Mère-Eglise–Fontenay–Rovenoville roads. He held this line with miscellaneous battle groups from the 243rd and 352nd divisions, as well as his own 709th. Most of these units had been badly damaged in the fighting of June 6 and 7, but the Americans were too busy at Isigny and Carentan to press their advantage on June 8, thereby giving Schlieben time to build a thin line to screen Cherbourg. Erwin Rommel, who had taken this port from the French in the campaign of 1940, realized that Cherbourg had to be Eisenhower's first strategic objective of the campaign. He wanted to reinforce Schlieben as rapidly as possible without jeopardizing Geyr's counterattack, so he ordered the 77th Infantry Division (then in Brittany) and the 17th SS Panzer Grenadier Division (which OKW had just released to him) to the left flank. The 3rd Parachute Division was also sent to the front, as was the Headquarters, II Parachute Corps, then in Brittany. It would take these units days to reach the front, but when they did arrive, Rommel placed the 17th SS Panzer Grenadier and 3rd Parachute divisions under General Eugen Meindl's II Parachute Corps on the left-center of the German line, with the mission of holding St.-Lô. Schlieben's makeshift force continued to hold the far left.

On June 8, German military intelligence scored three important, if lucky, victories. About noon a bundle of captured documents was turned over to intelligence officers at LXXXIV Corps. They had been retrieved from a shell-riddled landing craft on the Normandy coast, where the body of an American naval beachmaster was found among the dead. The interpreters went to work immediately, and soon the Germans had the entire operations plan of the U.S. V and VII Corps, as well as that of the adjacent British XXX Corps, including their day-by-day tactical objectives on the Cotentin Peninsula! The documents also revealed what Rommel had already guessed: Cherbourg was the strategic objective of the American landings.

Elsewhere on the front, SS men took a map from a knocked-out Canadian tank. On it, Nazi positions were accurately marked, even down to individual light machine-gun positions. This document indicated the efficiency of the intelligence network against which the Germans were operating. From another damaged tank an Allied radio code book was lifted, and it gave the code names for all the German positions in the British zone. Inexplicably, the British continued to use this book long after it had been compromised and thus allowed the Germans to see at least a portion of the Allied tactical plans.

Although these finds were of great value, they could not be taken advantage of to the maximum extent, for despite the mounting evidence, Hitler still insisted that the invasion would come at Pas de Calais. The fortunate triumphs of the German intelligence officers were largely thrown away by the High Command.

On June 9 General Geyr was at last ready to launch the long-delayed German panzer counterattack—at least two days too late. That morning he conferred with SS Colonel "Panzer" Meyer at the Ardenne Abbey, outside Caen. Meyer brought up the subject of how Germany could win the war by repelling the invasion. Geyr cut him short by saying: "My dear Meyer, the war can only be won now by political means."[29] Nevertheless, he ordered the attack. The 21st Panzer on the right flank would attack out of the Caen area, accompanied by the 12th SS Panzer in the center. On the German left, Bayerlein's Panzer Lehr Division would retake Bayeux. The overall objective was to force a breakthrough to the coast along a wide front. Further planning would depend on the development of this thrust. Meanwhile, Montgomery, Dempsey, and Bradley met and made some plans of their own. As the senior ground commander, Montgomery ranked above both Dempsey and Bradley, and he ordered a double envelopment of Caen. The British 6th Airborne Division, the 51st Highlander Division, and the 4th Armoured Brigade would provide the left hook east of the city. Their objective was to capture the village of Cagny and pin down the German reserves. The main blow would be to the west, where the XXX Corps, spearheaded by the 7th Armoured Division, would take Villers-Bocage and Evrecy. When the two spearheads reached their final objectives, the British 1st Airborne Division would be dropped between them and complete the encirclement of Caen.[30] It was a bold plan, though decidedly overly ambitious.

The German and British plans were in diametric opposition, and their timing was virtually identical. The result was a head-on collision all along the line.

On June 9 the 21st Panzer Division attacked into the British airborne bridgehead on the Orne, just as the 51st Highlander Division prepared to attack out of it. The 12th SS Panzer struck north along the Caen-Bayeux road, just as the Canadian 3rd Division prepared to move south along the same road. Panzer Lehr, advancing on Bayeux from the south, ran directly into the British 7th Armoured Division, which was advancing out of Bayeux in the opposite direction. The Germans were forced to commit their reserves far too early in the battle. On the other side, the British had their tanks well forward and initially did not have enough infantry up front to give them adequate protection. Panzer Lehr penetrated to within three miles of Bayeux, but a hasty Allied counterattack forced Bayerlein to a halt. Meanwhile, the four eastern Allied bridgeheads linked up and the gap between Utah Beach and the rest narrowed appreciably.

That night, Dietrich ordered Bayerlein to withdraw his division to defend the Tilly area, which now became the focus of British attention. Meanwhile, with Rommel's consent, General von Geyr went over to the defensive. He was ordered to regroup, await the arrival of the II Parachute Corps, and prepare to launch another attack.

Tactically, the fighting of June 9 was inconclusive. Strategically, it was a major Allied victory, which was completed the next evening when Allied radio intelligence and the "Ultra" codebreakers in London pinpointed Panzer Group West Headquarters in an orchard 12 miles southwest of Caen, because Geyr—a general of the Eastern Front—had never faced a tactically sophisticated enemy who possessed complete air supremacy, and he failed to make any attempt at camouflaging his command post. "Four large wireless trucks and several office caravans and tents stood in the open, and, to leave the passing pilots in no doubt as to the importance of this array, Geyr himself and his general staff officers, with resplendent red stripes down their trousers, came out with their fieldglasses from time to time to watch the RAF at work," Wilmot wrote later.[31] A saturation bombing raid pulverized the HQ and nearly wiped it out. General von Geyr was only slightly wounded, but Major General Ritter und Elder Sigismund-Helmut von Dawans, his chief of staff, was killed, along with the group's operations officer, the entire operations section, and other key personnel.[32] Only a few of the staff escaped injury. The Desert Fox himself barely escaped; he had just finished conferring with Geyr and left his HQ only an hour before the bombs fell. Ironically, Geyr's last words to Rommel as he left were to warn him to watch out for low-flying enemy aircraft!

The raid that knocked out the headquarters of Panzer Group West was a turning point in the Battle of Normandy. After this, all German planning concentrated on the defense, and all serious talk of large-scale offensive action was silenced. No German counterattack of the magnitude of June 9 was ever again launched in Normandy.

Rommel, in his *Papers*, listed five reasons for the Allied success up to June 10. First and foremost was Allied air superiority. Rommel estimated that the American and Royal air forces flew up to 27,000 sorties a day, and even the slightest daytime movement of the smallest German formation invited immediate aerial reprisals by the Allies. Movement, therefore, was restricted to night. In the short June nights of France, this often meant about nine hours. The flow of men and ammunition to the front was thus severely limited, especially when the disastrous state of the road and rail networks are taken into account. Second, the Allied heavy naval fire covered much of the Cotentin Peninsula. The Royal and American navies had 640 heavy guns; several valuable German units, including all three available panzer divisions, had been injured by these monsters. Third, the equipment of the Allies (whose industry was largely intact) was much superior to the worn German equipment. Much of Rommel's material was captured foreign stock, dating back to the early 1930s, and even the better portion of the German-manufactured equipment had been used extensively on the Eastern Front; as a result, breakdowns were common and repairs were difficult. Fourth, the Allies had an almost unlimited supply of ammunition, while Rommel's few stockpiles were dwindling fast. Fifth, the Allied use and threatened use of glider and paratroop units forced Rommel to hold back several units in critical sectors to secure his rear from these elite forces. Otherwise he could have moved these men to the front.[33]

Rommel's list is incomplete, probably because he feared that his papers might fall into the hands of the Gestapo. Therefore, criticisms of Hitler and his close associates are usually veiled, indirect, or omitted altogether. Nevertheless, the orders of the High Command hamstrung the Field Marshal's operations almost as much as the Allied air forces did. For instance, on June 9 Hitler and OKW issued a warning that Belgium was due to be invaded the next day and withheld the powerful 1st SS Panzer Division (now rebuilt to 21,000 men after returning from Russia) from Army Group B.

On June 10 the Desert Fox reported that owing to Allied air superiority, the enemy forces on the beachhead were building up faster than the reserves behind the German front. Rommel himself was very much aware of the enemy's aerial intervention, for he drove forward to Sepp Dietrich's headquarters that day. He was forced to abandon his car and take cover 30 times because of the fighter-bombers; he never did manage to reach the I SS Panzer Corps. Radio contact was also next to impossible. As of June 8, 16 of Dietrich's 20 radio sets had been knocked out, all or almost all by fighter-bombers or aerial-directed artillery fire. Not only were the pilots keeping Rommel's orders from being obeyed, they were preventing him from issuing orders altogether!

Enemy air power made it impossible to bring up the I SS Panzer Corps, the 7th Nebelwerfer Brigade, Panzer Lehr, the III Flak Corps, or the II Parachute Corps in time to launch an effective, prepared counterattack. Those elements that did arrive more or less intact had to be thrown into the line as soon as they were available. No forces remained with which to establish a mobile reserve. Rommel's report of June 10 was a veiled admission of defeat. His dispatches would grow less and less subtle as the situation in Normandy grew more and more desperate. In the days ahead he demanded the evacuation of the entire Brittany Peninsula, stating that it was strategically impossible to hold and was now almost useless as a U-boat base anyway. By mid-1944 most of the German submarines had been sunk, and their gallant crews were dead. Rommel also demanded the evacuation of the Channel Islands, which had 35,000 soldiers on them. He also insisted that southern France be abandoned. Here the LVI Panzer Corps, with its 9th, 11th, and 2nd SS Panzer divisions, lay inactive. If sent to Normandy, these units might well have been able to form the mobile reserve Rommel needed so badly. However, neither Hitler, OKW, nor OB West would approve any of these demands.[34] Also, the mythical Allied army group of George Patton continued to pin down the 15th Army in the vicinity of Pas de Calais, at a time when Rommel's front cried out for infantry. Hitler was still sure the real invasion would come here. This pigheadedness would eventually have the most disastrous results when the Normandy front broke.

Almost a year later, in May 1945, the Channel Island garrison (i.e., the 319th Infantry Division) surrendered. Except for a raid or two, it had not fired a shot in anger. Southern France and Brittany were overrun, with little loss to the enemy. Just as in North Africa, lack of support for Rommel's ideas was resulting in the defeat of the German armed forces; only the scale had changed.

After a badly shaken Baron von Geyr left the Western Front to recuperate from his wounds, Sepp Dietrich assumed temporary command of Panzer Group West and postponed all counterattacks indefinitely. Rommel's good friend and naval advisor, Admiral Ruge, wrote of this decision: "The Third Front had become a fact, and the fate of the Third Reich sealed."[35] Both Rommel and von Rundstedt realized now that it was hopeless to try to hold a line so far west. The prudent thing to do was to retreat into the interior of France, out of the range of the huge Allied naval guns, before Eisenhower could build up his armored pursuit forces. The need to retreat would be especially acute if Cherbourg fell, which appeared likely unless 7th Army received massive reinforcements immediately. On June 11 von Rundstedt vocalized this notion to Hitler, stating that the situation would require "fundamental decisions" if the Cotentin port was lost. Rommel said virtually the same thing to Keitel the same day. Both field marshals were ignored. Two days later, Rommel made yet another plea for infantry divisions and regimental combat groups from Pas de Calais. Again his request was rejected.[36]

The Allies continued their offensive in both the American and the British sectors without letup; however, they had failed to take advantage of the so-called "Caumont Gap," which lay between the 7th Army on Rommel's left flank and Panzer Group West/I SS Panzer Corps on his right. On June 10 this gap was loosely plugged by Baron Hans von Funck's XXXXVII Panzer Corps. Initially, Funck had only the 17th SS Reconnaissance Battalion, part of the 2nd Panzer Division, and his own GHQ troops to close the hole, but he was able to conduct a skillful delaying action in the sector until June 13, when the 2nd Panzer at last completed its march from the Abbeville-Amiens sector. Funck was also reinforced with a strong battle group of panzer grenadiers from the 2nd SS Panzer Division, which he threw into action against the Americans west of Caumont. Despite the thinness of his line, the highly competent Funck was able to launch a series of local counterattacks and even succeeded in retaking Hill 174 from the British 7th Armoured Division, bringing its advance to a halt. Under Baron von Funck, the German center was secure for the rest of the campaign.

Elsewhere, the battle was not developing so satisfactorily. Colonel von der Heydte still held the Carentan position, which prevented the U.S. VII Corps on Utah Beach from linking up with the rest of the 21st Army Group, but was gradually pushed back to the Vire-Taute Canal, which effectively sealed off the town to the east. That night, in a rare performance, the Luftwaffe sent a flight of Ju-52s to Normandy. They dropped desperately needed mortar and machine-gun ammunition to the paratroopers. The next day, fresh American troops launched heavy attacks and pushed back all sectors of the 6th Parachute Regiment's overextended perimeter. By noon they had gained a foothold in the town, and von der Heydte's exhausted men were unable to throw them out. That afternoon, von der Heydte made a reconnaissance in the hills southwest of the town to select defensive positions in case a retreat became necessary. He ran into SS Major General Werner Ostendorff, the commander of the 17th SS Panzer Grenadier Division, and his operations officer.[37] The SS men were also on a reconnaissance. Ostendorff informed von der Heydte that the 6th Parachute Regiment was attached to his division for an attack against the Americans, scheduled for the next day. Heydte asked for reinforcements, but Ostendorff turned him down. He wanted the colonel to hold out at Carentan until he could mass his division for the attack. The two officers argued briefly. Ostendorff discussed his experiences on the Eastern Front, and concluded, "Surely those Yanks can't be tougher than the Russians." "Not tougher," replied von der Heydte, "but considerably better equipped, with a veritable steamroller of tanks and guns." Ostendorff was not impressed. "Herr Oberstleutnant," he snapped curtly, "no doubt your parachutists will manage until tomorrow."[38]

Heydte had no choice but to return to Carentan. When he arrived, he found that his command post had been overrun and that the pinchers from the U.S. 101st Airborne Division were closing in behind him. He then decided to disobey orders and abandoned the critical position that evening, retreating to positions about a mile south of the town and avoiding the American encirclement.

The fall of Carentan allowed the U.S. forces from Utah and Omaha beaches to link up, which meant that the Anglo-Saxons now controlled a single large beachhead, extending from the British airborne bridgehead east of the Orne River all the way to the Montebourg area, 16 miles southeast of Cherbourg.[39]

The U.S. Army's official history stated that the withdrawal was a "blunder," but this conclusion has been the subject of dispute. There is no doubt, however, that the unauthorized retreat was a severe blow to the German Army in Normandy, and that Hitler and a great many in the High Command of the Armed Forces were furious at von der Heydte. The regimental commander reportedly escaped court-martial only because of his previous record. Ostendorff tried to retake the town on June 12 and 13, before his division had completed its assembly, but failed.[40]

The victory at Carentan gave the American beachhead the depth it needed so badly, and Bradley was now in a position to cut across the Cotentin Peninsula and isolate Cherbourg to the northwest. This was the next stage of the American part of the campaign. However, events elsewhere assumed predominance, at least momentarily. On the other flank, General Montgomery was about to resume his offensive, which had been temporarily checked by Geyr's counterattack.

It will be remembered that Montgomery planned a double envelopment of Caen. The "left hook" was to be delivered from the airborne bridgehead east of the Orne. The "right hook" was to be launched from the Bayeux area, and it was much stronger.

The left hook was, in fact, never delivered. The battlefield east of the Orne was initially the responsibility of 15th Army's LXXXI Corps (General of Panzer Troops Adolf Kuntzen), which was made responsible for the destruction of the British airborne bridgehead. It included the 346th Infantry Division (which ferried across the Seine on the night of June 6/7), the 711th Infantry Division, remnants of the 716th Infantry Division, and Battle Group Luck of the 21st Panzer Division. (General of Infantry Hans von Obstfelder's LXXXVI Corps, which was called up from southwestern France, took charge of this sector on or about June 21.) The Germans launched several counterattacks east of the Orne, beginning on June 7.[41] Battle Group Luck (*Kampfgruppe* or KG Luck) and Lieutenant General Erich Diestel's 346th Infantry Division were particularly aggressive, and their operations assumed all the aspects of a spoiling attack.[42] The German combat teams tied up the British 6th Airborne and 51st Highlander divisions, along with the 4th Armoured Brigade, until June 16. As a result, Monty's left hook never got out of its assembly areas. However, the price was high for the Germans. KG Luck lost all but eight of the panzers loaned to it by the 100th Panzer Regiment. The battle grew so fierce that hand-to-hand fighting took place in several spots.[43]

Montgomery's right hook was initially more successful. It was, however, facing groups of veteran soldiers who were rapidly gaining experience at fighting in hedgerow country. The German infantry set up in good defensive positions behind the hedges and in sunken lanes. Their elements set up in echelon, with overlapping zones of fire. The panzers often operated individually, with the infantry, as defensive weapons. They made superb armored machine-gun nests and frequently spearheaded local counterattacks against Allied footholds. On the other hand, they were knocked out by Allied fighter-bombers with almost equal frequency.

On June 11 the British 7th Armoured Division attacked through the 50th Infantry Division and began an attempt to encircle Panzer Lehr. This mission was ambitious in the extreme, because Bayerlein's division was perhaps the best equipped in the Nazi Army, with its fast, reliable PzKw IVs and Panthers. On the other side, the old desert soldiers of the 7th Armoured had left their reliable Shermans in Italy and were now equipped with Cromwells, a tank that was excellent in pursuit but inferior to the PzKw IVs and Vs in a tank battle, particularly if the fight became a slugging contest.

The 7th Armoured Division started the battle by capturing the village of Verrieres-Lingevres. It fell quickly, but Panzer Lehr counterattacked just as quickly and soon a major armored battle raged around the village. In the center of the German line the British 6th Armoured Regiment, supported by the Canadian infantry, launched a second attack against the remnants of the 12th SS Panzer Division at Le Mesnil-Patry. The British tankers ran right into a nest of 88mm anti-aircraft guns and were slaughtered. Thirty-seven tanks were knocked out, and only three NCOs and a handful of men ever came back. Every officer in the regiment was either killed, seriously wounded, or captured. The Canadians were also repulsed in savage fighting, although they did fare better than the 6th Armoured. The battle for Le Mesnil-Patry continued until June 14, but the SS line held.[44]

Meanwhile, at Tilly, Fritz Bayerlein discovered that he was being outflanked. While the bulk of the 7th Armoured Division pinned down his reduced force, a brigade-sized combat group from the Allied armored division penetrated as far as Villers-Bocage and took the pivotal village during the afternoon of June 12. This place was located on high ground well in the rear of the German line, in the void between the American and British sectors, which were still only loosely joined. Panzer Lehr's deep left flank was in grave danger, and Bayerlein had already committed his reserves. There was nothing he could do but call for help. Fortunately for Panzer Lehr, help was not far off.

On the morning of June 13 the Allied combat group, which consisted of the 22nd Armoured Brigade, the 5th Royal Artillery Regiment, and the 1st Infantry Brigade, continued its advance toward Hill 213 (near Villers-Bocage), which controlled the vital road to Caen. They were spotted by SS Lieutenant Michael Wittmann, the commander of the 2nd Company, 101st SS Heavy Panzer Battalion.[45] Wittmann was no ordinary lieutenant. He had already personally destroyed 119 tanks and armored vehicles on the Russian Front and wore the Knight's Cross with Oak Leaves, a decoration normally reserved for generals who had distinguished themselves by directing major operations involving large units. It was only rarely awarded to enlisted men or company-grade officers.

Wittmann noticed at once that the British vehicles were too close together and that there were high hedges on either side of the road, so the British would be unable to turn around if attacked. He therefore did not wait for the rest of his company to come up but immediately attacked the British with his own Tiger tank. He destroyed half-track after half-track with his machine guns, while shell after shell from the Cromwells struck the huge PzKw VI but bounded off its thick armored hull. The British tanks, on the other hand, were no match for his 88mm main battle gun. Within five minutes the SS lieutenant had knocked out 25 British armored vehicles, bringing his personal total to 144. Soon the rest of Wittmann's company (three Tigers and a PzKw IV) joined in the fight, in which a total of 25 British tanks, 14 half-tracks, and 14 Bren carriers were destroyed. The spearhead of the flanking column was annihilated.[46] Map 3.1 shows this Battle of Villers-Bocage.

The British combat group's troubles were just beginning. The weather had turned bad, and the RAF was grounded, leaving the 22nd Armoured Brigade and its supporting units badly isolated. At just that moment the vanguard of Lieutenant General Baron Heinrich von Luettwitz's 2nd Panzer Division, en route to reinforce Panzer Lehr, arrived and joined in with Wittmann near Villers-Bocage instead.[47] Also, Bayerlein had managed to scrape together a reserve and immediately dispatched it to the village, where the 22nd Armoured was soon trapped; before it could make a getaway, the British brigade was severely mauled. Sixteen officers and 176 men were killed, and dozens of others were wounded and/or captured. The 1st Infantry Brigade left 4 officers and 60 men on the battlefield as well. The flanking column—or what was left of it— limped back to British lines. Montgomery's right hook had been blocked.

Meanwhile, on June 14 British military intelligence located the command post (CP) of the 12th SS Panzer Division. The Royal Navy quickly opened up on this chateau with its heavy guns. When one of the huge 16-inch shells landed in front of the building and another landed behind it a few moments later, General Witt knew that he was being bracketed. He and his orderly ran from the house and jumped into foxholes, which had been dug for just such an eventuality, but a shell landed right beside Witt's slit trench, killing him instantly. When he learned of Witt's death, Sepp Dietrich remarked; "That's one of the best gone. He was too good a soldier to stay alive for long." He was succeeded by Kurt "Panzer" Meyer, who, at the age of 33, became the youngest division commander in the German Wehrmacht.[48] Needless to say, the investigation into the Abbaye Ardenne atrocity was dropped—at least by the Germans.

Ironically, had Witt stayed put, he would have lived. The chateau that served as his command post survived the naval bombardment intact.

Meanwhile, on June 11 Rommel and von Rundstedt met and found themselves in complete agreement. They decided to report separately and independently to the Fuehrer and to state that the panzer divisions must be pulled out of the line before an effective counterattack could be launched. This meant, they concluded, that infantry reinforcements must be sent to Normandy to man the front and relieve the armor.

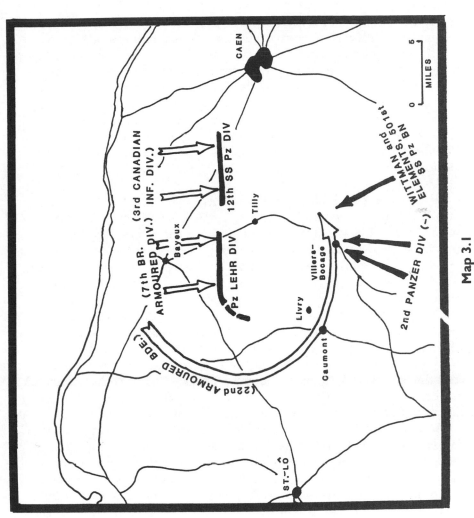

Map 3.1

THE BATTLE OF VILLERS-BOCAGE

Hitler responded to Rundstedt's report (he did not receive Rommel's report until the next day, June 12) by transferring the II SS Panzer Corps (9th and 10th SS Panzer divisions) from the Eastern Front to Normandy. He also ordered that the British airborne bridgehead be attacked and destroyed at once in order to free the 346th Infantry Division.

Rommel realized that this order would be impossible to carry out, because the II SS would not arrive for some time and the 346th Infantry Division had already suffered heavy casualties in earlier counterattacks. He therefore requested permission to pull his main defensive lines in the northeast back behind the flooded Dives River; with the troops thus gained, he proposed to attack the bridgehead from the south, using the 346th Infantry, Battle Group Luck, and the 7th Mortar Brigade.

Hitler rejected this strategy out of hand. "Every man shall fight and die where he stands!" he shot back. The stalemate east of the Orne continued.

Sir Bernard Law Montgomery was nothing if not persistent. Faced with four panzer divisions (including Luettwitz's previously undetected 2nd Panzer), he realized that he did not have the strength to carry out an offensive everywhere at the same time. Consequently he decided to go over to the defensive in front of Caen and launched an all-out frontal attack on the battered Panzer Lehr and Hitler Jugend divisions to the west of the city. On June 15 Montgomery's second major thrust began with a massive aerial and artillery bombardment. Then the 50th Infantry Division, reinforced by new armored units, attacked the Panzer Lehr. The village of Lingevres fell, but the grenadiers held Tilly, thanks primarily to their excellent use of the Panzerfaust. At the same time that the 50th struck, the newly arrived British 49th Infantry Division attacked the 12th SS Panzer Division at Putot-Brouary, on the Panzer Lehr's right flank. Once again the teenage SS men held fast.[49]

The battle continued on June 16. The British took Hottot and cut the Tilly-Balleroy road, but Bayerlein launched an immediate counterattack, and the 902nd Panzer Grenadier Regiment, supported by 15 Panthers, retook the village in furious fighting. Despite his heavy casualties, Montgomery attacked Tilly a third time on June 18. The bulk of the British VIII Corps took part in the battle for the ruins of the village. The RAF, the Royal Navy, and several fighter-bomber squadrons plastered the area, but to no avail: They were repulsed again. However, Panzer Lehr and the 12th SS Panzer Division were being bled white. It was only a matter of time before they would be annihilated. The German ground forces called in vain for support from the Luftwaffe. It was simply not forthcoming. The German Air Force had been driven from the skies, never to return. In mid-June, General Guenther Korten, the chief of the

General Staff of the Luftwaffe, and 3rd Air Fleet reported that the Allied fighter-bombers were systematically smashing all ground installations; that the 3rd Air Fleet was outnumbered 20 to 1 during normal operations and twice that much during major operations, and that German fighter operations were now only conditionally possible over the invasion area. The Allies already had 30 operational airfields in the beachhead area.[50]

While Erwin Rommel's men continued to hold on to their Cotentin line by their fingernails, the first V-1 weapon was fired on June 13 and was a fiasco. On June 16, however, an effective V-1 salvo was launched. Traveling at 400 miles per hour, the V-1s crossed the English Channel and landed in the London area. Utter confusion resulted. "The Rocket Age had begun," Paul Carell wrote.[51]

Hitler intended to break England's spirit by employing these new weapons against her population. German scientists would win the war for the Reich, he said. The men of the Western Front would simply have to hold on until that day. Rommel protested that they could not and demanded that the High Command send representatives to Normandy to see for themselves what the true situation was. He commented on June 14 that both army and SS troops were fighting with great courage, but the balance of strength was remorselessly shifting more and more against them each day. The Desert Fox was very depressed, reminiscent of those dreadful days in the desert after El Alamein, when it seemed as if Panzer Army Afrika would not make good its escape to Tunisia.[52]

Much to Rommel's surprise, Hitler acceded to his demand to meet with the leaders of the Western Front. Perhaps Hitler saw this meeting as an attempt to rally the spirit of his marshals; in any case, he ordered Rommel and von Rundstedt to meet him on the morning of June 16 at Margival, a Fuehrer HQ constructed in 1940. It was from here that Hitler had planned to direct the invasion of Great Britain. Those days seemed a long time ago indeed. Rommel was off visiting the battlefield and the grave of General Marcks (who had recently been killed by a fighter-bomber) when the order arrived at his headquarters. He returned to La Roche-Guyon at 3:00 A.M. on the 16th, after a 21-hour trip to the front lines. Now he had to endure a 140-mile ride over damaged roads to Hitler's bunker. There was no time to make any preparations at all for the conference.[53]

Early the next morning Hitler and Jodl arrived at Margival. Rommel, who had only managed to snatch two hours of sleep, was in an ugly mood. Hitler looked pale, sleepless, and ill. He toyed nervously with his glasses and some colored pencils, while sitting hunched on a stool, as the marshals stood in front of him. All his former hypnotic powers were gone. Bitterly he denounced Rommel and von Rundstedt for the success of the Allied invasion to date. Then it was the soldiers' turn to speak. After a few introductory remarks, von Rundstedt turned the conference over to Rommel. With what General Speidel later called "merciless frankness," Erwin Rommel pointed out the hopelessness of the German position.[54] He dismissed as a lie a BBC report—which Hitler had all too readily accepted as an authentic fact—that the defenders of the Atlantic Wall had been captured "in their sleep and their underwear" on D-Day. "Officers and men . . . have done all that duty could require of them," Rommel added with some heat. "They have simply been overwhelmed by Allied air and naval bombardment supremacy, as well as by conventional field artillery." Hitler's face flushed with anger as Rommel called the Cherbourg fortress "useless" and proceeded to denounce Hitler's whole concept of fortress-defense in the same, uncompromising terminology. "Cherbourg will fall in a week," he declared categorically.

Then the Desert Fox predicted what the Allies would do next: breakthrough from the Caen-Bayeux area and the Cotentin Peninsula, at first to the south, then in the direction of Paris. A secondary operation would attack past Avranches to cut off the Brittany Peninsula. Germany had no way to prevent this in the long run. Montgomery's 21st Army Group now had 22–25 mobile and armored divisions on shore, with 2 or 3 arriving each week. Rommel's dangerously understrength forces were being bled white and could not hold on indefinitely. The tough Swabian categorically stated that there would be no secondary landing north of the Seine, and pointedly demanded freedom of maneuver. "I propose pulling back our forces in Normandy out of the range of Allied naval guns," he declared.[55] While the infantry retreated behind the Orne, the panzer divisions would cover them and strike the Allied pursuit columns on the flanks. He conceded that the plan had only a one-to-four chance of succeeding, but attempting to hold the present line would eventually lead to disaster. Field Marshal von Rundstedt supported his subordinate's demands.[56]

Hitler did not want to listen to the unpleasant truth. He called upon his generals to keep their heads. If they could only hold in the East and defeat the Allied invasion, he declared, Britain would sue for peace because of the V-weapons.[57] He promised that they would cause "mammoth destruction" and that "these weapons will bring England to its knees!"[58]

Rommel and Rundstedt requested that the V-1s be used against the Allied beachheads, but General of Artillery Erich Heinemann, the officer in charge of V-weapons,[59] pointed out that this was not feasible because the margin of error in the rockets' guidance systems was too great. The weapons usually landed within 9 to 12 miles of where they were aimed, but they could not be accurately fired at tactical targets. The marshals then suggested that the weapons be turned on the port cities of southern

England, but Hitler vetoed this idea too. He wanted to destroy London to make the British sue for peace.

Somehow the commanders got the conference back on track. Rommel gave an account of the destructive powers of Allied weapons, but Hitler refused to believe his former favorite. Rommel then bluntly pointed out that no person of authority in Hitler's entourage had yet visited the front. Decisions were being made in the dark, he said, without firsthand knowledge. "You demand our confidence, but you do not trust us yourself," Rommel snapped at Hitler. The Nazi dictator flushed at this reprimand but said nothing.[60]

An Allied air raid forced the conference to adjourn to an air-raid shelter. While there, Rommel continued to press his points to Hitler. Finally, Rommel predicted that the Western Front would soon collapse and that similar collapses could be foreseen on the Eastern and Italian Fronts as well. Then he declared: "It is urgently necessary to end the war!"

"Don't you worry about the future decision of the war," Hitler shouted back. "You take care of your own front!"[61]

The Margival conference lasted from 9:00 A.M. to 4:00 P.M., with an hour break for lunch. During this period Hitler gobbled down a plate of vegetables, several pills, and small glasses of various medicines. The discussions ended without a single positive result. The next morning an off-course V-1 rocket exploded near the bunker, and a shaken Hitler departed immediately. This reaction was a far cry from that of the Fuehrer whom Major General Rommel had guarded in the Polish campaign of 1939, when it seemed he enjoyed being under fire. Behind him, Hitler left an order. Victory, it said, was to be gained by "holding fast, tenaciously to every square yard of soil."[62]

NOTES

1. Ruge, "Invasion," p. 336; MacDonald and Blumenson, "Recovery," pp. 85–88. Estimates of German casualties are so varied as to be useless. They probably lost 5,000–6,000 men.

2. Ruge, *Rommel*, pp. 178–79.

3. Ellis, I, p. 217.

4. Carell, p. 85.

5. Ibid., pp. 95–96.

6. Ibid., p. 96.

7. Hart, II, p. 550; Toland, p. 1076.

8. Fritz Bayerlein was born in Wuerzburg in 1899 and entered the army as a Fahnenjunker in 1917. He joined the Reichsheer as an enlisted man in the early 1920s and was commissioned second lieutenant in the 21st Cavalry Regiment in 1922. He served as Guderian's Ia during the Polish and French campaigns (1939–40) and became the chief of staff of the Afrika Korps in

September 1941. He became chief of staff of Panzer Army Afrika after General Gause was wounded in the Battle of the Gazala Line (1942), and he temporarily commanded the corps in the retreat from Egypt after its commander was captured in the Battle of El Alamein. Bayerlein was named chief of staff of the 1st Italian-German Panzer Army in early 1943 but was evacuated back to Europe after being wounded in Tunisia in April 1943. He led the 3rd Panzer Division on the Eastern Front (October 1943–early January 1944) before assuming command of the Panzer Lehr Division on January 10, 1944.

    9. Carell, p. 112.

    10. Sepp Dietrich was born in the village of Hawangen, Swabia, on May 28, 1882, the son of a master meat packer. He dropped out of school after eight years to become an agricultural driver and then a baker's errand boy. He joined the 7th Bavarian Field Artillery Regiment when World War I broke out and was wounded at Ypres in 1914 and in the Battle of the Somme. He ended the war in one of Germany's few tank units.

    Dietrich joined the Freikorps to fight the Poles in Silesia in 1920 and then became a member of the Bavarian Landespolizei (provincial or "Green" police), but he was abruptly discharged after taking part in Hitler's Beer Hall Putsch of 1923, which ended in a firefight—with the Nazis and their supporters (including Dietrich) on one side and the Green Police on the other.

    In the 1920s, Dietrich held a number of low-wage jobs (waiter, gas station attendant, etc.); he also became a favorite of Adolf Hitler and his personal bodyguard. After the Nazis took power in 1933, Dietrich was given the task of forming an SS unit for the protection of the Reichschancellery. He formed a unit of 177 men on March 17, 1933. From this modest beginning sprang the 1st SS Panzer Division "Leibstandarte Adolf Hitler," which Dietrich led until 1943, seeing action in Poland (1939); the Netherlands, Belgium, and France (1940); Yugoslavia and Greece (1941); and the Russian Front (1941–43). After two years on the Eastern Front, Dietrich assumed command of the I SS Panzer Corps on July 27, 1943.

    Later, Dietrich was promoted to SS colonel general and commanded the 6th (subsequently 6th SS) Panzer Army in the Battle of the Bulge and on the Eastern Front, which was now in Hungary and Austria (1945). He was sentenced to 25 years in prison for war crimes in 1946 but was paroled in 1955. West German courts then gave him another 18-month sentence for executions he directed during the purge of the SA (Storm Troopers or Brownshirts) in 1934. He served only 5 months, however, due to a serious heart condition. He died in Ludwigsburg (apparently in his sleep) of a massive heart attack on April 21, 1966, at the age of 73.

    11. Carell, pp. 114–15. Besides Pickert and Rommel, a number of other key German officers were absent all or part of D-Day, including Sepp Dietrich, who was on a hunting trip in Belgium. Three divisional commanders whose troops were in the Cotentin Peninsula (Lieutenant General Heinz Hellmich of the 243rd Infantry, Major General Wilhelm Falley of the 91st Air Landing, and Lieutenant General Karl Wilhelm von Schlieben of the 709th Infantry) were en route to the war game at Rennes, and Major General Edgar Feuchtinger, the commander of the 21st Panzer Division, was away without leave (AWOL). Colonel Hans Georg von Tempelhof, Rommel's operations officer, and Colonel

Wilhelm Meyer-Detring of OB West's operations staff were on leave. Admiral Theodor Krancke, the chief naval officer in the West, was in Bordeaux on an inspection trip, and Grand Admiral Karl Doenitz was on his first leave of the war. So many key officers were absent from their posts that Hitler ordered an investigation to see if the British Military Intelligence had anything to do with it.

12. Ellis, I, pp. 237–38.

13. Luck, p. 161.

14. The 30th Mobile Brigade (Schnelle Brigade 30) was created in March 1943. It included the 505th, 507th, 513th, 517th, and 518th Mobile Battalions. It was officially disbanded on September 5, 1944 (Tessin, Volume 4, p. 286).

15. Harrison, p. 338.

16. Kurt Adolf Wilhelm "Panzer" Meyer was born on December 23, 1910, in the village of Jerxheim, 20 miles southeast of Brunswick, into a family of very modest means. He joined the Nazi Party in 1925 (at age 15), became a shopkeeper's assistant in 1928, and then joined the Mecklenburg police. An ardent Nazi, he was a member of the SS by 1931 and joined the Leibstandarte in late 1933. By December 1937 he was an SS captain and commander of the regiment's 14th Company—the motorcycle unit. He fought in Poland, France, the Balkans, and on the Eastern Front with the 1st SS Panzer before being transferred to the Hitler Youth Division.

Meyer was captured by Belgian partisans in September 1944 and was turned over to the Allies. After the war, he was sentenced to death by a military tribunal presided over by his former opponent, Harry Foster. Meyer was not executed, as we have seen, and was eventually pardoned. He died in Hagen on December 23, 1961—his 51st birthday. His funeral was attended by thousands of former SS men.

17. Foster, p. 322.

18. Ibid., p. 316; McKee, pp. 70–71.

19. Foster, pp. 320–21. This was the testimony of SS Private Jan Jesionek of the 15th Company, 26th SS Panzer Grenadier Regiment, after the war. His testimony was largely responsible for Meyer's being convicted and sentenced to death.

20. Ibid, pp. xiv–xv.

21. Stephen L. McFarland, "Air Combat," in David G. Chandler and James L. Collins, Jr., eds. *The D-Day Encyclopedia*. (New York: Simon and Schuster, 1993), pp. 10–12.

22. Alfred Price, "II Air Corps," in *The D-Day Encyclopedia*, pp. 487–90.

23. Werner Junck was born in 1895. A fighter pilot in World War I, he shot down five airplanes before the Armistice. He joined the secret Luftwaffe in 1934 and commanded the 53rd Fighter Wing (JG 53) in the first weeks of the war. He fought in the Battle of Britain and later directed the small Luftwaffe contingent that supported Iraq in its unsuccessful rebellion against the British. He later commanded the 3rd Fighter Division (headquartered in Metz, France) before assuming command of the II Fighter Corps. After being relieved of his command, he served as chief of the aviation units' organizations office in OKL. He was promoted to lieutenant general on December 1, 1944, but was discharged from the service at the end of the year. He died on August 6, 1976. See

Absolon, p. 44, and Alfred Price, "II Fighter Corps" and "Werner Junck," both articles in *The D-Day Encyclopedia*, pp. 130–31, 325.

24. Albert Price, "IX Air Corps" and "X Air Corps," *The D-Day Encyclopedia*, pp. 390–91, 545–47.

Alexander Holle (born February 27, 1898) joined the Imperial Army as an infantryman in 1915 and survived the Battle of Verdun. Then he became a balloon observer and was shot down three times. He escaped by parachute on each occasion. He was selected for the Reichsheer in 1920, joined the Luftwaffe in 1935, and fought in Spain with the Condor Legion. He was chief of staff of IV Air Corps during the Polish campaign and led a fighter command in Norway against Allied shipping (1941–43). He led the X Air Corps from the summer of 1943 until it was dissolved in July 1944. He ended the war as Luftwaffe Commander, Denmark.

Dietrich Peltz was born in 1914 and joined the Luftwaffe in 1935. He commanded a Stuka (dive-bomber) squadron in Poland and France and a Ju-88 bomber group in the Battle of Britain. He fought in Russia and the Mediterranean before being named inspector of bomber units in December 1942. He took charge of Attack Command England in 1943. Later he commanded the II Fighter Corps in the Battle of the Bulge.

25. Carell, p. 23.

26. Ibid., p. 136.

27. Harrison, pp. 351–53.

28. Harrison, p. 356; Carell, pp. 132–33.

29. McKee, p. 78.

30. Ibid., pp. 78–80.

31. Wilmot, p. 303.

32. Major General Ritter und Elder von Dawans was born in 1899 and was commissioned second lieutenant in the infantry in 1918. Discharged in 1919, he managed to join the Reichsheer in 1924 and was on the staff of the I Corps when World War II broke out. He served as Ia, 19th Panzer Division (1940–41); chief of staff, XIII Corps (1941–42); chief of staff, III Panzer Corps (1942–43); and chief of staff, 4th Army (1943). He became chief of staff of Panzer Group West in December 1943. Most of his service had been on the Eastern Front.

After the RAF attack, Dawans and 16 others were buried together in a mass grave, located in one of the bomb craters.

33. Rommel, pp. 476–77.

34. Rommel, p. 476; Speidel, pp. 82–83.

35. Ruge, p. 337.

36. Liddell Hart, II, p. 551; Irving, *Hitler's War*, p. 640; Ruge, p. 337.

37. Werner Ostendorff was born in Koenigsberg, East Prussia, on August 15, 1903. He served in the army as an enlisted man in the 1st Infantry Regiment during the interwar years and briefly was a member of the Luftwaffe before joining the SS in 1935. He was a tactics instructor at the SS Junker School at Bad Toelz in 1939. He worked as a General Staff officer with the SS-Verfuegung-division in the Western campaign of 1940. In 1941 he was on the General Staff of the 2nd SS Panzer Division during Operation "Barbarossa," where he was awarded the Knight's Cross.

Ostendorff remained on the Eastern Front until 1944 and was named chief of staff of the SS Panzer Corps (later II SS Panzer Corps) in 1943. He assumed command of the 17th SS Panzer Grenadier Division "Goetz von Berlichingen" in January 1944. He held this post until June 16, when he was severely wounded. He was succeeded by SS Colonel Otto Binge (June 16–18), SS Colonel Otto Baum (June 18–July 30), Binge again (August 1–29), SS Colonel Dr. Eduard Deisenhofer (missing in action, September 1944), and SS Colonel Gustav Mertsch.

Ostendorff resumed command of the 17th SS Panzer Grenadier on October 21 and held it until November 15, when he was apparently wounded again. He did not return to duty until February 4, 1945, when he assumed command of the 2nd SS Panzer Division "Das Reich," which was now on the Eastern Front. Now an SS lieutenant general, Ostendorff was critically wounded on March 9 and died in the hospital at Bad Aussee, Austria, on May 1, 1945. See E. G. Kraetschmer, *Die Ritterkreuztraeger der Waffen-SS*, 3rd ed. (Preussisch Olden-dorf: Verlag K. W. Schuetz KG, 1982), pp. 186–89. Also see Roger James Bender and Hugh P. Taylor, *Uniforms, Organization and History of the Waffen-SS* (Mountain View, Calif.: R. James Bender Publishing, 1971).

38. Carell, pp. 133–34.

39. Breuer, *Cherbourg*, pp. 140–41.

40. Harrison, pp. 360–66. The 17th SS Panzer Grenadier Division "Goetz von Berlichingen" was a full-strength unit (more than 17,000 men) but was poorly equipped. Four of its six grenadier battalions were supplied with impro-vised transport (mostly Italian vehicles), and two were mounted on bicycles. Its tank battalion (the 17th SS Panzer Battalion) had no tanks, but its antitank battalion (also numbered 17) had 37 modern, self-propelled guns. See James Lucas, "17th SS Panzer Grenadier Division," in *The D-Day Encyclopedia*, p. 505.

41. Ellis, I, p. 227. General of Panzer Troops Adolf Kuntzen was born in Magdeburg in 1889. He entered the Imperial Army as a senior officer cadet in 1909 and was commissioned second lieutenant in the 1st Hussar Regiment in 1910. After serving in World War I, he remained in the Reichsheer and was commander of the 3rd Light (subsequently 8th Panzer) Division from 1938 to 1941. Later he led the LVII Panzer Corps on the Russian Front. He was named commander of Corps Command XXXII in 1942. This headquarters was up-graded to the LXXXI Corps. Kuntzen was relieved on September 4, 1944, and was discharged from the service at the end of 1944. He retired to Abbensen and was still alive in 1958 (Keilig, p. 193).

42. Erich Diestel was born in Deutsch-Eylau in 1892, was educated in various cadet schools, and joined the Imperial Army as an officer-cadet in 1912. He was commissioned second lieutenant in the elite Brandenburg 35th Fusilier Regiment and served on the Western Front in World War I. He remained in the Reichsheer and was commander of the I Battalion/68th Infantry Regiment when World War II began.

Diestel later commanded the 188th Infantry Regiment in Luxembourg, Belgium, and France (1940) and on the Eastern Front (1941–42). In 1942 he was named commander of the 101st Light Division and led it in the capture of Rostov and in the Caucasus campaign. Then he returned to Germany and, on

August 1, 1942, assumed command of the newly formed 346th Infantry—a
static division—at Bad Hersfeld. Many of its soldiers were Osttruppen—Eastern troops of questionable loyalty.

The 346th Infantry Division had lost more than half of its combat troops by
June 13; it nevertheless remained in the line. Diestel led it well and particularly distinguished himself during the Battle of the Scheldt. For reasons not
made clear by the records, however, he was sacked on October 11, 1944, and
was never reemployed. He died in 1973.

43. McKee, pp. 82–83.

44. Ibid., p. 87.

45. The 101st (later 501st) Heavy Panzer Battalion was a GHQ unit of the
I SS Panzer Corps.

Michael Wittmann was born on April 22, 1914, at Vogelthal in the Oberpflaz
district. He graduated from high school and then worked for his father (a
farmer) until October 1934, when he was accepted into the 19th Infantry
Regiment of the Reichsheer. Discharged as a corporal in 1936, he joined the
Waffen-SS in 1937 and was assigned to the Leibstandarte Adolf Hitler (the
LAH).

The quiet, unassuming Wittmann was a sergeant in the LAH's assault gun
battalion when the war broke out. He fought in Poland, France, Belgium, and
the Balkans. He did not come into his own until 1941, when he began to knock
out Soviet tanks at an incredible pace. In 1942 he attended the SS-Junker
School at Bad Toelz and was commissioned second lieutenant at the end of the
year. He assumed command of a company of Tiger tanks on the Eastern Front
in 1943; he destroyed 30 Soviet tanks and 28 guns in the Battle of Kursk alone.
He took charge of the 1st Company/501st SS Heavy Panzer Battalion in April
1944.

For the action at Villers-Bocage, Wittmann was decorated with the Swords
to the Knight's Cross with Oak Leaves and a few days later was promoted to
captain. He was reported missing in action on August 8, 1944. When last seen,
his lone Tiger was engaged in a fierce battle with five Shermans. In 1987 a
French highway crew was widening a road near Cintheaux when it unearthed
an unmarked grave. Inside they found the remains of Michael Wittmann, the
greatest tank ace of all time. He is now buried in the Soldiers' Cemetery at La
Cambe.

46. McKee, p. 94; Carell, pp. 157–58.

47. Baron Diepold Georg Heinrich von Luettwitz—called Heinrich—was
born in Krumpach, Silesia, on December 6, 1896, and enlisted in the Imperial
Army in 1914, when World War I broke out. After attending a quick officers'
training course in 1915, he was commissioned second lieutenant in the 48th
Infantry Regiment. An avid horseman, he secured a transfer to the 1st Ulan
Regiment in 1917. Luettwitz fought on the Western Front throughout the war
and joined the Reichsheer as a second lieutenant in the 8th Cavalry Regiment
in 1919. Although he remained an avid equestrian all of his life, he quickly
recognized the potential of motorized forces and assumed command of I Battal-
ion/8th Cavalry (the regiment's motorized battalion) in 1931. In 1935 he commanded the 3rd Motorized Battalion, which was equipped with PzKw I tanks.

Luettwitz was captain of the German equestrian team during the 1936 Olympics. The team won several medals, but not the elusive gold, earning Hitler's animosity for several years. He was transferred back to a horse unit against his will in 1936. Eventually he was able to take command of the 1st Reconnaissance Battalion in East Prussia but was severely wounded in the Polish campaign. The 1st Recon was left in Poland during the French campaign in 1940. Luettwitz remained in professional exile until the Russian campaign. A supernumerary officer on the staff of Army Group North when the invasion began, he assumed command of the 59th Rifle Regiment of the 20th Panzer Division after its commander was killed in action in late June. Luettwitz distinguished himself on the Eastern Front and rose from the rank of lieutenant colonel to lieutenant general, successively commanding the 20th Rifle Brigade (1942), 20th Panzer Division (1942–43), and 2nd Panzer Division (1944).

Transferred to the Western Front in March 1944, he performed well and succeeded Baron von Funck as commander of the XXXXVII Panzer Corps in September. His performance as a corps commander left much to be desired. His unauthorized efforts to bluff the American commander at Bastone into surrender provoked the reply "Nuts!" and almost led to Luettwitz's relief by the 5th Panzer Army commander, Baron Hasso von Manteuffel. He nevertheless led the XXXXVII Panzer until April 1945, when it was trapped in the Ruhr Pocket and was forced to surrender. Released from prison in 1946, he retired to Neuberg, Bavaria, where he died on October 9, 1969, at the age of 73.

48. Ellis, I, pp. 258–60.
49. Carell, pp. 158–59.
50. Ibid., p. 164.
51. Ibid., p. 159.
52. Irving, p. 385.
53. Speidel, p. 89.
54. Ibid., pp. 91–92.
55. Breuer, *Cherbourg*, p. 158; Speidel, p. 91.
56. Rommel, p. 479.
57. Carell, p. 162.
58. Breuer, *Cherbourg*, p. 158.
59. General of Artillery Erich Heinemann was born in Duesseldorf in 1888 and retired from the army in 1937. Recalled to active duty in 1940, he commanded Harko 302 (the 302nd Higher Artillery Command) on the Eastern Front before assuming command of the LXV Corps (and the German V-1 program) on December 1, 1943. Later this program was taken over by the SS, and Heinemann was relieved on February 28, 1945. Never reemployed, he died in Berlin in 1956 (Keilig, p. 133).
60. Speidel, pp. 92–93.
61. Breuer, *Cherbourg*, pp. 158–59; Speidel, pp. 93–94.
62. Rommel, p. 479.

Field Marshal Erwin Rommel, the "Desert Fox," commanded the 7th Panzer Division, the Afrika Korps, Panzer Army Afrika, and Army Group Afrika between 1940 and 1943. Named Commander of Army Group B in the latter part of 1943, Rommel was in overall command of German forces in Normandy until he was seriously wounded on July 17, 1944. In October 1944, he was forced to commit suicide, due to his part in the conspiracy to depose Adolf Hitler. (U.S. War College)

Hitler decorates Rommel, 1942. Major General (later General of Infantry) Rudolf Schmundt, the Chief of the Army Personnel Office, is in the background. Schmundt was blinded and critically wounded in the Stauffenberg assassination attempt on July 20, 1944, and died on October 1, 1944. (U.S. Army Archives)

Field Marshal Gerd von Rundstedt, Commander-in-Chief of OB West, 1942 to July 1944, and September 1944 to March 1945. An officer of the "Old School," Rundstedt commanded considerable respect, although his ideas concerning mobile warfare and panzer tactics were very much out of date by 1944.

Wilhelm Mohnke, commander of a panzer grenadier regiment in Normandy and later commander of the 1st SS Panzer Division. Mohnke was apparently responsible for the murder of several Canadian prisoners of war during the Normandy campaign. He was commandant of the Fuehrer's Headquarters during the Battle of Berlin and was captured by the Russians. Released in 1955, he was living in a suburb of Hamburg at last report (1991).

General of Panzer Troops Baron Leo Geyr von Schweppenburg, Senior Armored Advisor to Field Marshal von Rundstedt and the Commander of Panzer Group West, 1944. A veteran of the Eastern Front, Geyr did not understand that Allied air superiority had rendered previous panzer tactics obsolete; therefore, his concepts for employing Germany's mobile reserves were in diametric opposition to those of Rommel.

Hugo Sperrle, the Commander-in-Chief of the 3rd Air Fleet, 1944. A capable officer when he commanded the Condor Legion in Spain in the 1930s, he had "gone to seed" by 1944, and his efforts to provide air support for Army Group B were totally inadequate. Hitler finally sacked him in September 1944, and he was never reemployed. (U.S. National Archives)

SS General Josef "Sepp" Dietrich, Commander of the I SS Panzer Corps, Normandy, 1944. He later commanded the 6th (later 6th SS) Panzer Corps during the Battle of the Bulge and on the Eastern Front (1944–45). (U.S. National Archives)

SS Colonel General Paul Hausser, the Commander of the II SS Panzer Corps, who replaced the late General Dollmann as Commander of the German 7th Army in Normandy. Hausser, who lost an eye while fighting on the Eastern Front, did a poor job as Commander of the 7th Army. He was seriously wounded in August 1944, and did not return to duty until January 1945, when he became Commander of Army Group G. (U.S. National Archives)

General Dwight D. Eisenhower, the Supreme Allied Commander in Europe. The Officer picking his nose in the back of the jeep is believed to be Lieutenant General Omar Bradley, who led the U.S. 1st Army in Normandy. (U.S. Army Institute for Military History)

British General Sir Bernard Law Montgomery (left) engages insincerities with U.S. General George Patton, Sicily, 1943. The rivalry between these two military giants is still legendary. Montgomery commanded the Allied ground forces during the Battle of Normandy, while Patton's U.S. 3rd Army was activated in early August 1944, shortly after Field Marshal Rommel was critically wounded. (U.S. National Archives)

General J. Lawton "Lightning Joe" Collins, the conquerer of Cherbourg and Commander of the U.S. VII Corps during the Battle of Normandy. Arguably the best Allied corps commander in France, Collins's tactical astuteness and decisiveness on the night of July 25/ 26 resulted in the Anglo-Saxon breakout, the collapse of the left flank of Army Group B, and the rapid liberation of France. This photo was taken in the 1950s, when he was Chief of Staff (i.e., Commander) of the United States Army. (U.S. Army War College)

A self-propelled assault gun, mounted on a PzKw III chassis. (U.S. Army War College)

A Panzer Mark III (PzKw III). (U.S. Army War College)

Utah Beach during the build-up phase, June 9, 1944. Sperrle's 3rd Air Fleet was unable to interfere with the Allied landings and subsequent build-up, nor to protect the German ground forces.

Allied fighter-bombers circle the battlefield in Normandy, June 1944. The aircraft on the ground are gliders.

Remnants of the U.S. artificial harbor off Omaha Beach, wrecked during the famous storm in June 1944. The piers of this harbor jutted out 2,800 feet from the beach. Its loss seriously hampered Eisenhower's re-supply efforts. (U.S. Army Photograph SC-198169; photograph dated June 21, 1944)

One of the German gun positions at Azeville, neutralized by American paratroopers on D-Day. (U.S. Army Photograph SC-275935)

This dead German soldier fell in the streets of Cherbourg. In his right hand he still clutches a hand grenade that he never got to use.

Lieutenant General Wilhelm Burgdorf, Chief of the Army Personnel Office and the "gravedigger of the German Officers' Corps." Acting upon Hitler's orders, Burgdorf presented the Desert Fox with a poison capsule and persuaded Rommel to take it. Burgdorf committed suicide in Berlin at the end of the war. His body was never found. (U.S. National Archives)

CHAPTER 4

CHERBOURG

As we have seen, Lieutenant General Wilhelm von Schlieben was defeated in his attempt to retake Ste.-Mère-Eglise. On June 9 he threw the 1057th Grenadier Regiment into an attack against the American airborne bridgehead west of the Merderet River and gave Brigadier General James M. Gavin, the deputy commander of the U.S. 82nd Airborne Division, some bad moments, but the "All-Americans" paratroopers prevailed in heavy fighting. Schlieben then retreated to a line overlooking the western edge of the American beachhead, where he assembled what troops he could find, and what units Rommel could spare, while Bradley and his lieutenants were preoccupied with the Battle of Carentan. Between June 9 and 12 he established a line manned by miscellaneous units from the 709th, 243rd, and 91st divisions, as well as the 7th Army Assault Battalion. Schlieben's main strength, however, was his artillery. Several field artillery units had survived D-Day at least partially intact, and von Schlieben gathered all he could: a battalion from the 243rd Artillery Regiment, the 456th and 457th Motorized Artillery battalions, a battery of six French 155mm guns from the 1261st Army Coastal Artillery Regiment, the remnants of the 1709th Artillery Battalion, five batteries from Flak Group Koenig, and part of Major Koenig's 100th Mortar Regiment. Despite his young age and relatively junior rank, Schlieben placed a fine officer, Major Friedrich Wilhelm Kueppers, in charge of the artillery forces.[1]

Utah Beach, on the east coast of the Cotentin, faced southwest, toward the interior of the peninsula. Sixteen miles to the northwest was Cherbourg, the strategic objective of the American landings. As soon as they established some depth to their bridgehead, Rommel knew that the Americans would turn on von Schlieben and go after this prize. However, he could spare little in the way of reinforcements for 7th Army, because he simply had to contain Montgomery in front of Caen and Bradley in front of St.-Lô, or the Allies would break out of hedgerow country and reach the more favorable terrain to the south. This would allow their offensive to pick up steam, and the end of the Third Reich would be in sight. Rommel succeeded in halting both these forces by committing all of his mobile reserves as soon as they arrived. Unfortunately, this tactical plugging left von Schlieben pretty much on his own.

It was June 12 before Bradley captured Carentan and reduced the most significant strong points still holding out in the American rear. Although these battles tied up most of his divisions, General Bradley did make some preliminary moves to the west before then. From June 8 to 10, von Schlieben's makeshift corps fought against the 4th Infantry and 82nd Airborne divisions, which gradually pushed it back toward its main defensive positions along the Montebourg-Quineville line. By the time this German withdrawal was completed, Carentan had fallen, as well as the coastal forts of Azeville, St.-Marcouf, and Crisbecq. These victories left Lieutenant General J. Lawton Collins's U.S. VII Corps free to attack the Cherbourg landfront. Schlieben, meanwhile, had at last received some additional reinforcements in the form of the 77th Infantry Division under Major General Rudolf Stegmann.[2] All other units in von Schlieben's command had been badly damaged since D-Day, but the 77th was fresh from Brittany and was still capable of offering prolonged resistance. When the Americans finally did advance on the "fortress" of Cherbourg, they faced a reasonably formidable combat force.[3]

On June 11 the U.S. VII Corps struck with the 90th Infantry and 82nd Airborne divisions. The newly arrived 90th was stopped almost immediately, but the veteran paratroopers scored a potentially decisive breakthrough. They attacked the 100th Panzer Replacement Battalion, a unit made up mainly of foreigners in German service, which broke and ran in its first clash with the enemy. A combat group from the 265th Infantry Division arrived just in time to stabilize the situation, but the tactically important village of Pont l'Abbé was lost, so von Schlieben fell back a short distance and dug in for the next onslaught.

Another major disaster overtook German arms on June 12, when General Erich Marcks, the tough and steady commander of the LXXXIV Corps (of which von Schlieben's command was a part), was caught by a fighter-bomber on the road west of St.-Lô. He was critically wounded (a shell struck him in the right leg) and bled to death before help could arrive. General of Artillery Wilhelm Fahrmbacher, the commander of the XXV Corps in Brittany, assumed temporary command of the LXXXIV Corps until a permanent replacement for Marcks could be named.[4] The man chosen for this thankless job was Lieutenant General Dietrich von Choltitz, a veteran of the Russian Front, who arrived two days later.[5] Fahrmbacher immediately surveyed his new command and reported that it could not hold against a determined American attack. There were too few men, too much mixing and splitting of units, too many stopgap measures, and not enough ammunition.

The defeat of von Schlieben's makeshift force was entirely predictable. The embattled veteran of the Eastern Front faced the U.S. 9th Infantry, 4th Infantry, and 82nd Airborne divisions, with the U.S. 79th and 90th Infantry Divisions known to be in the VII Corps reserve. Clearly von Schlieben was facing heavy odds, even if Anglo-American air superiority and naval support were not taken into account.

On June 15, after two days of skirmishing, the U.S. breakthrough came, with the 82nd Airborne spearheading the penetration. German artillery slowed down the American advance by adopting a new tactic: It raked them with highly concentrated barrages of short duration. This method made it difficult for the ever-present fighter-bombers and spotter aircraft to pinpoint the location of the well-camouflaged German gun positions. At night especially, all Kueppers's guns would open up at once—but at different targets. As a result the attackers were suffering casualties, while German artillery units remained pretty much intact.[6] Such was not the case for the infantry units, however. By June 16 the Nazi defenses were beginning to deteriorate. General Collins launched a two-pronged offensive down two east-west running roads, heading past the small Douve River to the sea. The 82nd Airborne spearheaded the northern attack, while Major General Manton Eddy's U.S. 9th Infantry Division led the southern thrust. The 91st Air Landing Division (commanded since June 10 by Colonel Eugen Koenig) was a shell.[7] The other units, except for the 77th Infantry Division, were also in remnants. It would be impossible to halt the retreat east of the Douve, the last barrier between U.S. VII Corps and the western coast. General Collins wasted no time in exploiting his victory and pressed on with all possible forces toward St. Sauveur and the coast, taking hundreds of prisoners (most of them Russians, Poles, and Czechs) as he went. His objective was obvious to anyone who could read a map: Collins wanted to cut the Cotentin and the LXXXIV Corps in half. Field Marshal Rommel recognized the danger as early as June 14, even before the Americans launched their major offensive, but there was little he could do about it. As of June 12, he had only 12 divisions (perhaps 120,000 men) to face 326,000 American and British soldiers.[8] The odds would get even worse in the days ahead, and the Desert Fox knew that he could not hold everywhere, so he ordered the 77th Infantry Division to break out of the trap before it was sprung. The 77th was almost the only cohesive force remaining north of Collins's probable route of advance, indicating that Rommel realized that Cherbourg was doomed and that he wanted to salvage all he could before the ultimate collapse of the northern half of the LXXXIV Corps. The other divisions in the enemy's path—the 91st,

243rd, 709th, and part of the 265th—were now of regimental size or less, burned out, shattered beyond hope, and probably too disorganized or too demoralized to make good their escape in any event. (Fortunately for Colonel Koenig, the main American attack came north of his positions, so the remnants of the 91st Air Landing Division and a fraction of the 243rd Infantry Division escaped the encirclement of Cherbourg.) On June 16, however, Hitler countermanded Rommel's order to Major General Stegmann. The 77th Infantry Division would defend Cherbourg to the bitter end.[9]

A few hours later the climax of the unequal battle was reached. The U.S. VII Corps flanked Montebourg to the south. Stegmann's 77th Infantry was unable to check the 82nd Airborne and 4th Infantry divisions, which reached the west coast of the Cotentin on June 17. Schlieben's men (now under the ad hoc Headquarters, Group von Schlieben) were virtually encircled. The condition of Group von Schlieben continued to worsen on June 16 and 17, a deterioration that was accelerated by the death of one of von Schlieben's best subordinates. On June 16 Lieutenant General Heinz Hellmich of the 243rd Infantry Division was killed by a 20mm shell from an American fighter-bomber.[10] That small part of his division south of the American thrusts was temporarily combined with the remnants of the 91st Air Landing to form a single unit under the command of Colonel Bernhard Klosterkemper.[11] Lieutenant Colonel Franz Mueller, the commander of the 922nd Grenadier Regiment and a veteran of the Eastern Front, took over the bulk of the division, which was now retreating towards Cherbourg.[12]

The death of General Hellmich ended Group von Schlieben's last, very slim chance it had of preventing the Americans from sealing off the Cherbourg landfront. At 5:05 A.M. on June 18 General Eddy's spearhead captured the tiny port of Barneville and looked down on the blue waters of the Atlantic. Cherbourg was cut off.

To defend the southern edge of the American corridor—which now extended all the way across the Cotentin peninsula—from German counterattacks, Bradley committed another U.S. corps: the VIII, under Major General Troy H. Middleton. Middleton was given the 82nd and 101st Airborne divisions and was ordered to cover Collins's rear as he advanced northward on Cherbourg. Like Rommel, General Stegmann realized that the Americans were turning north to wipe out the Cherbourg pocket. Unlike Rommel, he decided that the 77th Division had to be saved, even if it meant flagrant disobedience of the Fuehrer's direct orders. On the evening of June 17 he turned south and struck out across the American corridor. At that moment the Allied front across the peninsula was far from solid; this situation, however, could not be expected to last for long. Stegmann decided to get his men out of the trap while he still had the chance. Although he saved much of his command,

General Stegmann could not save himself. Near the village of Bricque-bec fighter-bombers destroyed his horse-drawn columns. As he tried to reorganize what was left, the aircraft attacked again and his body was ripped apart by 20mm shells. He died instantly.[13]

Colonel Rudolf Bacherer, the commander of the 1049th Infantry Regiment, assumed divisional command and continued with Steg-mann's plan. Late on June 17 he surprised an American infantry battalion and took 250 prisoners. With his remaining 1,500 men (some sources say he had 1,700), he broke through the corridor and reached the southern front of LXXXIV Corps near La Haye-du-Puits the next day.[14]

Meanwhile, the jaws closed inexorably on Cherbourg. Hitler commanded the troops to hold their present positions at all costs. This command was meaningless, for the Americans were already in von Schlieben's rear, and the escape of the 77th stripped his right flank of troops. If the Americans discovered this (as they surely would), they could swing north along the western coast of the peninsula and bag the entire force before it even reached Cherbourg. Rommel therefore changed Hitler's order to read that Cherbourg was to be held at all costs.

By mid-1944, Hitler's insanity was far advanced, and he lived in a dream world. His grasp of reality was steadily slipping as the military situation got more and more out of control. He even went so far as to order Rommel to counterattack and relieve von Schlieben. "Fancy ordering me to attack Cherbourg!" Rommel exclaimed to Admiral Ruge later, as they went on one of their walks near the Chateau La Roche-Guyon. "I was glad enough to have managed to piece together even a semblance of a defensive front."[15]

To defend the Cherbourg landfront, General von Schlieben reorganized his command into four main combat groups. Battle Group Mueller included most of the remnants of the 921st and 922nd Grenadier Regiments of the 243rd Infantry Division under Colonel Mueller. Combat Group Kiel, which was led by a lieutenant colonel of that name, included the 919th Grenadier Regiment of the 709th Infantry Division and the 17th Machine Gun Battalion, as well as elements of the 922nd Grenadier Regiment. Kampfgruppe Rohrbach (Colonel Helmuth Rohrbach) consisted mainly of Luftwaffe and naval security personnel, as well as elements of the 729th and 739th Infantry Regiments of the 709th Infantry Division, and KG Koehn consisted of most of what was left of Colonel Walter Koehn's 739th Infantry Regiment and remnants of the 709th Infantry Division. The light antiaircraft elements of the 25th Flak Regiment were also assigned to the battle groups.[16]

On June 19, after a pause of less than 22 hours, the Allied advance on Cherbourg resumed. (General Collins was not nicknamed "Lightning Joe" for nothing.) The Germans resisted at Montebourg on the eastern flank against the U.S. 4th, 9th, and 79th Infantry divisions, until the artillerymen fired all the ammunition they could not carry with them in their limited transport; then the surviving infantrymen retreated as rapidly as they could into the fortress. Most of them reached the city by the end of the next day.

The siege of Cherbourg began on June 21. General von Schlieben realized that he could not hold out indefinitely and that there was little chance for relief. His objective, then, was time. Time to allow the sailors and engineers to destroy the harbor; time to enable Rommel to establish a solid defensive line to the south; always time!

He did not have much left with which to fight. The units involved were already smashed, most of them were well below 50 percent of their original strength, and Schlieben's perimeter was 31 miles long—much more than he had hoped to successfully defend with his largely disorganized and demoralized command. Nevertheless, he issued an order to all of his commanders: "Withdrawal from the present positions is punishable by death. I empower all leaders of every grade to shoot on sight anyone who leaves his post because of cowardice. The hour is serious. Only willpower, readiness for fighting and heroism to the death can help."[17]

Despite his desperate order, Schlieben must have known that his position was hopeless from the beginning. A major storm did give the trapped garrison some respite, even though it also underlined to the enemy the necessity of taking Cherbourg as soon as possible.

The weather began to change on June 20. A gale was brewing. It was what Montgomery later called "the most famous gale since the Armada." For three days breakers rolled across the beaches. They held up landings for several days and endangered the success of the invasion.[18] British Squadron Leader Hill remembered: "On the beach just west of where I was at Juno, there was utter chaos; literally hundreds of small craft were washed ashore by the gale at high tide and lay on the road which traversed the beach, rather like a cargo of timber logs."[19]

The smaller Allied landing vessels, such as LSTs and LCMs (Landing Ship, Tank, and Landing Craft, Mechanized, respectively), were particularly hard hit. Off Omaha Beach alone 90 ferrying vessels were lost, and the British lost another 250 such vessels. Eight hundred small vessels were grounded on the beaches and left stranded when the water receded.[20] Many of these had to be written off.

The storm, labeled by the British official historian as the worst June storm to hit the Channel in 40 years, wrecked the two artificial harbors on which the Allied High Command depended. The British harbor was eventually repaired, but the American harbor off Omaha Beach was totally destroyed. Omar Bradley was left with only three days' supply of ammunition, which meant that he had to delay his planned attacks in the St.-Lô region. Likewise, Montgomery's June 22 attack on Caen had to be postponed.

To add to the Allies' supply problems, the Luftwaffe began night drops of a new type of mine into the waters off the beachhead. It was a pressure or "oyster" mine, which was activated by the pressure change caused by a ship's hull moving through the water and was unsweepable by any method known in 1944.

German submarines also became active, although there were few of them left in the Navy of the Third Reich. Forty-three of them left bases in Norway, Germany, and the Bay of Biscay region, with orders to attack the Allied ships off the Normandy coast. A dozen of these had to return prematurely because of mechanical defects or damages inflicted by depth charges. Ten were sunk before they could reach the area of operations and eight more were destroyed while there. Only 13 of those engaging the Royal and American navies ever returned. In this "last hurrah" of the Nazi Navy, U-boats destroyed seven warships, two LSTs, one LCI (Landing Craft, Infantry) and 13 transport ships totalling 50,000 tons, while 6 other transports (totaling 49,000 tons) were damaged. The German submariners had suffered a major defeat in this, their last major battle of World War II. There were simply not enough of them to disrupt the Allied invasion, in the face of Allied technological superiority in the field of naval warfare.[21] The oyster mines did almost as much damage to the Allies' shipping as did the German Navy. In the week of June 22–29 alone they sank four warships, as well as four other vessels, and seven other warships were damaged. One oyster mine blew up the *Derry Cunihy*, with the British 43rd Reconnaissance Battalion on board. Of its 500 men, 150 were killed and 180 wounded, and all its equipment was lost. The 43rd was eliminated as a combat force even before it reached the mainland.[22]

In Cherbourg, however, nothing could save the doomed garrison. On June 22, even before the storm had completely dissipated, approximately 1,000 aircraft (mainly P-51s, P-47s, and rocket-firing Typhoons) pulverized the defensive positions of Group von Schlieben. Twenty-four of them were shot down by German antiaircraft gunners. The cornered soldiers resisted stubbornly that day, and the Americans gained little ground, but the next day resistance began to weaken. The U.S. VII Corps established four wedges in the fortified line. Hitler ordered von Schlieben "to defend the last bunker and leave the enemy not a harbor but a field of ruins."[23] This work had been in progress for some time. On June 9 Field Marshal von Rundstedt had told his staff that he did not believe Cherbourg could be saved. Later that night he issued the order: "Begin at once to destroy the Cherbourg harbor." By June 24, the destruction process was in an advanced stage of completion.[24]

On the morning of June 24 Wilhelm von Schlieben reported that he had no more reserves and that the fall of the fortress was inevitable. Nevertheless he ordered his men to resist until the last cartridge, even though some of them showed little inclination to do so. German morale collapsed altogether in some units, although others continued to fight it out with grim tenacity.

The next day the Americans took Fort du Roule and entered the suburbs of Tourlaville and Octeville, thus putting the headquarters of Group von Schlieben in the immediate front of the battle. Schlieben signaled Rommel that his battle groups had been smashed and his few remaining troops were exhausted, nearly out of ammunition, and had their backs to the sea. The harbor installations, he reported, had been effectively destroyed. Because the loss of the city was now unavoidable, he asked the Desert Fox if there was any use in having his last forces wiped out and urgently requested instructions. Rommel replied, "In accordance with the Fuehrer's orders, you are to continue fighting to the last round." "Is that all?" von Schlieben asked his radio operator. "That was all," the operator replied.[25]

Erwin Rommel, it seems, had temporarily been cowed by the pressure from Hitler and the High Command. He spent the entire day moping about La Roche-Guyon in a state of abject depression.[26] Schlieben had no way of knowing that even as Cherbourg went through its death agonies, the commander of Army Group B was involved in a plot to bring about the end of the Nazi dictatorship.

At 7:00 P.M. on June 25, naval demolition teams under Captain Witt blew up the remains of the harbor with 35 tons of dynamite. Ten minutes later von Schlieben burned his secret papers. The Americans were within 100 yards of his command bunker.

The defenders held the bunker until 1:30 P.M. the next day. Then Schlieben turned to Rear Admiral Walther Hennecke, the Naval Commander, Normandy, and announced that he intended to act in accordance with his own conscience. This was the second time in his career von Schlieben had defied orders. As the commander of the 18th Panzer Division in Russia he had led his men out of encirclement against orders. (This may explain why he was commanding a fourth-class static infantry division instead of a panzer division in 1944—he had definitely been demoted.) Now he gave the command to surrender.[27] Some 842 Germans poured out of the underground command bunker, their hands in the air. Hitler later denounced Schlieben as "A disgrace to his uniform and the lowest form of German general!"[28]

Schlieben's order involved only his own headquarters. The leaders of the various sectors were left on their own to surrender or keep fighting as they saw fit. The city commander, Major General Robert Sattler, capitulated the next morning, along with 400 of his men. Naval Captain Witt (the harbor commander), Major Kueppers, and others continued to resist. It was a hopeless struggle, however, and the agony was soon over. The energetic and resourceful Kueppers (who had run out of ammunition) surrendered the powerful Fort Osteck on June 28 to General Barton of the 4th Infantry Division, and the last pockets of resistance (at Cap de la Hague, on the northwest corner of the peninsula) were overcome on July 1—more than two weeks behind Eisenhower's schedule.[29] Lieutenant Colonel Kiel was the last to surrender.

The fall of Cherbourg released thousands of men in mobile forces, who would soon be sent against the left flank of Rommel's Normandy front. However, the prize the U.S. VII Corps had fought so hard for turned out to be of much less value than expected. Colonel Alvin G. Viney, the American engineer officer charged with the task of rehabilitating the port, reported: "The demolition of the port of Cherbourg is a masterful job, beyond a doubt the most complete, intensive, and best-planned demolition in history." The U.S. Army's official history recorded that "the whole port was as nearly a wreck as demolitions could make it." Three weeks would elapse before the Americans could get the slightest use out of the fortress-harbor, and it would remain essentially unusable until September. Hitler was so pleased that he awarded Admiral Hennecke the Knight's Cross, even though he was in captivity.[30]

The collapse of resistance in the northern Cotentin ended a major phase of the Normandy campaign. The Allies had achieved their first strategic objective and had liberated the first major city in France. During the Cherbourg campaign, Collins's VII Corps had lost 22,000 men, including 2,811 killed, 13,564 wounded, and 5,665 missing. German losses were estimated at 47,070 killed, wounded, or captured, including 826 officers and six generals.[31] They no longer had to worry about Cherbourg holding out in their rear, and they could now turn their full attention to the south, where Erwin Rommel had established a thin line in hedgerow country. Against the Americans in the western half of the Cotentin Peninsula, he now had four fewer divisions and 39,000 fewer men with which to defend "Fortress Europe."[32] As of June 18 he faced approximately 600,000 enemy soldiers, and by July 1 the total number of Allied troops who had landed in Europe stood at 929,000, or about three times what Rommel could muster. In addition, the Allies were increasing their strength at a rate of two to three divisions per week.[33] If they could force the Desert Fox out of hedgerow country, the German armies in the West would be facing annihilation. The floodgates were creaking on the Western Front.

NOTES

1. Harrison, pp. 385–95; Carell, p. 167.

2. Rudolf Stegmann was born at Nikolaiken, East Prussia, in 1894 and entered the Imperial Army as a Fahnenjunker in 1912. Commissioned in the 141st Infantry Regiment in 1914, he helped scatter the Czar's armies at Gumbinnen and Tannenberg. He spent 1915–18 on the Western Front and was selected to join the Reichsheer. A major when World War II started, he led the II Battalion/14th Motorized Infantry Regiment in Poland and commanded the regiment (part of the 5th Panzer Division) in Belgium, Luxembourg, France, Yugoslavia, Greece, and on the Russian Front. The records are not clear as to whether Stegmann collapsed from exhaustion or was wounded during the Battle of Rzhev; in any case, he was forced to give up command of the 14th Motorized on February 5, 1942, and was without an assignment for seven months. In September 1942 he was named commander of the 2nd Panzer Grenadier Brigade (of the 2nd Panzer Division) back in the Rzhev salient. In April 1943 he was named commander of the 36th Panzer Grenadier Division and was given the task of demotorizing it and converting it into the 36th Infantry Division. He led his new command on the Russian Front until the fall of 1943, when he was seriously wounded near Bobruisk. He was given command of the 77th Infantry Division on May 1, 1944 (see Samuel W. Mitcham, Jr., and Gene Mueller, *Hitler's Commanders* [Lanham, Md: Scarborough House, 1992]).

3. Harrison, pp. 385–95.

4. Wilhelm Fahrmbacher was born in Zweibruecken in 1888. He joined the Bavarian Army in 1907 and was commissioned second lieutenant in the 4th Bavarian Field Artillery Regiment in 1909. He fought in World War I, served in the Reichsheer, and was a lieutenant general commanding the 5th Infantry Division when World War II began. Fahrmbacher later commanded the VII Corps on the Russian Front, before assuming command of the XXV Corps in France on May 1, 1942.

After briefly commanding the LXXXIV Corps in Normandy, General Fahrmbacher returned to his own corps in Brittany. Here he checked the U.S. 3rd Army at Lorient, a fortress and U-boat base that he held until the end of the war. Fahrmbacher retired to Garmisch and died on April 27, 1970.

5. Dietrich von Choltitz was born in 1894 and entered the Imperial Army in 1914. He served in World War I and the Reichsheer and was a lieutenant colonel commanding the III Battalion/16th Infantry Regiment when World War II broke out. Choltitz advanced rapidly, to colonel (1941), major general (1942), lieutenant general (1943), and general of infantry (August 1, 1944). He commanded the 16th Infantry Regiment (1940–42) and the 260th Infantry Division (1942), served on the General Staff at OKH (1942), was deputy commander of the XXXXVIII Panzer Corps (late 1942), was acting commander of the XVII Corps (1942–43), and commanded the 11th Panzer Division (1943). He was again named deputy commander of the XXXXVIII Panzer Corps, a post he held until August 30, 1943, when he was wounded in action. He did not hold another post until June 15, 1944, when he took command of the LXXXIV Corps (Keilig, p. 60).

After the Americans broke the German line in Normandy in late July 1944, Choltitz was relieved of his command by Field Marshal von Kluge, who needed yet another scapegoat and who (completely without justification) held Choltitz partially responsible for the disaster. Almost immediately after he was relieved as corps commander, Choltitz was promoted to general of infantry and was named Wehrmacht Commander of Greater Paris on August 7. Despite Hitler's orders that the city be razed, Choltitz surrendered it intact on August 24, 1944.

    6. Carell, pp. 167–68, 184.

    7. Eugen Koenig was born in Trier on September 19, 1896. He joined the Imperial Army as a war volunteer in 1915 and earned a reserve commission in the infantry in 1917. Discharged in 1920, he rejoined the army in 1936 as a first lieutenant in the reserves. He nevertheless rose to the rank of lieutenant general in the Second World War, earning the Oak Leaves to the Knight's Cross in the process. After the 91st Air Landing Division was disbanded, Koenig commanded the 272nd Volksgrenadier Division until it was forced to surrender at the end of the Battle of Ruhr Pocket in April 1945. He was living in Bitburg in 1958 (Keilig, p. 178).

    8. Montgomery, p. 54.

    9. Harrison, pp. 413–14.

    10. Carell, pp. 184, 167–68. Lieutenant General Heinz Hellmich was born in Karlsruhe on June 9, 1890, and entered the Imperial Army as a Fahnenjunker in 1908. Commissioned in the 136th Infantry Regiment in 1910, he fought in World War I, where he was captured on the Eastern Front. He remained in the service after the armistice and was one of the "rising stars" in the Wehrmacht when World War II broke out.

Hellmich was named quartermaster general of the 7th Army in August 1939 and was promoted to quartermaster general of Army Group B in October 1939. On June 1, 1940, he was named commander of the Berlin-Brandenburg 23rd Infantry Division—an elite unit that was considered one of the prize commands in the army. Hellmich led his division with considerable skill in the early stages of the Russian campaign, but during the Battle of Moscow his nerves and health collapsed in January 1942, and he had to be sent back to Germany, ruining a promising career. When he returned to duty that spring, he was given command of the 141st Mobilization (later Replacement) Division at Insterburg, East Prussia—a definite demotion. Later he was named inspector of Eastern Troops and was not given another combat assignment until he took command of the 243rd Infantry Division in January 1944.

    11. Bernhard Klosterkemper was born in Coesfeld in 1897 and joined the army as a Fahnenjunker in 1916. He was commissioned in the 78th Infantry Regiment in February 1918 and was selected to remain in the Reichsheer. Only a major when the war began in 1939, he took charge of the III/272nd Infantry Regiment in September 1939. Later he served on the staff of the XXIII Corps and became commander of the 920th Grenadier Regiment of the 243rd Infantry Division and took charge of the remnants of the unit when General Hellmich was killed. After the division was dissolved in September 1944, Klosterkemper was given command of the 180th Reserve (later Infantry) Division. He fought in Holland and in the Ruhr Pocket, where he and his surviving men surrendered to the Americans on April 18, 1945. He died in Bremen on July 19, 1962.

12. In August 1944 the remnants of the 243rd Infantry Division were absorbed by the 182nd Reserve Division.

13. Carell, pp. 169–70.

14. Colonel Bacherer and the remnants of the 77th Infantry Division were later captured in the Mons Pocket in September 1944.

15. Irving, p. 392.

16. Hayn, pp. 63–64; Carell, p. 167; Harrison, pp. 385–95. Also see Breuer, *Cherbourg*. The 191st Engineer Battalion, 91st Air Landing Division (Captain Bonenkamp) was also cut off in the Cherbourg debacle (Hayn, pp. 63–64).

17. Breuer, *Cherbourg*, p. 181.

18. McKee, p. 126.

19. Ibid., p. 126. Also see Carell, pp. 172–74; Montgomery, p. 62.

20. Harrison, p. 426.

21. Ruge, p. 342.

22. McKee, pp. 128–29.

23. Harrison, p. 430; Carell, p. 181.

24. Breuer, *Cherbourg*, p. 114.

25. Carell, p. 179.

26. Irving, p. 391.

27. Carell, pp. 185–211; Speidel, p. 88; Montgomery, p. 63. Schlieben retired to Giessen where he died on June 18, 1964.

28. Breuer, *Cherbourg*, p. 235.

29. Harrison, p. 441.

30. Rear Admiral Walther Hennecke was born in Bethelm/Hanover on May 23, 1898. He entered the navy as a war volunteer in 1915 and received his commission as an ensign in 1917. He spent most of his career on line ships and commanded the obsolete battleship *Schleswig-Holstein* (May–October 1941); however, he spent most of World War II as commander of the Ship Artillery School. He assumed command of his Normandy post on May 6, 1943, was promoted to rear admiral on March 1, 1944, and was captured on June 26, 1944. Admiral Hennecke was released from captivity on April 18, 1947. He died on New Year's Day, 1984 (Hildebrand and Henriot, Volume 2, pp. 59–60).

31. Harrison, pp. 441, 447.

32. Breuer, *Cherbourg.*, p. 252.

33. Montgomery, p. 63.

CHAPTER 5

THE CRUMBLING FORTRESS

As the U.S. VII Corps advanced on Cherbourg, Erwin Rommel desperately hung on to the hedgerow country against the sledgehammer-like blows of the British 2nd and American 1st Armies. He held out pretty much with his own resources, for little help was sent by Berlin. From D-Day to the third week in July, Rommel lost 2,722 officers and 110,357 men, of which only 10,078 were replaced. In the same period the Allies lost 117,000 men. These casualties were more than fully replaced.[1]

As resistance in Cherbourg deteriorated from furious to weak, more German divisions sat idle between the Seine and the Scheldt than were fighting in Normandy. The reason for this situation was that, even at this late date, Adolf Hitler refused to believe that the invasion had come! As incredible as it may seem, the Fuehrer and OKW still believed that the Normandy landings were a diversion, and that the main blow would come at the Pas de Calais. Even more incredibly this view had considerable support from the Abwehr—OKW's military intelligence service, which had recently been taken over by the SS.

As we have seen, the German intelligence estimates on the potential sites of the Allied landings were based on little more than educated guesswork. At the same time, Allied security and intelligence countermeasures were extremely effective, and Luftwaffe reconnaissance flights over England were now little less than suicide missions. In addition, the Allied deception plan was brilliant. German intelligence estimated that General Patton's 1st Army Group had a strength of about 25 divisions. In reality, it did not control a single combat unit. All of its forces were bogus, as was the fictitious radio traffic between its "divisions." In early 1944 the Abwehr estimated that there were 90 Allied divisions and 22 independent brigades in the United Kingdom. Actually,

Eisenhower had only 37 divisions available for action at that time. On D-Day, he would have 2,876,000 men in 45 full-strength divisions, all of which were fully mobile.

Colonel Baron Alexis von Roenne, the chief of German Army intelligence in the West, was only too eager to accept Patton's bogus army group as a genuine force. For months he had been deliberately exaggerating the strength of the Allied forces massing in England. It will never be known whether von Roenne, a strong anti-Nazi, was engaging in high treason or whether he was merely trying to introduce some reality into strategic planning at Fuehrer Headquarters. He was deeply involved in the July 20 attempt to assassinate Adolf Hitler, so his true motivations will probably never be established with certainty. In any case, on June 6, he estimated that Patton's army group had 25 divisions and was being held in reserve for a second invasion. These fictitious divisions played a major role in the subsequent campaign, for it proved much easier for von Roenne to add divisions to the German estimation of the Allied Order of Battle than for anyone to ever take them off again. As late as June 26, under the influence of Roenne's falsified data, Army Group B's intelligence section (Lieutenant Colonel Staubwasser) estimated that there were 67 enemy divisions in England, of which 57 were fit for use in France. Actually, Eisenhower had only 15 divisions in England at that time, and they were awaiting transport to Normandy. As was not particularly unusual, the German intelligence services were of much greater value to the Allies than to the Germans in the Normandy campaign.

As a result of the grossly inaccurate Wehrmacht intelligence reports and Hitler's insistence that there would be a second invasion, a force equivalent in strength to an army group, with 24 infantry divisions, five Luftwaffe field divisions, and two panzer divisions, sat motionless. Meanwhile, in the American sector alone, Rommel faced four full corps of 14 divisions, against which he could field only three intact divisions, three decimated divisions of approximately regimental strength, and a few miscellaneous formations. On July 3 OKW estimated that the Allies had landed 225,000–250,000 men with 43,000 vehicles. Actually, they had landed 929,000 men, 177,000 vehicles, and 586,000 tons of materiel. Rommel was outnumbered roughly 3 to 1.[2] On June 20 the High Command ordered von Rundstedt and Rommel to launch a massive armored counterattack and hurl the Allies into the sea. This order was ridiculous in the extreme. It was far too late for that and probably had been since June 7. Three of the panzer divisions earmarked for the participation in this attack (the 1st SS, the 9th SS, and the 10th SS) had not yet arrived and would be delayed even longer by the U.S. and Royal air forces, as was the case with other units en route to the front. A week later, for example, a battle group from the 265th Infantry Division was assigned to 7th Army to replace a battle group from the same division that was destroyed at Cherbourg. It took the new unit five days to cover the 180 miles to the front, but it took seven days to transport its heavy equipment 100 miles by railroad; then it had to proceed by highway.[3] As a result of such delays, two of the panzer divisions in the line—the Panzer Lehr and 12th SS—could not be taken out, because the two infantry divisions sent from southern France to replace them at the front (the 276th and 277th Infantry) were also seriously delayed by enemy aircraft. Neither the Panzer Lehr nor Hitler Jugend could properly be called a division in any case, inasmuch as half their men or more had become casualties since June 6. Only SS Lieutenant General Heinz Lammerding's 2nd SS Panzer Division "Das Reich" was in a position to launch the ordered attack, and a single division would be easily repulsed.[4] Besides all this, the Allied aerial domination had reduced Rommel's resupply effort to a trickle. The Field Marshal had approximately 637 guns, but they only had a few shells each, not even enough for the batteries to carry out all of their defensive fire missions. Counterattack was, of course, out of the question. As von Rundstedt's chief of staff, General Blumentritt, said, "As he [Hitler] would not modify his orders, the troops had to continue clinging on to their cracking line. There was no plan any longer. We were merely trying, without hope, to comply with Hitler's order that the line Caen-Avranches must be held at all costs."[5]

By now, the thin German line had more or less solidified. East of the Orne lay Hans von Obstfelder's LXXXVI Corps, covering Rommel's far right flank. On its left lay I SS Panzer Corps, defending the critical city of Caen with three panzer divisions. The German center was held by Baron von Funck's XXXXVII Panzer Corps, and the II Parachute Corps held St.-Lô. The German far left flank was held by the LXXXIV Corps, on the west coast of the Cotentin. Table 5.1 shows the German Order of Battle on June 21.

Montgomery had brought a new corps ashore by June 18: the British VIII. He planned to close on Caen with another pincer attack, this time nearer to the city. The fresh VIII Corps would provide the main punch. It was scheduled to begin on June 22 but was delayed three days by the gale. Meanwhile, Battle Group Luck launched its last counterattack. Its objective was the village of St. Honorine, three miles northeast of Caen, which had just been taken by the British 51st Infantry Division, but it was stopped by British artillery and naval gunfire. The battle group's tank contingent was reduced to seven panzers.[6] Like so many units before it, the group was now burnt out. Nevertheless, its survivors remained in the line.

Table 5.1
The German Order of Battle, Army Group B
June 21, 1944

Panzer Group West[1]	British 2nd Army Sector
LXXXVI Corps	Orne River Sector
716th Infantry Division	
346th Infantry Division	
7th Mortar Brigade	
KG Luck	
I SS Panzer Corps	Caen Sector
21st Panzer Division	
12th SS Panzer Division	
Panzer Lehr Division	
7th Army	
XXXXVII Panzer Corps	Caumont Gap
2nd Panzer Division	
17th SS Reconnaissance Battalion	U.S. 1st Army Sector
Elements, 2nd SS Panzer Division	
II Parachute Corps	St.-Lô Sector
3rd Parachute Division	
Elements, 353rd Infantry Division	
Remnants, 30th Mobile Brigade	
KG, 352nd Infantry Division	
LXXXIV Corps	West Coast
17th SS Panzer Division[2]	
6th Parachute Regiment	
Elements, 353rd Infantry Division	
KG, 265th Infantry Division	
KG, 77th Infantry Division	
KG, 91st Air Landing Division	
KG, 243rd Infantry Division	

NOTES
1. Reactivated on June 29
2. With KG, 275th Infantry Division, 635th Ost Battalion, and 7th Army Assault Battalion attached
KG = *Kampfgruppe* (a battle group or a division at regimental or battle group strength)

Sources: Hayn, pp. 69–71; Tessin, various volumes.

On June 22 Montgomery attacked again. Even though this assault was not his major offensive, it was serious enough. His objective was the vital Hill 112, which dominated the city of Caen. The attack was spearheaded by the newly arrived 11th Armoured Division, which faced the nearly exhausted survivors of the 12th SS Panzer Division. The

Hitler Youth still continued to resist with fanatical courage, and the struggle for the hill became one of the most bitter small battles of World War II. Even the divisional commander, SS Oberfuehrer Kurt Meyer, manned a Panzerfaust (antitank weapon). A counterattack by a small force of Tiger tanks ended the battle. The teenage SS men continued to hold the vital position.

Shortly after the repulse of the 11th Armoured Division, Montgomery launched a night attack further east and broke through the positions of the 192nd Panzer Grenadier Regiment of the 21st Panzer Division. However, Major General Feuchtinger immediately counterattacked with his reserve and again closed the road to Caen. For the next two days heavy skirmishing continued all along the Caen front, particularly between the 11th Armoured and 12th SS Panzer Divisions. On June 25 Montgomery's long-delayed offensive, code-named "Epsom," began. The plan was relatively simple: The XXX Corps would start by attacking east of Tilly to pull in the German reserves. The next day, Major General Sir Richard O'Connor's British VIII Corps, with one armored and two infantry divisions, would pass through the Canadian 3rd Division and attack east of Caen, from the Orne bridgehead. Its objective was the area around St. Mauvieu, southeast of the city. If it was reached, Montgomery would be out of bocage (hedgerow) country. Meanwhile, the British I Corps would engage in a flanking attack even further to the east, while the Canadians again tried to take the airfield at Carpiquet. Map 5.1 shows the "Epsom" offensive.

The XXX Corps attack was spearheaded by the 49th Division with the 8th Armoured Brigade attached. It struck toward the critical Fontenay and Rauray ridges, where it was met by the remnants of Bayerlein's Panzer Lehr Division. The battle here grew fierce. McKee wrote: "Germans and British became inextricably intermingled in the fog and bitter hand-to-hand fighting developed where no quarter was given on either side."[7] The British 49th Division suffered heavy casualties against the Panzer Lehr and only managed to secure a small foothold on the western end of Fontenay Ridge.

The VIII Corps struck the next day as planned. This force alone included 60,000 men, 600 tanks, and 300 guns. They were further supported by 400 guns from the XXX and I Corps on their right and left flanks, respectively. Three cruisers from the Royal Navy and 250 RAF bombers also pounded German positions. The greatly reduced 12th SS Panzer Division opposed the advance of the VIII Corps, which included the 15th Scottish Infantry, 11th Armoured, and 43rd Wessex Infantry divisions, along with the 31st Army Tank and 4th Armoured brigades. In addition, the Canadian 3rd Infantry Division of the British I Corps supported the main drive by launching yet another attack on Carpiquet Airfield. The Germans were outnumbered at least six to one. To make

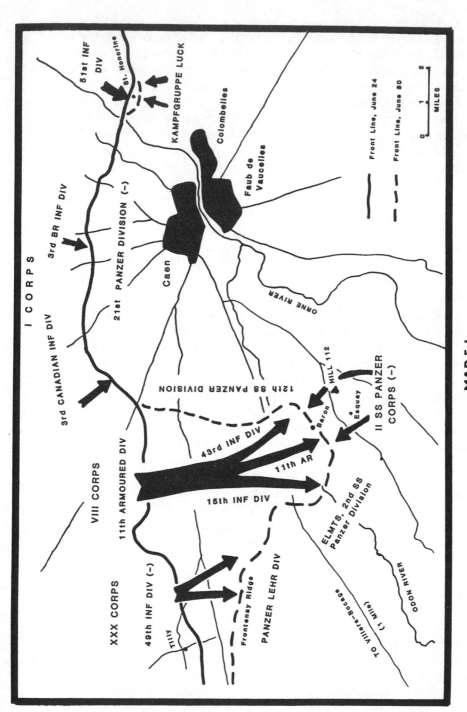

MAP 5.1
THE EPSOM OFFENSIVE

matters worse, Sepp Dietrich, whose I SS Panzer Corps controlled both the Panzer Lehr and the "Hitler Jugend" divisions, committed his last reserves prematurely. "Panzer" Meyer of the 12th SS objected, but to no avail. As a result, the 12th SS Panzer Engineer Battalion (which was fighting as infantry, like most of the German engineer battalions in Normandy) was left unsupported at 7:00 A.M. on June 26, when the massive British barrage struck its line, concentrating on a sector only two miles wide. Then the bulk of the British VIII Corps fell on its positions. The battalion was overrun, as was much of the 26th SS Panzer Grenadier Regiment. "The Scotsmen were now through the thin main line of defense," Major J. J. How wrote later,

but so well had many of the positions been camouflaged that they passed by without seeing them. The Hitler Youth grenadiers were coming to life in the rear of the assaulting infantry. Troops overrun are usually so demoralised that they give themselves up. Not so with these Hitler Youth soldiers. . . ."Snipers!" was the warning on every tongue.[8]

The British allowed the snipers and the German artillery to separate their infantry from their armor, and the attack bogged down. SS Major Siegfried Mueller, the commander of the SS engineers, turned his headquarters into a strong point and held out well into the night before slipping away to the west with the last seven survivors of his headquarters company.

The stubborn resistance of the SS men gave the 7th Army time to take countermeasures. Dollmann rushed most of the Army's reserves to the threatened sector, including three battalions from the 2nd SS Panzer Division, the entire 7th Mortar Brigade, much of the 8th Mortar Brigade, and a small battle group from the 21st Panzer Division. Sepp Dietrich also sent in his reserve: the Tigers of the 101st SS Heavy Panzer Battalion. Most of these units attacked the left or right flank of the British bulge, seriously slowing down the British drive but not stopping it. Rommel also took a hand in the battle. He ordered the II SS Panzer Corps (9th and 10th SS Panzer divisions), which was just arriving from Russia, to head for the Caen sector. This unit, however, was still en route from Paris and was under heavy aerial attack. Its arrival would be delayed until June 29. Rommel also sent in that part of the 2nd SS Panzer Division that was in Army Group reserve. The Desert Fox considered the situation so serious that he halted all supply movement on the roads and gave the armor emergency priority of movement.

Late on the afternoon of the 26th, "Panzer" Meyer led a desperate counterattack on the right flank of the British spearhead. He struck with everything he could lay his hands on, including a small battle group from the 21st Panzer Division. The SS were met by the 15th Scottish and 11th

Armoured divisions and were beaten back. They had, however, achieved their objective: The British advance was halted, at least temporarily.

On June 27 the Allies got their attack going again, but at a much slower pace. The British 11th Armoured and 15th Scottish divisions suffered heavy losses against well-placed German artillery fire, not to mention antitank gunners hidden in the hedgerows. Brigadier Hilton, the Scottish division's artillery commander, was wounded by a Panther and later died of his injuries, but the fighting continued. The Scots finally managed to break the thin SS line and establish a bridgehead over the Odon River near Baron. The fighting reached General Meyer's headquarters at Verson before the evening had ended. (Meyer had refused to withdraw it earlier on the grounds that it would be bad for morale.) Slowly the British and Scots continued to inch toward Hill 112.[9]

That night, Meyer moved his division HQ back two miles to Louvigny. Meanwhile, he was reinforced with the 54 multiple-tube-mortars of the 83rd Mortar Battalion (part of the 7th Mortar Brigade) and Kampfgruppe Weidinger (two panzer grenadier battalions of the 2nd SS Panzer Division, led by SS Major Otto Weidinger).[10]

On the morning of June 28 the men of the British VIII Corps struck again, and again they slowly pushed "Panzer" Meyer back, before he was reinforced by a company from the 100th Panzer Regiment of the 21st Panzer Division. He threw them into battle immediately, along with a few SS grenadiers and a Panther or two. Again there was heavy fighting, and again an Allied breakthrough was halted by the last German reserves, but they could not prevent the British 11th Armoured Division from capturing Hill 112. Casualties were heavy on both sides, but the Anglo-Saxons could afford them—the Germans could not. On June 27, for example, the 12th SS Panzer Division had only 56 operational tanks left—about 25 percent of its authorized strength. Only 53 of Panzer Lehr's tanks were operational as of June 26. It had begun the battle with 190 less than three weeks before.[11]

During the night of June 28/29, the vanguard of the II SS Panzer Corps began to arrive. It was led by SS General Paul Hausser, who had retired from the Army as a lieutenant general before joining the SS.[12] His 9th SS and 10th SS Panzer divisions, nicknamed "Hohenstauffen" and "Frundsberg" respectively, were made up entirely of veterans, toughened by months of combat on the Eastern Front. In April they had broken the Russian spring offensive before being sent into reserve at Tarnopol. On June 13 they entrained at Tarnopol and moved directly to Normandy. Most of their combat units were up by June 29. Hausser immediately grouped his men for a counterattack; however, Montgomery caught this "Eastern General" in his assembly areas and subjected the II SS Panzer Corps to a massive aerial, naval, and artillery bombardment. By the time Hausser regained his balance, Hill 112 had fallen.

June 29 was another day of desperate fighting. Hill 112 had to be retaken, or Caen was doomed. Meyer slugged at the vital position with all his remaining artillery. Meanwhile, General Geyr von Schweppenburg prepared for an immediate counterattack with all the forces he could throw together. Geyr's Panzer Group West Headquarters, which was upgraded and redesignated 5th Panzer Army a few days later, had been reactivated the day before and took over the right flank of Rommel's Normandy Front. His forces included the XXXXVII Panzer, I SS Panzer, II SS Panzer, and LXXXVI Infantry corps, the last of which was en route from the 1st Army in southern France. Dollmann's 7th Army was transferred to the western (St.-Lô) sector, where it commanded the LXXXIV and II Parachute corps. These dispositions indicate that Erwin Rommel felt Geyr was his best tactical commander, for he entrusted him with his most critical and dangerous sector. Unfortunately for the general, he took over a battle already in progress with practically all his reserves committed. Rommel was unable to help, because local American attacks had forced him to commit his last reserve (a battle group from the 2nd SS Panzer Division) to prevent the collapse of his left flank.[13] To make matters worse, Fuehrer Headquarters ordered Geyr to throw the newcomers from the II SS Panzer Corps into the battle before they were ready. "By this order the Panzer Group is already sold out!" von Geyr snapped bitterly.[14] The results were predictable: The attack began in the afternoon and had been defeated by nightfall. Hill 112 remained in British hands.

Meanwhile, Rommel lost yet another senior commander. Colonel General Friedrich Dollmann, chief of the 7th Army since 1940, died of a heart attack on June 29.[15] Hitler had wanted to sack him for some time, but Rommel had insisted that he be allowed to remain at his post. The Desert Fox, who had had no idea that Dollmann's health was so bad, had appreciated the fact that Dollmann was loyal, even if he was not the best tactical commander in the world. Hitler finally overrode Rommel and issued the order relieving Dollmann of his command; however, the 7th Army leader dropped dead before it reached his headquarters.[16] Rommel recommended that Kurt von der Chevallerie, the commander of the 1st Army, replace Dollmann. Instead, Hitler named SS General (soon to be SS Colonel General) Paul Hausser commander of the 7th Army, a move that did not please Erwin Rommel. The SS man had been a General Staff officer and was able, courageous, and energetic, but his record as a corps commander had been uneven, and he was definitely a Nazi. SS Lieutenant General (soon General of Waffen-SS) Wilhelm "Willi" Bittich, the leader of the Hohenstauffen Division, succeeded to the command of the II SS Panzer Corps.[17] Bittich was a fine leader in his own right. He had been a Luftwaffe officer but joined the Waffen-SS in order to gain faster promotions. Already he had commanded the 2nd SS Panzer Division in Russia and the 8th SS Cavalry Division in the Balkans, but his most famous victory lay ahead of him: Bittich would all but annihilate the British 1st Parachute Division at Arnhem the following September. SS Colonel Thomas Mueller, the commander of the 20th SS Panzer Grenadier Regiment, became acting commander of the 9th SS Panzer Division when Bittich moved up.

On June 30, his first day as a corps commander, Bittich won a major victory by recapturing Hill 112 from the British 29th Armoured Brigade. His trump card was the 7th Mortar Brigade (a unit supplied by 7th Army Headquarters), which trained 300 tubes on the heights. Before the Battle of Normandy was over, this unit fired some 8,000 tons of mortar-shells at the Allies.

While the II SS retook Hill 112, Panzer Lehr Division beat back attacks from Montgomery's 49th and 50th Infantry and 2nd Armoured divisions a few miles to the west.[18] The German line had been bent and pushed back, but it had not broken.

A dangerous gap had existed on the left (western) flank of the Panzer Lehr Division for several days. Field Marshal Rommel was aware of this fact but was too occupied with the battle for Hill 112 to do anything about it. Fortunately for him the British 2nd Army failed to detect it. On June 30 a battle group from the 2nd SS Panzer Division was finally available to fill the hole. The relatively fresh 2nd SS and the nearly exhausted Panzer Lehr were now placed under the command of Baron von Funck's veteran XXXXVII Panzer Corps Headquarters, which soon exerted a real control over the battlefield. The Allies had missed a golden opportunity to score the decisive breakthrough.[19]

The reason for the British failure at Hill 112 was that despite their overwhelming air superiority, which crippled German movement, they were still too slow. They had suffered heavy casualties on the road to the hill, but they failed to bring up reinforcements for the 29th Armoured Brigade when it finally took the key position. The Germans under Rommel, on the other hand, threw everything into the breach as soon as it became available. It had been just barely enough to prevent the decisive breakthrough.

General Speidel, the chief of staff of Army Group B, called the Battle of Hill 112 "tactical patchwork" and "unsound in every respect."[20] He was right, of course, but there was little else his chief could do. Rommel's emergency measures had prevented a catastrophe once more—but only by a hair.

While the all-important Battle of Hill 112 was reaching its climax, Erwin Rommel was hundreds of miles away, waiting. He and his immediate superior, Field Marshal von Rundstedt, sat at Hitler's Bavarian residence from late morning until early evening, a total of roughly six hours. Rundstedt was heard to mutter something about how this would be a good way to kill an old man. Rommel also let his feelings show, declaring to von Rundstedt that they both believed the war should be ended now, and that he intended to make no secret of their views when they spoke with the Fuehrer. He also spoke with Goebbels and Himmler, both of whom agreed to support his position in the Fuehrer conference. Rommel was optimistic when Hitler at last decided to see them. The conference took place in front of a large audience, which included the unemployed Field Marshal Guenther von Kluge, who had just recovered from injuries suffered on the Eastern Front some months before. Rommel and von Rundstedt twice requested a private audience with Hitler and were twice rejected. Rommel finally cleared his throat and tried twice to discuss the overall situation in the West, beginning with the political situation, but Hitler cut him off both times. "You will deal with your military situation, and nothing else," the Fuehrer ordered emphatically.

After this exchange, Rommel tried to give him a realistic report, but Hitler did not want to listen. The Nazi dictator reprimanded Rommel for failing to launch a relief attack on Cherbourg as he had commanded. He also bluntly informed von Rundstedt that Army Group B would not be allowed to withdraw behind the Seine and that southern France would not be evacuated as the Prussian marshal had suggested. Rommel would not be given any of the 15th Army's divisions, Hitler continued, for they would all be needed when the real invasion came. The Desert Fox was to concern himself with holding his present line, to prevent the enemy from reaching open country and driving on Paris.[21] Then, in a discussion General Blumentritt described later as "fantastic,"[22] Hitler lapsed into a monologue about his miracle weapons, such as the jet airplane and the V-1 and V-2 rockets, which would bring the Allies to their knees. Finally, weary of this tirade, Rommel asked Hitler point-blank how he imagined the war could still be won, and he called on the others in the room to express their views.

Goebbels and Himmler maintained a guilty silence. Even without the promised support, the Field Marshal faced Hitler with a courage the dictator was not accustomed to from his generals. He again said that he could not leave without addressing the subject of Germany.

"Field Marshal," Hitler replied, "be so good as to leave the room. I think it would be better that way."[23] Rommel turned on his heel and left Hitler's presence, never to see him again.

After the conference, Rommel said to Field Marshal Keitel: "A total victory, to which Hitler is still referring even today, is absurd in our rapidly worsening situation, and a total defeat can be expected."[24]

Even Keitel, Hitler's notorious yes-man and longtime enemy of the Desert Fox, agreed. "I too am aware that there is nothing more to be done," he said. He promised to present the situation to Hitler along the lines Rommel described. However, it is highly doubtful that he ever attempted to do so.[25]

Despite all that had happened, Hitler still refused to believe that the major Allied invasion had come. He repeated his orders to Rommel and von Rundstedt to hold every inch of ground at all costs. Any thought of mobile warfare was to be forgotten. "Why must our battles be directed by idiots far from the scene who have no conception of what's going on in Normandy?" Rommel snapped bitterly to General Speidel and Admiral Ruge.[26] When Rommel returned to La Roche-Guyon, he was given an estimate of the situation, written by Geyr and 7th Army's new chief, SS General Hausser. They both called for the evacuation of the Caen pocket and a retreat to the shorter Orne River–Bully–Avenay–Villers-Bocage–Caumont line. This retreat would at last place the German forces out of range of Allied naval guns and allow Rommel to create an armored reserve; however, it would also put the Allies on terrain favorable for armored operations. Obviously these proposals were in complete opposition to the orders Hitler had just issued. Rommel approved the plan anyway, then unilaterally placed all Luftwaffe and naval units in his zone of operations under the command of the German Army,[27] and hastily forwarded Geyr's recommendations to Rundstedt at OB West Headquarters in Paris. The reason for the sense of urgency was that both field marshals expected to be relieved of their commands as a result of the Berchtesgaden conference. The documents arrived in Paris a few minutes after midnight on July 1. Rundstedt quickly endorsed them and requested a free hand in the evacuation of Caen. Jodl recommended the rejection of these ideas and brought the matter before Hitler. The Nazi chieftain turned down the proposals as expected and again ordered OB West to hold every position presently occupied and to halt every Allied breakthrough by local counterattacks.

Hitler's reaction to the insubordination of his top generals was quick in coming. Geyr was placed in Fuehrer Reserve (i.e., was dismissed from active service) on July 2. Hitler blamed him for the failure of the counterattack of June 29 and considered him a defeatist. Rommel protested his removal but was brushed off by Keitel. Fifth Panzer Army was turned over to General of Panzer Troops Heinrich Eberbach, who had commanded the 4th Panzer Division on the Eastern Front.[28] Eberbach's chief of staff was Major General Alfred Gause,[29] the former chief of staff of Panzer Army Afrika and of Army Group B. At the same time as Geyr's dismissal, Colonel Heinrich Borgmann, one of Hitler's army adjutants, entered von Rundstedt's command post. With considerable deference, he presented the aging field marshal with the Oak Leaves to the Knight's Cross and a handwritten letter from Hitler. It was a polite note ordering von Rundstedt into retirement on the grounds of age and health.

Rundstedt's reaction was one of relief. "I thank God that I won't be in command during the coming catastrophe!" he told Field Marshal Rommel.[30] "I shall be next," Rommel remarked when he heard the news. Of the top German commanders on the Western Front six weeks before, only he remained.

Although Rommel was by seniority next in line for the post, Hitler named Field Marshall Guenther von Kluge the successor to von Rundstedt as Commander-in-Chief of OB West. The 61-year-old von Kluge, called "Clever Hans" in top army circles because of his skills as a political end-fighter, was in no way prepared for what he would be facing in Normandy. He had served in World War I as an artillery officer and rose to command the VI Corps in prewar Germany but had lost this command when the Nazis purged Army Commander-in-Chief General Baron Werner von Fritsch and his allies in 1938. Kluge was recalled to active duty in January 1939, when he commanded the 6th Army Group in Hanover. He later led the 4th Army in Poland and the French campaign of 1940, where Rommel had been one of his divisional commanders. Since then his services had been entirely in the East, where he led the 4th Army on the drive toward Moscow. In December of that year Hitler relieved Field Marshal Fedor von Bock of the command of Army Group Center and named von Kluge to succeed him. Kluge soldiered here, without particular distinction, until he was injured in an automobile accident on a snow-covered Russian road in October 1943. Now he faced his greatest challenge. Kluge was a non-Nazi, as opposed to being an anti-Nazi, and he had no idea of what he was up against in the West.[31]

In the East, Kluge had shown a definite talent for finding scapegoats. In his first few weeks as an army group commander, he had sacked—among others—Heinz Guderian, Erich Hoepner and Adolf Strauss, the commanders of the 2nd Panzer, 4th Panzer, and 9th armies, respectively. He had already been influenced against Rommel at Fuehrer Headquarters, where Hitler, Keitel, and Jodl spoke of him as being disobedient and a defeatist. Kluge spent several days at Berchtesgaden, where he let himself be convinced that the disasters on the Western Front were attributable solely to poor generalship. Consequently he was overly optimistic when he arrived at Rommel's headquarters on July 5, intent on "straightening out" the Desert Fox. At first the conference was chilly as von Kluge listed Rommel's sins: He was too pessimistic and too easily influenced by the "allegedly overpowering effect of the enemy's weapons," both in France and in North Africa. Rommel was too obstinate and did not carry out the Fuehrer's orders as wholeheartedly as he should. He advised Rommel that even he must obey orders without question or reservation from now on.

Rommel grew angry and then furious. He had never been the type to take unwarranted criticism (or even warranted criticism) lying down. The insult was doubly humiliating because Dr. Speidel and Colonel von Tempelhoff were present. The Swabian heatedly demanded that Kluge draw conclusions only after he had visited the front. He denounced Hitler's criticisms of him as unjustified and proceeded to censure the High Command itself in no uncertain terms. The argument grew so violent that von Kluge ordered everybody to leave the room except Rommel and himself.[32]

Their departure did nothing to abate the fury of the argument, which ended with Kluge crying that, up to now, Rommel had not really commanded anything larger than a division, and with Rommel howling back that Kluge had yet to meet the British in battle. (Neither remark was true.) The Desert Fox insisted that von Kluge withdraw his accusations and apologize in writing. This the new OB West refused to do, and the two were at loggerheads. After this meeting, there was an intense resentment between them; it did not completely dissipate even after von Kluge had come around to Rommel's viewpoint.[33]

Kluge told his staff that he felt sure he had scored more points than Rommel in their shouting contest and that the Desert Fox would not try to go over his head and deal directly with Hitler, as he had done under Field Marshall Kesselring in North Africa and under von Rundstedt in the West. Even as he spoke, Rommel was sending another ten-page letter directly to the Fuehrer, listing his previous demands and requesting that the appropriate conclusions be drawn.[34] He also dispatched a letter to Kluge, demanding that he inform him of the grounds the OB West had for making his earlier accusations. Rommel also submitted an attached document, which had already been forwarded to Hitler, that was a severe indictment of the way the Nazi High Command had conducted the war in Normandy to that date. It started out with the statement that the Normandy garrison was too weak to begin with, its equipment outdated, ammunition stocks too small, construction of fortifications too much in arrears, and "the supply situation . . . utterly inadequate."[35]

The report went on to give a laundry list of the reinforcements and countermeasures he had requested, and how he had been turned down almost every time. Rommel spared no one, including the Quartermaster General Eduard Wagner,[36] Jodl, the Navy, and the Luftwaffe. He was, however, at least diplomatic enough to make his criticism of Hitler himself implied or indirect rather than blatant and personal.

Meanwhile, Kluge was coming round to Rommel's view of the military situation. Of his new commander, the Chief of Staff of OB West wrote: "Field Marshal von Kluge was a robust, aggressive type of soldier. At the start he was very cheerful and confident—like all newly appointed commanders. . . . Within a few days he became very sober and quiet. Hitler did not like the changing tone of his reports."[37]

It took Kluge only one inspection of the front to make him realize that he was wrong on the Rommel question. He reversed himself completely and even acknowledged the justification of a memorandum that the Desert Fox had written to Hitler at the end of June, in which Rommel had commented: "The enemy's command of the air restricts all movement in terms of both space and time, and renders calculation of time impossible."[38] Kluge also promised not to meddle in the affairs of Army Group B in the future.

The supply situation, already at the crisis stage, reached astronomical proportions by July 2. Colonel Lattmann, the army group's artillery officer, reported that he needed a minimum of 3,500 tons of supplies per day, but he was not even getting 350 tons. Rundstedt's old supply officer had already been sacked, but the new one could do no better,[39] in view of the total Allied control of the air.

The Allies did not give Army Group B any respite while the Germans tried to work out their supply problems, command structure, and personality and policy conflicts. Montgomery continued his strategy of continuous alternation of the center of gravity between the British on his left flank and the Americans on his right. This method forced the Germans to rush their armored forces from one crisis point to another. They grew steadily weaker without seriously challenging the Allied foothold in Europe, because there were simply not enough reserves to permanently deal with both the Caen and the St.-Lô sectors at the same time. Rommel asked of OKW in early July: "How can they expect me to hold out with a quarter of a division when three American divisions are attacking?"[40]

Throughout his last campaign, Rommel naturally chose to concentrate most of his armor against the British in the eastern (Caen) sector rather than against the Americans on his left flank. The reasons were fundamental: If the Americans broke through, the Battle of Normandy would be lost, but Army Group B would still be in a position to retreat across the Seine. If the British broke through, they would be between the Germans and the Seine, in a position to cut the Army Group off from its bases, Paris, and the Reich. At best the 7th and 5th Panzer armies would be routed and most of their heavy equipment would be lost. They would then be unable to prevent the Allies from overrunning France and thrusting into Germany itself, possibly into the Ruhr industrial area.

The Third Reich would have lost whatever feeble chances it had left of staving off defeat. For these reasons, Rommel's left wing was always weaker than his right, although many of the Americans sloughing their way through the hedgerows would have questioned this fact in 1944.

The key position in the American sector was St.-Lô. It was a road center rivaling Caen, and its capture would give Bradley the additional lateral communications he needed, as well as road routes to the south, out of hedgerow country. Methodically he plotted his next offensive.[41] Map 5.2 shows the Normandy Front on July 1, 1944, two days before the U.S. offensive began.

The American offensive was launched in corps attacks by echelon. The VIII Corps on the American right (coastal) flank attacked the far left flank of the LXXXIV Corps on July 3. The next day, July 4, the VII Corps in the right-center of the American line jumped off. Three days later, the newly committed U.S. XIX Corps went over to the offensive against the right flank of von Choltitz's LXXXIV Corps and the left flank of Meindl's weak II Parachute Corps. The fourth and final U.S. thrust was launched by their V Corps, which attacked on July 7, on the far left of the American line, against the right flank of Meindl's corps.

On the western coast of the Cotentin, the U.S. VIII Corps massed thousands of men, including the 8th Infantry, 79th Infantry, 82nd Airborne, and 90th Infantry divisions. Against this huge force, von Choltitz could commit only the understrength 353rd and the greatly understrength 243rd and 77th Infantry divisions.

The Americans were confident of victory and General Middleton's VIII Corps was expected to advance 20 miles against light German resistance. One U.S. Army Intelligence estimate, dated June 28, stated that "the German division unit as such . . . has apparently ceased to exist." However, as the American official history pointed out, this may have been true in the last week of June, but it was certainly not the case in the first week of July.[42]

The Germans were badly outnumbered, and each American division, except the 82nd Airborne, was at or near its full authorized strength of 14,000 men. Colonel Eugen Koenig's 91st Air Landing Division, on the other hand, was fairly typical of the German units on July 3. It had only 3,500 effectives, and this figure includes the remnants of the 243rd Infantry Division and a battle group from the 265th Infantry Division, as well as other miscellaneous formations. Colonel Bacherer's 77th Infantry Division, which had been mauled in its breakout two weeks before, had fewer than 3,000 troops. The German command in this sector had also suffered heavy losses. Both the 77th and the 91st divisions had seen their commanders killed in recent actions, and their army commander was also dead, while LXXXIV Corps now had its third leader since D-Day.

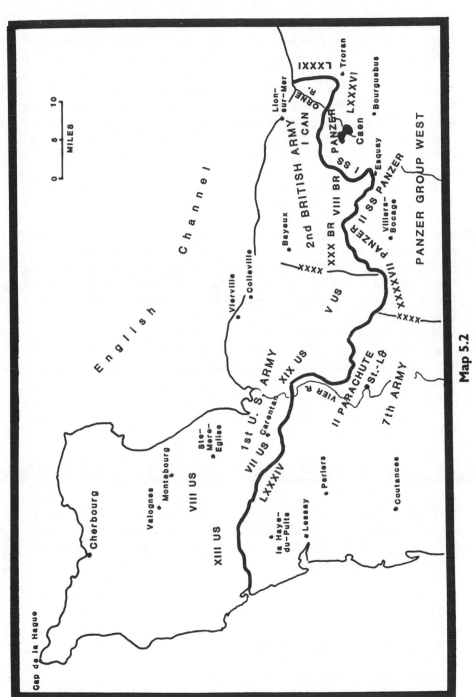

Map 5.2
THE NORMANDY FRONT: July 1, 1944

Despite its staggering losses, the LXXXIV again rose to the occasion. Its men, well dug-in in the hedgerows, gave ground slowly and only after bitter fighting. The U.S. 82nd Airborne managed to advance only four miles in three days. Although it did take the tactically important Poterie Ridge, the 82nd's casualties were tremendous. The strongest company left in its 325th Glider Infantry Regiment, for example, now numbered only 57 men. One company could field only 12—the normal size of an augmented squad! The division had lost more than half its men since D-Day. Now it was withdrawn from the line and returned to England to rebuild and get a well-deserved rest.[43]

There was no rest for Rommel's divisions, no matter how much they deserved or needed it. Major General Middleton sent the 90th Division of his VIII Corps against the important heights of Mont Castre, in the main effort of his corps. This attack was backed with the heaviest artillery support and was stubbornly opposed by two of Koenig's battalions, the remnants of the 77th Infantry Division, and a battalion from the 353rd. On July 3, the first day of the attack, the Americans gained less than a mile, at the cost of more than 600 casualties. The next day they advanced two more miles, with even higher casualties. Finally Middleton captured the high ground on July 6, only to face immediate counterattacks. Rain prevented the U.S. air power from intervening as SS General Hausser threw the fresh 15th Parachute Regiment, just up from Brittany, into the struggle.[44] The fighting in and around Mont Castre lasted for three more days, before the advanced American combat group was wiped out. When the battle ended, the U.S. 90th Infantry Division held only a part of the reverse slope of the heights. In five days it had advanced four miles, at a cost of more than 2,000 men.

On the extreme left flank of Rommel's line, the U.S. 79th Division attacked along the Atlantic coast against the remnants of the 243rd Division. Its objective was the high ground in the vicinity of La Haye-du-Puits. In five days it suffered over 2,000 men killed, wounded, and captured. Hausser had to commit two battalions of the 2nd SS Panzer Division to prevent a breakthrough, but by July 8 the 79th had stalled, and the VIII Corps offensive had failed all along the line.

Meanwhile, the U.S. VII Corps began its attack on July 4, America's Independence Day. The victors of Cherbourg found themselves in swampy terrain, with inadequate space to commit all their forces. It was hoped that they could quickly reach the Periers–St.-Lô highway, for south of this the ground was drier, and the corps could fan out and commit the bulk of its infantry.

Although American Lieutenant General Collins had the 4th, 9th, and 83rd Infantry divisions under his command, he could commit only the 83rd initially, because of the terrain. His attack was met by the survivors of von der Heydte's 6th Parachute Regiment and elements of the 17th

SS Panzer Grenadier Division. The attack started badly. The commander of the American spearhead was killed before he could advance 200 yards. The 83rd Division lost 1,400 men on the first day. The slaughter was so bad that Colonel von der Heydte returned captured American medical personnel so that they could aid the wounded. The terrain—swampy, hedgerow country—could hardly have been less suitable for offensive action, and the rainy weather eliminated the Allies' air cover, but the U.S. forces attacked again on July 5. The VII Corps managed to gain a mile along the Carentan-Periers road at the cost of another 750 casualties.

Despite the narrowness of the front, General Collins threw his veteran 4th Infantry Division into the battle, but it also failed. The paratroopers and SS men were generally of a very different character, but they possessed a common toughness and fought with bitter determination. Although Hausser was forced to send part of Lammerding's 2nd SS Panzer Division (which was now being split and scattered all over the battlefield) into the fight, the Americans were halted by July 7. They had advanced less than 2 1/2 miles in four days.

With the U.S. VIII and VII corps decisively engaged in heavy hedgerow fighting, the U.S. XIX Corps started its offensive on July 7. It was approximately 11 miles due north of St.-Lô when it began its drive on the city. Initially it had three infantry divisions: the 30th on the right, the 29th on the left, and the 35th in the center.

To the surprise of the American leadership, Major General Charles Corlett's corps made rapid headway. The reason for this was simple: The Allies' tactic of continually shifting the center of gravity was paying off. Rommel and Hausser had been forced to commit all of 7th Army's and Army Group B's reserves to halt the attacks of the U.S. VIII, U.S. VII, British XXX, British VIII, and British I corps all along the line from the Orne bridgehead to the west coast of the peninsula. These attacks by more than half a million men had come within a four-day period. All that remained to defend St.-Lô was KG Heinz: a battle group from the 275th Infantry Division, consisting of the much-reduced 984th Grenadier Regiment; the 275th Fusilier Battalion; and a three-battery artillery battalion. It faced three full-strength American divisions. At 3:30 A.M. on July 7, eight field artillery battalions, including one of heavy 8-inch guns, blasted Colonel Heinz's positions. By 6:00 A.M. the Americans had a foothold across the small Vire River, a position that U.S. Army Intelligence expected to be strongly held. Only one machine gun fired on the American infantry as they crossed the stream. By nightfall the bridgehead across the Vire was definitely established. General Bradley decided that the time had come to commit his armor for the decisive thrust toward St.-Lô, so he sent the 3rd Armored Division into the battle.[45]

Erwin Rommel's line was reeling. Not only was his St.-Lô sector threatened with immediate collapse, but Caen was also in imminent danger of falling. On July 2 Rommel (in hopes of forming some kind of mobile reserve) had taken the battered Panzer Lehr Division out of the line and replaced it with the newly arrived 16th Luftwaffe Field Division, which had just come down from the Netherlands. The next day Montgomery struck with his veteran British 3rd Infantry Division at the exact point Panzer Lehr had vacated. Despite the support of the 12th SS Panzer Division—itself a mere skeleton—the green air force unit broke and ran. It was a complete rout. The Luftwaffe unit lost 75 percent of its men (mostly captured) and almost all of its artillery. The remainder of the unit was so demoralized that Rommel attached it to the 21st Panzer Division, probably in the hope that the latter could restore some fighting spirit to the survivors. The divisional commander, Major General Karl Sievers, wandered about the battlefield on July 3, vainly trying to restore some cohesion to his disintegrated command.[46]

The Luftwaffe Field Division reflected one of the worst aspects of Nazi Germany's military system: the personal empire. The rout of the 16th Field Division is an excellent example of the results of such a system. These men were not cowards but highly trained and skilled air force personnel, perfectly competent when it came to repairing Messerschmitts, building airfields, or directing air traffic. As the Reich's air power declined, however, they became excess baggage. Instead of transferring them to the army, where they could have been properly retrained for ground combat, Reichsmarschall Hermann Goering insisted on keeping them under his personal control and persuaded Hitler to create the Luftwaffe Field divisions for that purpose. They would serve as infantry—but under Luftwaffe leadership and command. As a result, both officers and men were insufficiently prepared for land battles, and the Allies smashed them in almost every encounter. Now, thanks to the collapse of the 16th Field, the British closed in on Caen. However, the fanatical 12th SS Panzer Division—no matter how greatly reduced— was still a force to be reckoned with.

No better example of the tenacity and blind courage of these young SS men can be found than their conduct at the Battle of Carpiquet. In peacetime this place was the airport for Caen; in 1944 it was the best-constructed and best-defended strong point in the whole Caen defensive network. On July 4 it was attacked by the Canadian 8th Infantry Brigade, two battalions of the British 79th Armoured Division, and a battalion of the Canadian 7th Infantry Brigade. The Canadians were supported by 428 artillery pieces, plus the 16-inch guns of the battleship *Rodney* and the 15-inch guns of the mortar ship *Roberts*. The airfield was defended by only 150 Germans, almost all of them in their teens. This was all that was left of the once impressive 25th SS Panzer Grenadier Regiment.[47]

When the division commander, SS Oberfuehrer Meyer, realized that an attack on Carpiquet was imminent, he rushed all his reserves to the threatened zone. This "divisional reserve" consisted of two or three worn tanks and one 88mm antiaircraft gun.[48] Clearly "Panzer" Meyer was also scraping the bottom of the barrel.

Remarkable as it may seem, the Allies came out of this battle second-best. The SS lost the village of Carpiquet but held the more critical airfield position against all comers. Even General Montgomery complimented them on their "stout fight."[49] The Canadians fell back with "relatively enormous losses." Neither side took prisoners in the desperate struggle. The Canadians tried to storm the airfield again the next day but were again turned back.[50] Erwin Rommel had picked the right unit to defend the all-important city on the Orne.

Meanwhile, the men of the U.S. XIX Corps had pushed their way across the Vire and were smashing Combat Group Heinz, the last force between them and St.-Lô. To prevent Rommel from pulling men out of his front lines to save St.-Lô, Omar Bradley ordered his U.S. 1st Army to attack all along the line. Troy Middleton committed the VIII Corps reserve—the fresh 8th Infantry Division—to the fighting, and on July 9 the village of la Haye-du-Puits finally fell. At last the weather broke, and U.S. fighter-bombers blasted German positions near the western coast of the Cotentin. Mont Castre fell on the evening of July 10. By July 13 German resistance on Rommel's extreme left flank had definitely weakened, and the U.S. VIII Corps had reached the high ground overlooking the Ay and Seves rivers. It had advanced across seven miles of hedgerow country in 11 days, at a cost of over 10,000 killed, wounded, or missing.

General Collins's U.S. VII Corps also kept up the pressure, but not as effectively as Middleton's men. From July 8 to 15 it attacked the 17th SS Division and the remnants of the 6th Parachute Regiment, now supported by panzers and artillery elements from the 2nd Panzer Division. The VII gained very little ground in spite of tremendous losses. Major General Raymond Barton's 4th Infantry Division alone lost 2,300 men from July 5 to 15, including three battalion and nine company commanders. The 83rd Division lost 5,000 men in a similar period, along with half of its attached tanks, and also failed to break the thin German line. "The Germans are staying in there just by the guts of their soldiers," General Barton commented. "We outnumber them 10 to 1 in infantry, 50 to 1 in artillery, and by an infinite number in the air."[51] Just as in North Africa, Erwin Rommel was getting the maximum possible effort from his men; just as in North Africa, it would not be enough.

At the same time, 200 miles away, the strong 15th German Army—more than half the combat forces in Army Group B—lay idle. Adolf Hitler even now clung to the notion that this was not the invasion. The Allies, he maintained, would come at the Pas de Calais. The 15th Army sat inactive while her sister 7th Army and the 5th Panzer Army bled to death in the hedgerows of Normandy.

Meanwhile, as we have seen, Omar Bradley committed the 3rd Armored Division into the Vire bridgehead north of St.-Lô while successfully pinning down all of Rommel's other forces in the U.S. zone. The order sending in the U.S. 3rd Armored could have been the key decision of the campaign if it had been made 24 hours later. On July 7, however, the bridgehead was not yet large enough to accommodate such a large tank force. The 3rd Armored was one of the two oversized American tank divisions. Like all U.S. tank divisions at this time, it had three main components: Combat Commands A, B, and Reserve (CCA, CCB, and CCR, respectively), but it had 232 tanks instead of the normal 168, and 16,000 men instead of the standard 12,000. In the congestion of the battle area, CCB strung out for 20 miles on the single, rain-drenched, dirt, approach road. This bulky column crossed the single engineer tank bridge on the night of July 7/8, maintaining radio silence as ordered. This was a serious error. By the time its crossing was completed, CCB was badly disorganized, and from that point on, almost everything that could go wrong did. Communications failed; coordination between tanks and artillery, and tanks and infantry was almost nonexistent; a hasty infantry divisional commander relieved the leader of CCB, thus further disrupting U.S. command channels; the commander of the XIX Corps fell ill; and the congestion on the single road south of the Vire severely restricted resupply efforts, to the point where the frontline infantry was soon running short of food and ammunition. The entire operation—which could easily have been a victorious march into St.-Lô—degenerated into a dreadful mess.

Erwin Rommel was quick to take advantage of his opponent's disorganization. He correctly judged the situation on the Vire to be more critical (at the moment) than that on the Orne, so he threw Panzer Lehr—his one reserve panzer division, which he had just taken out of the line—into the contest. Rommel shifted this formation laterally across the rear area of the battle zone (a tricky maneuver), toward the crumbling sector. He also sent into the battle that part of the 2nd SS Panzer Division not yet engaged. This particular SS combat group amounted to a battalion of infantry and a company of tanks. Its mission was to slow down the Americans until General Bayerlein's armor arrived for the counterattack.

Rommel's desperate measures should not have worked, but they did. The Americans had penetrated the Vire River against minimal opposition on July 7. Rommel put his counterattack plans into operation the same day. The U.S. forces that had brushed aside Combat Group Heinz had a clear shot for St.-Lô late on the 7th, but the hasty commitment of the 3rd Armored Division had paralyzed their advance. It was July 10—2 1/2 days later—before the confusion caused by this premature commitment abated, and the resupplied American drive could start up again. By that time the opportunity was lost, for the vanguard of Panzer Lehr had arrived on the battlefield.[52]

Bayerlein's attack, delivered in poor weather, knocked the breath out of the renewed American thrust for St.-Lô. Unhindered by the U.S. Air Force, Colonel Joachim Gutmann's 902nd Panzer Grenadier Regiment, supported by 20 tanks, struck the U.S. 30th Infantry Division. On Gutmann's left Colonel Scholze's 901st Panzer Grenadier Regiment, supported by a dozen Panther tanks, mauled a regiment from the U.S. 9th Infantry Division. By 6:30 A.M. Panzer Lehr had pushed the Americans back two miles. The attack began to weaken before noon, however. The panzer division, down to one-third of its June 6 strength, proved too weak to defeat the combined efforts of the 3rd Armored, 30th Infantry, and 9th Infantry divisions. Bayerlein lost more than 500 men and 32 tanks in the attempt, but American casualties were also high. The U.S. breakthrough was sealed off and the stalemate reimposed—at least temporarily.[53]

Rommel's days must have seemed to run together as crisis followed crisis, almost without letup. Each day he was relatively weaker than the day before. Eisenhower now had a million men in Europe. Rommel had probably fewer than 250,000. The 15th Army still idly guarded its unthreatened sector, while Hitler and his lackeys vacillated in East Prussia.

In Normandy, the front was on the verge of collapse. Bradley and Montgomery ruthlessly threw fresh reserves into the cauldron, and Rommel met them with the same jaded forces. He knew that the day was rapidly approaching when they would break, and he said so. As usual, the Nazi High Command viewed him as an alarmist and ignored his pleas. Yet, he continued to hold off the invaders with all the genius and force of will he could muster.

The American offensive was not really defeated on July 11—it was simply checked for the moment. Meanwhile, with Panzer Lehr out of the line, Montgomery had launched yet another massive offensive against Caen. It began on the evening of July 7, the same day the American XIX Corps began its attack north of St.-Lô. First a massive artillery bombardment virtually leveled the city, and then 500 RAF four-engine bombers dropped 2,560 tons of high explosives on the ruins. The bombings lasted from 9:50 P.M. to 10:30 P.M. and killed an estimated 5,000

French civilians. Monty's ground attack began six hours later. The British general ignored the advice of General Bradley, who recommended that he attack immediately after the last bomb fell. "Rush it and you'll get it," were his exact words.[54] Instead, Montgomery—showing the periodic excessive caution that was his only major weakness as a military commander and for which he has been severely criticized (perhaps too severely, especially in American circles)—allowed the men of the 21st Panzer and Hitler Jugend divisions six hours to recover. When he struck at dawn, they were ready and waiting for him.[55]

About all the massive aerial and artillery bombardments had accomplished was to tip off the Germans that the offensive was coming. At 4:20 A.M. on July 8 General Dempsey's British 2nd Army attacked with 115,000 men, spearheaded by the fresh 59th (Staffordshire) Infantry Division, supported by the 3rd Armoured Division and two Canadian tank brigades.[56] The 3rd Canadian Infantry Division advanced on the right of the 59th Infantry, while the British 3rd Infantry attacked on the Staffordshires' left. They drove on the city in a contracting semicircle. By July 9 the 12th SS Panzer Division had been pushed back about two miles, and there was fighting in the northern suburbs. Hitler's orders were uncompromising: Caen was to be defended to the last man. The SS men responded, and bitter house-to-house fighting took place. The I Battalion of the 26th SS Panzer Grenadier Regiment particularly distinguished itself. The 1st Flak Battery of the 12th SS Flak Battalion knocked out a large number of Sherman tanks before it was overwhelmed. Obeying Hitler's order to the letter, it was completely wiped out.[57]

Fighting of this nature was too much, even for a hardened veteran like "Panzer" Meyer. He requested permission to evacuate the city, but his corps commander, Sepp Dietrich, turned down the request on the grounds that Hitler had forbidden it. Meyer retreated anyway. Later he said, "We were meant to die in Caen, but one just couldn't watch those youngsters being sacrificed to a senseless order."[58] That night he fell back south of the Orne to the industrial suburbs of Colombelles and Faubourg de Vaucelles. The infantry regiments of the formerly elite Hitler Jugend Division were down to the strength of a battalion, and the divisional antitank battalion had lost more than half of its guns.[59] Most of Caen was now in British hands. The next morning, July 9, the British 3rd Division entered the city from the east and linked up with the Canadian 3rd Division, advancing from the west. By the end of the next day, the last cutoff pockets of German resistance had been mopped up. Montgomery had his prize, which was now a sea of rubble. It had taken him more than four weeks to advance 10 miles. The British 2nd Army had suffered more casualties than the British General Staff had projected for the entire balance of the war, and yet the German line was still intact. Rommel reestablished a front along the east bank of the Orne, and most of his men were still in the hedgerows. The British still had not reached tank country, but they were only a river crossing away and in a position to establish themselves on the flat ground southeast of Caen. From there they could threaten the communications centers of Falaise and Argentan, which were critical to Army Group B; they could also threaten the Seine basin, Paris, and/or Rouen and Le Havre, and would also be in a position to drive a wedge between the 5th Panzer and 15th armies.[60] Rommel had no choice but to defend this flat ground with the bulk of his surviving armor, at the expense of his western flank.

To the west of the burning city the Battle of Hill 112 was renewed on July 10. Meanwhile, a few miles away, Erwin Rommel met with Eberbach's chief of staff, Major General Gause. He and Rommel had served together from July 1941 until March 1944, except for about half of 1942 when Gause was recovering from wounds suffered in the Battle of the Gazala Line. Early in the spring of 1944 they had a personal falling out, apparently because their wives could not get along, and Rommel had replaced him as chief of staff of Army Group B. The Desert Fox continued to respect his former subordinate, however, and had asked Lieutenant General Rudolf Schmundt, the Army's chief personnel officer, to give Gause command of the next available panzer division—a move that would have resulted in a promotion for Gause, had Schmundt obliged. Their personal differences now seemed to be entirely forgotten. Gause told Rommel that 5th Panzer Army was critically short on shells, but this was nothing new—all of Rommel's units were short on supplies of every description. The Allied air forces had totally disrupted the army group's rear area: bridges were down, railroads cut, barges sunk, transport destroyed, facilities demolished, depots smashed, and cities in rubble. Germany still had supplies, but it simply could not get them through to Army Group B. Gause told Rommel that troop morale remained high, but "courage alone won't be enough against the enemy's sheer weight of metal."[61]

Even without the city, the high ground of Hill 112 was of great significance, because it still controlled the terrain between the Odon and the Orne. South of the Orne the bocage ended; therefore, to keep his right flank in good defensive territory, Rommel needed to hold this vital terrain feature. Paul Hausser, the 7th Army commander, considered Hill 112 to be the key to Normandy. General Bittich, leader of the II SS Panzer Corps, apparently agreed, because he committed the 102nd SS Heavy Panzer Battalion to the struggle. This elite group included the best of the SS tankers, mostly drafted into the unit from the Eastern Front. They were equipped with the PzKw VI (Tiger) tank, arguably the best in the German arsenal. It was fortunate for the Germans that Bittich placed them here, for on July 10 the British hurled the 43rd

Wessex Division, the Canadian 3rd Division, the 46th (Highland) Brigade, the 4th Armoured Brigade, and the 31st Army Tank Brigade into the struggle for the hill. By midnight the situation was critical, despite the skill of the defenders. Each side occupied half of the hill by that time.[62]

The next day the grenadiers of the 9th and 10th SS Panzer divisions (II SS Panzer Corps) launched a counterattack. They gained some ground, but not much. Both sides suffered heavy losses in hard fighting. In the next week the battle tottered back and forth in a real slugfest. On July 12 the British took the hill, but the SS took it back the next day. By July 15 the Tiger battalion was isolated on the crest, but they held on, despite the cost. The next day they were rescued by the 9th SS Panzer Division.[63]

Meanwhile, the British I Corps, led by the 51st Infantry Division, attempted to take Colombelles (across the river from Caen) but was thrown back. At last, the Allies gave up the contest and regrouped. Montgomery reorganized, committing the Canadian II Corps (2nd and 3rd Canadian Infantry divisions) and the British XII Corps to the line. The Germans also took advantage of this short lull by digging in. The SS panzer troops entrenched themselves on Hill 112 so well that they held it until the end of July.[64]

In Washington and London, top-level staffs and politicians spoke of the crisis in Normandy. Even General Eisenhower was worried. It seemed that Hitler's "hold at all costs" strategy was working. Montgomery's invasion force was pinned down by Field Marshal Rommel. It occupied a narrow bridgehead 10–20 miles deep—hardly a fifth of what Eisenhower and his Supreme Headquarters planned for it to hold by that date. It was feared that the Germans might bring up their reserves and hold the Allies in the Cotentin until the onset of winter. This would be a disaster of unforeseeable magnitude. Winter weather would deny the Allies the use of their most important weapon: air power. Also, it was by no means certain that they could continue to supply their huge 21st Army Group throughout the winter. Cherbourg was still virtually useless, and the winter storms would doubtless wreck the surviving artificial harbor. With no other port facilities, the supply situation could conceivably grow very bleak indeed. Rommel might even succeed in pushing the Allies back into the sea.[65]

At last Hitler and his advisors were weakening in their insistence that the Normandy landings were not the real invasion. In the first and second weeks in July, they released four infantry divisions from the 15th Army at Pas de Calais. Three of these were earmarked for the Caen sector, where elements of the 5th Panzer Army could expect some relief at last. It might even be possible for Rommel to establish a significant mobile reserve.[66] Montgomery was certainly concerned about this possibility. He wrote later:

There were two very disquieting developments in the enemy situation during the first week in July. The identification of the 2nd SS Panzer Division in the American sector . . . showed the enemy's determination to strengthen his resistance in the west in spite of 2nd [British] Army's endeavours to prevent it. Moreover, we had identified fresh infantry divisions on the eastern sectors, which were relieving Panzer formations in the line; during the week 1st SS, 2nd SS, Lehr and 21st Panzer Divisions were known to have been withdrawn wholly or partially into reserve.[67]

The situation was not quite as dark as this passage might suggest, for all these German units were wholly or largely burned out. Still it was a dangerous trend: The Desert Fox was trying not only to stall the invasion but to seal it off in depth. Despite all obstacles, he was beginning to meet with some success; however, Rommel was not going to form a strong mobile reserve if the Americans could prevent it. Doggedly, they launched another series of attacks near St.-Lô, using their XIX and V corps. Major General Gerow's V included the 1st Infantry, 2nd Infantry, and 2nd Armored divisions. Corlett's XIX Corps still had the 29th, 30th, and 35th Infantry divisions. Again they faced the II Parachute Corps of General Eugen Meindl.[68] He had an assortment of battered and understrength units, which were formed up in two very mixed divisions. On the left flank, a battle group from each of the 266th, 352nd, and 353rd Infantry divisions was placed under the operational control of the 352nd Infantry Division Headquarters. On the right flank stood the reduced 3rd Parachute Division. The 12th Assault Gun Brigade was in support. Panzer Lehr, which was exhausted, was transferred to the LXXXIV Corps and occupied a sector of the front line further west. Meindl had almost no tanks and very few reserves.

The Americans began to close in on St.-Lô on July 11, when the V Corps attacked Hill 192, which overlooked the St.-Lô–Bayeux road east of the city. The hill was defended by a single parachute battalion. It was attacked by the entire U.S. 2nd Infantry Division. The 2nd's divisional artillery alone fired 20,000 rounds that day. In all, 45 tons of high-explosive shells were hurled at the position. The battle began at 6:00 A.M., and the hill fell at noon. Only 15 paratroopers surrendered.

Hausser ordered Meindl to retake the hill at all costs. That paratroop general, however, was more concerned with holding his disintegrating front together than with trying to obey an order that no longer made sense. He had almost nothing in reserve and certainly not enough to eject the entire U.S. 2nd Infantry Division. He was very much relieved when the Americans did not press their success by continuing to attack southward. Had they done so, they might have achieved their decisive breakthrough then and there.

Bradley was more concerned with St.-Lô at this moment than with a long-range breakthrough. Indeed, the capture of this ruined departmental capital preoccupied the minds of the American political and military leaders at this time. They badly needed a victory—for propaganda reasons if nothing else. They also needed the road network of which St.-Lô was the major junction; in addition, the high ground near the city dominated a considerable stretch of hedgerow country. However, St.-Lo was not as important as Caen in the strategic sense, because the bocage country did not end just south of the city but continued for several miles beyond.

While the U.S. V Corps took Hill 192, U.S. XIX Corps also began a major thrust toward the city, which lay barely four miles south of its front line. They struck out toward Hill 112, the key position north of St.-Lô and second only to Hill 192 in tactical importance. (This Hill 112 should not be confused with the other Hill 112, located near Caen.) Unfortunately, attacking toward this hill meant that they would be confronted by dozens of hedgerows, defended by veteran soldiers. Six battalions of U.S. heavy artillery—155mm, 4.5-inch, and 8-inch guns— blasted Meindl's line. The attack did not begin until afternoon, when it was reasonably certain that Panzer Lehr would not renew its offensive. Had the Americans attacked here 24 hours earlier, before Bayerlein filled the gap, Rommel's center would have been penetrated and the entire German front might have come unglued. There was no way they could have known this, however. Now a brutal fight ensued, and both sides suffered heavy losses. The battle became general all along the line. By nightfall the 3rd Parachute Division was reduced to 35 percent of its previous strength. The 353rd Division's battle group had lost around 800 men, about 80 percent of its original force, and the 352nd Infantry Division amounted to less than a peacetime battalion. Meindl was forced to commit his last reserves to prevent a disaster.

Eugen Meindl called SS General Hausser at 7th Army HQ and requested reinforcements. Specifically, he wanted the regiment of the 5th Parachute Division, which was just arriving from Brittany, but Hausser refused to turn it over. He believed that the defeat of Panzer Lehr's recent counterattack placed the LXXXIV Corps' sector west of St.-Lô in even greater danger of collapse than Meindl's. The airborne commander did not argue but tartly remarked that someone was going to have to come up with a brilliant plan very soon if the Americans were to be countered.

The German resistance had also taken its toll. The American spearhead, the 29th Infantry Division, was unable to keep up the pressure the next day. It continued to attack on July 12–13 but gained little ground. Seeing that this tough outfit was temporarily exhausted, General Corlett shifted the burden of the attack to the 35th Infantry Division. It gained ground on the right flank of the German 352nd Division and soon threatened to cut it off in a bend of the Vire River. The 352nd, in battle since D-Day, had met 40 American attacks in the last three days. Now it finally wavered, but the Americans were again too slow. Meindl had finally received some reinforcements in the form of the remnants of the 30th Mobile Brigade and a battle group from the 266th Infantry Division, both of which he immediately committed to the threatened zone. This move again slowed the American momentum but did not stop it entirely. The remnants of the 352nd escaped, but three days later, on the morning of July 16, the U.S. 1st Army captured Hill 122, just 3,000 yards north of St.-Lô. The fall of the city was now just a matter of time.[69]

The next day, July 17, Hausser requested permission to abandon the city. His chief of staff, Major General Max Pemsel, telephoned Rommel's operations officer at Army Group B Headquarters. Pemsel wanted the request forwarded to OB West and then on to OKW, which meant Hitler. Colonel Tempelhoff thought this was impractical, for he knew what the reply would be. "You take whatever measures you think are necessary," he told Pemsel. "If you have to withdraw, go ahead, just report to us afterwards that the enemy penetrated your main line of resistance in several places and that you barely succeeded in reestablishing a new line to the rear."[70] Rommel had chosen his staff well. Using this formula, the II Parachute Corps escaped annihilation, despite Hitler's order.

The city fell on July 19. However, Meindl still occupied the heights a mile south of St.-Lô. Bradley had captured only a large mass of ruins, at the cost of over 5,000 casualties in six days. Since its attacks began on July 3, the U.S. 1st Army had lost 40,000 men.[71] The Americans were still bogged down in hedgerow country, and the German front was still intact.

While the Americans slugged their way toward St.-Lô, Rommel faced another threat on his right flank. With typical determination he pivoted to meet it. This turned out to be his last battle. Appropriately, it was against his old foe from North Africa, Sir Bernard Law Montgomery.

The fall of that part of the Caen urban area north of the Orne had improved Monty's overall position only a little. As long as the Germans held the southern suburbs, they still held the neck of the Caen bottle. The end of the hedgerow country was in sight, but Montgomery still could not get there. Therefore, in view of the overall deterioration of the Allies' strategic position, he decided to launch yet another offensive on July 15, with the big punch coming on July 17. It was code-named "Goodwood" and had the objective of breaking free into the tank country south of Caen. Table 5.2 shows the Order of Battle of the opposing forces when the battle began.

Table 5.2
Opposing Forces, British Sector
July 15, 1944 (left to right)

Panzer Group West	British 2nd Army
Caumont Sector	
XXXXVII Panzer Corps	XXX Corps
276th Infantry Division	49th Infantry division
2nd Panzer Division[1]	50th Infantry Division
	59th Infantry Division
	8th Armoured Brigade
	33rd Army Tank Brigade
Odon Salient (Hill 112 Sector)	
II SS Panzer Corps	XII Corps
271st Infantry Division[2]	15th Infantry Division
10th SS Panzer Division[2]	43rd Infantry Division
277th Infantry Division	53rd Infantry Division
102nd SS Heavy Panzer Battalion	4th Armoured Division
9th SS Panzer Division[3]	31st Army Tank Brigade
	34th Army Tank Brigade
Caen Sector	
I SS Panzer Corps	II Canadian Corps
272nd Infantry Division[4]	2nd Canadian Infantry Division
101st Heavy Panzer Battalion	3rd Canadian Infantry Division
KG, 12th SS Panzer Division[3]	2nd Canadian Armoured Brigade
Lower Orne Sector	
LXXXVI Corps	I British Corps
KG, 711th Infantry Division	3rd British Infantry Division
KG, 346th Infantry Division	6th Airborne Division
KG, 16th Luftwaffe Field Division	51st Infantry Division
KG, 21st Panzer Division	27th Armoured Brigade
103rd Heavy Panzer Battalion[3]	1st Special Service Brigade
	4th Special Service Brigade
Panzer Group West forces	British 2nd Army Reserves
disturbed throughout the battle zone:	VIII Corps
3 regiments of III Flak Corps	Guards Armoured Division
7th Mortar Brigade	7th Armoured Division
8th Mortar Brigade	11th Armoured Division
9th Mortar Brigade (-)	
654th Heavy Anti-Tank Battalion[5]	

NOTES

1. The 326th Infantry Division was en route from Boulogne to relieve the 2nd Panzer Division.
2. 271st Infantry Division was in the process of relieving the 10th SS Panzer Division.
3. In Reserve.
4. 272nd Infantry Division was in the process of relieving the 1st SS Panzer Division.
5. A *Jagdpanther* unit, equipped with superb Jagdpanther tank destroyers.
KG = *Kampfgruppe* (a battle group or a division at regimental or battle group strength).
(-) = Elements of this unit had been detached and sent elsewhere.

The initial thrust came on the British right flank and was launched by their XXX and newly committed XII Corps. It was aimed at the high ground south of Villers-Bocage, but its real objective was apparently to pin down the German reserves. The Allies lost more than 3,500 men, gained very little ground against the XXXXVII Panzer and II SS Panzer Corps, and were three miles west of Tilly when nightfall came. However, they had tied down the 1st SS, 10th SS, and 2nd Panzer divisions and had forced the Germans to commit the 9th SS Panzer Division to counterattacks.[72]

The offensive on the British left began on the night of July 16/17, when their 53rd Infantry Division took the village of Cahier north of the Orne. Fifth Panzer Army retook it the next day in heavy fighting, but another threat posed itself almost immediately: The British I Corps attacked Colombelles, and Eberbach had to throw the 21st Panzer Division back into the battle (even though it had only 47 tanks left) to prevent them from overrunning the suburbs south of Caen. Montgomery believed that his attacks had left Rommel with only one panzer division uncommitted: the burnt-out 12th SS, which was licking its wounds in the woods south of Falaise. By dawn on July 18, Montgomery's attacks had pinned down the 10th SS Panzer Division near Esquay and the 9th SS Panzer near Evrecy and Maltot, as well as the 21st Panzer at Colombelles. Now Monty unleashed his main attack: It came from the Allied far left flank, out of the airborne bridgehead east of the Orne River. This sector had huge drawbacks. First, its assembly areas were visible to the German positions at Bois de Bavent and Colombes. Second, it was constricted, with a narrow frontage. The armored divisions Montgomery committed from here would have to advance in file instead of on line, which would greatly reduce their effectiveness. Third, the Germans had a string of fortified villages and outposts all along the left flank of the route of advance. These were coordinated, prepared positions, with overlapping fields of fire. The British left flank would be exposed throughout the length of its initial advance. Fourth, the bridgehead was too small to allow for the maximum employment of artillery. Fifth, the road network was small and in poor condition, at least partially resulting from Allied shelling. Traffic congestion would be a major problem.[73]

General Montgomery had three British armored divisions available for the attack: the 7th, 11th, and Guards, all under British VII Corps. In addition, 500 reserve tanks were already in Normandy, and the Canadian 4th Armoured and Polish 1st Armored divisions, now in England, stood ready for embarkation to the continent. Heavy losses, therefore, would be acceptable if the decisive breakthrough could be made.

As previously mentioned, the British armored divisions would have to advance in file (that is, one behind the other) instead of on line.

Montgomery picked Major General "Pip" Roberts's veteran 11th Armoured to lead the way, followed by the Guards and 7th Armoured. The Canadian infantry would cover the left flank, the British the right. This scheme of operations was not a very satisfactory arrangement, but Montgomery felt sure that his spearheads would be able to reach the Orne Canal, bridge it, brush aside the remnants of the 12th SS Panzer Division, and capture Falaise to the south. If successful, the offensive would destroy three German divisions, unglue Rommel's whole front, and open the gates to Paris.[74]

The British counted on air power to pave the way. The bombardment represented the greatest air concentration in history to that date. A thousand British Lancaster and Halifax heavy bombers and 1,500 U.S. Fortress and Liberator heavy bombers, followed by 600 British and American medium bombers, would saturate an 8,000-yard sector with 12,000 tons of bombs—5,000 tons of which would fall in less than 45 minutes. They would be supported by more than 2,000 fighters. British Air Vice Marshal Harry Broadhurst, commander of this vast armada, remarked: "I don't really know what bit of air will be left unoccupied when the show starts."[75] In addition to the aerial blitzkrieg, naval gunfire and 720 field artillery pieces, which had 250,000 rounds to fire, would blast the German strong points. The Canadian 2nd and 3rd Infantry divisions would attack into the gap thus created and secure its flanks. An entire armored corps would then attack through the hole in Rommel's line—into tank country! Paris and the destruction of Army Group B seemed within Montgomery's grasp.

Unfortunately, as Major General J.F.C. Fuller wrote, "The Germans . . . had seen through these clumsy tactics."[76] Rommel met with Sepp Dietrich and Wilhelm Bittich, the commanders of the I SS and II SS Panzer corps, respectively. They concluded that the Allied offensive was imminent and would come in the zone of the 16th Luftwaffe Field Division, the worst combat unit in the army group. It had already been routed once, it will be recalled, and there was no reason to believe that it would perform any better now. Accordingly, Rommel brought up two fresh formations to meet the Allied thrust. These were the newly arrived 272nd Infantry and 1st SS Panzer Division "Leibstandarte Adolf Hitler," commanded by Major General Friedrich-August Schack and SS Major General Theodor Wisch, respectively.[77] Montgomery thought that the SS panzer division was fully committed near Esquay, but he was mistaken.[78] Rommel also concentrated a few remaining Tiger tanks, 194 field guns, 272 of the six-barreled Nebelwerfer rocket launchers, and 78 88mm antiaircraft guns at Bourguebus Ridge. This position was out of the range of British artillery but in the Allies' suspected route of advance.

The U.S. 8th Air Force was supposed to bomb this general area, but apparently Allied intelligence failed to detect the camouflaged positions of the 88s. In any event they were completely missed by the bombs and were ready when Monty unleashed his tanks.

The carpet bombing began at 5:00 A.M. on July 17. Over the next two days, the Allies fired more than 100,000 shells into the zones of the LXXXVI and I SS Panzer corps alone, and pounded their positions with 7,800 tons of bombs from 2,200 bombers.[79] The 16th Luftwaffe Field Division was almost totally destroyed; all of its original battalion commanders were now killed, wounded, or missing. The last 50 tanks of the 100th Panzer Regiment, 21st Panzer Division, were bombed in their positions near Emieville. All of them were hit, and most of them were destroyed. To the shock of the Allies, however, the Desert Fox had established not one but five defensive zones to deal with the offensive. Each consisted of a line of infantry to absorb the initial shock, a supporting line of tanks immediately behind it, a line of strong points with antitank guns, strong artillery concentrations in concealed positions, and a second line of strong points with mobile reserves (including panzers) some miles behind. "Twelve thousand tons of bombs did not succeed in cracking this formidable obstacle," Admiral Ruge wrote.[80]

The main attack ran right into Rommel's flak nest at Bourguebus Ridge, where it immediately bogged down. The II SS Panzer Corps quickly committed its Tiger companies, along with elements of the newly attached 1st SS Panzer Division. The British armored spearhead, which expected only scattered resistance, was halted in confusion. At nightfall SS General Wisch, the commander of the Leibstandarte, launched a counterattack with his Panthers. They alone shot up 80 British tanks. The British 11th Armoured Division lost 126 tanks that day—over half its total strength. The Guards Armoured Division lost another 60 on the Caen-Vimont road, all victims of the flak nest. In all, Montgomery lost 200 tanks on the first day of the offensive.[81] "Goodwood" had been stopped in its tracks, its back broken. There was even some talk of relieving Montgomery of his command for the abject failure of this offensive.[82] Erwin Rommel had won a major victory. He did not know it, however, for he was lying unconscious in a field hospital—and was not expected to live.

NOTES

1. Ruge, p. 343.
2. Ibid., p. 342; Carell, pp. 201–2.
3. Ruge, p. 340.
4. Harrison, pp. 442–43.
5. B. H. Liddell Hart, *The Other Side of the Hill* (London: Cassell, 1951), p. 409.
6. McKee, p. 122; Montgomery, p. 64.
7. McKee, p. 133.

8. J. J. How, *Hill 112* (London: William Kimber, 1984) pp. 61–65 (hereafter cited as "How"); McKee, pp. 133–41.

9. Ibid.

10. How, pp. 61–65; Harrison, p. 444; McKee, pp. 144–45; Carell, p. 207; Montgomery, pp. 64–65.

11. McKee, pp. 154–58; Craig W. H. Luther, *Blood and Honor: The History of the 12th SS Panzer Division "Hitler Youth," 1943–1945* (San Jose, Calif.: R. James Bender Publishing, 1987), p. 197

12. Paul Hausser, who was perhaps the single greatest influence on the military development of the Waffen-SS, was born in Brandenburg on October 7, 1880, the son of a Prussian officer. He was educated in various military prep schools and graduated from Gross Lichterfelde (located in Berlin-Lichterfelde), Imperial Germany's equivalent of West Point, in 1899. Guenther von Kluge was one of his classmates.

Hausser was assigned to the 155th Infantry and served eight years of regimental duty. He became a member of the General Staff in 1912. He held a number of General Staff positions in World War I and also commanded an infantry company. After the war, he served in the Freikorps (against the Poles) and joined the Reichsheer. He retired as a major general in 1932, with an honorary promotion to lieutenant general.

Paul Hausser joined the SS in 1934, when Himmler offered him the job of training his SS-Verfuegungstruppe (SS-VT or Special Purpose Troops)—the embryo of the Waffen-SS. He soon became responsible for the military training of all SS troops, except Theodor Eicke's "Death's Head" concentration camp guards. In late 1939 he was named commander of the SS-VT Division, which he led in France in 1940. This unit later became the 2nd SS Panzer Division "Das Reich," which he led until October 1941, when he was badly wounded on the Eastern Front and lost his right eye. After he returned to active duty in 1942, Hausser was named commander of the SS Panzer Corps, which later became the II SS Panzer Corps. Hausser led the corps on the Eastern Front in 1943–44, with uneven results.

Hausser turned out to be a poor to mediocre army commander. He led 7th Army until he was severely wounded during the breakout from the Falaise Pocket. (Hausser was rescued and escaped, but two-thirds of his command did not.) He was not able to return to active duty until late January 1945. He was nevertheless given command of Army Group G, which he led until the end of March. By now he was thoroughly disillusioned with the Nazi leadership and was sacked because he objected to one of Hitler's senseless hold-at-all-costs orders.

Despite his prominence in the Waffen-SS, SS Colonel General Hausser was not subjected to a long imprisonment after the war. A staunch defender of the Waffen-SS until the end, he died on December 28, 1972, at the age of 92.

13. Ibid., pp. 161–63; Carell, p. 209; Ruge, p. 341.

14. Harrison, p. 444.

15. Speidel, pp. 103–4.

16. Most sources place the date of Dollmann's death as June 29; some, however, cite the 28th. Years after the war, General Pemsel stated that Doll-

mann committed suicide, but this assertion is unconfirmed, and—frankly—I doubt if it is true. Dollmann was not the type.

17. Ellis, I, p. 323. General of Infantry Kurt von der Chevallerie was born in Berlin in 1891 and had had a distinguished career on the Eastern Front, commanding the 99th Light Division and LIX Corps. He was named acting commander of the 1st Army in southwestern France on June 2, 1944. Politically unacceptable to the Nazis and unjustly held responsible for the collapse of the German forces in southwest France, he was relieved of his command on September 5, 1944, and was never reemployed. He was in Kolberg when it fell to the Russians in 1945. He was arrested by the Soviets and never seen again.

Willi Bittrich was born in Wernigerode in the Harz Mountains on February 26, 1894. He served as an aviator in World War I and then fought against the Poles in the Eastern marshlands. Between the wars he remained a pilot and was involved in training aviators at the secret German base in Russia. In 1934 he joined the SS-VT and by 1940 was commander of the SS-Regiment Deutschland. He took charge of the 2nd SS Panzer Division in 1941 after Paul Hausser was wounded. In 1942 he organized the SS-Cavalry Division and later was in charge of building up the 9th SS Panzer Division "Hohenstaufen," which he successfully commanded on the Eastern Front.

In September 1944 Bittrich smashed the British 1st Airborne Division at Arnhem. He surrendered to the Americans but was handed over to the French, who held him until 1954; then he was tried for war crimes at Bordeaux and acquitted. See Jost W. Schneider, *Verleihung Genehmigt!*, Winder McConnell, ed. and trans. (San Jose, Calif.: R. James Bender Publishing, 1977), pp. 35–37.

18. Carell, pp. 209–10. The 7th Mortar Brigade included the 83rd and 84th Mortar regiments and was commanded by Colonel Tzschoekell.

19. Speidel, pp. 88–89. Despite the tactical skill with which he fought on both the Eastern and Western Fronts, Normandy was Baron Hans von Funck's last campaign. He was sacked by Hitler on September 1, 1944, and would never have been reemployed had it not been for General of Infantry Walter Schroth, the commander of Wehrkreis XII (the XII Military District). Schroth gave Funck command of Reserve Panzer Command XII in Wiesbaden. In October 1944 Schroth was killed in an automobile accident; in January 1945 General Burgdorff, the army personnel officer (see Chapter VI), forced Funck into retirement and dismissed him from the army at the end of February. Funck was captured by the Soviets at the end of the war and spent 10 years in prison. He died in West Germany on February 14, 1979 (Friedrich von Stauffenberg, "Panzer Commanders of the Western Front," unpublished manuscript in the possession of the author.)

20. Ibid., p. 89.

21. Speidel, p. 89; Toland, pp. 1080–81; Irving, *Hitler's War*, pp. 649–50; Irving, pp. 397–98; Rommel, p. 480.

22. Toland, p. 1081.

23. Irving, p. 399.

24. Speidel, pp. 101–2.

25. Ibid.

26. Speidel, pp. 103–4.

27. Seaton, *Fortress*, p. 118.

28. Geyr's forced retirement lasted only a few weeks. On July 21, the day after the failure of the attempt on Hitler's life, his friend Heinz Guderian was named chief of the General Staff. The following month, Geyr succeeded Guderian as inspector of panzer troops. Captured by the Americans at the end of the war, he became a prolific writer about military affairs, although his views were largely discounted by the West German Army. Until the end, he contended that he was right and Rommel was wrong on the question of the employment of strategic reserves in the Normandy campaign. Baron Leo Geyr von Schweppenburg died in Irschenhausen on January 27, 1974.

Heinrich Eberbach was born in Stuttgart in 1895. He joined the Imperial Army in 1914 and was commissioned second lieutenant of infantry in 1915. He was taken prisoner on the Western Front and was held captive for more than a year. After the war, he joined the police and was active in developing motorized, paramilitary police forces. He returned to the army as a major in the panzer branch in 1935 and became commander of the 35th Panzer Regiment in 1938. He led this unit in Poland and in the Western campaign of 1940. He successively led the 5th Panzer Brigade, 4th Panzer Division, and XXXXVIII Panzer Corps on the Eastern Front (1941–44), before becoming commander of the 5th Panzer Army (nee Panzer Group West). Eberbach was commanding the 7th Army during the retreat from France on August 8, 1944, when he was captured by the British. He was still alive in West Germany in the 1970s.

Upon assuming command, Eberbach studied Geyr's recommendations and wrote a dispatch to OB West, stating that he agreed with them entirely. Field Marshal von Kluge, however, did not forward Eberbach's views to OKW (Foster, p. 332).

29. Alfred Gause became chief of staff of the 6th Panzer Army in September 1944 but was relieved in November and not reemployed until April 1945, when he was named commander of the II Corps, which was isolated in the Courland Pocket in western Latvia. He surrendered to the Soviets on May 9, 1945, and spent 10 years in Soviet prisons. He then retired to Karlsruhe, where he was living in 1957 (Keilig, p. 101).

30. Breuer, *Cherbourg*, p. 256.

31. Christopher Chant, Richard Humble, William Fowler, and Jenny Shaw, *Hitler's Generals and Their Battles* (New York; Chartwell Books, Inc., 1976) p. 86.

32. Speidel, pp. 105–6.

33. Ibid.

34. Irving, p. 403.

35. Rommel, p. 481.

36. Eduard Wagner was born in Kirchenlamitz in 1894 and entered the Bavarian Army as a Fahnenjunker in 1912. Commissioned second lieutenant in the 12th Bavarian Field Artillery Regiment when World War I broke out, he remained in the Reichsheer after the war. A branch chief at OKH when the war broke out, he became quartermaster (chief supply officer) for the army on August 1, 1940. He held this post until July 23, 1944 (Keilig, p. 359).

37. Hart, 1951, p. 413.

38. Ibid., p. 485.

39. Irving, pp. 401–2.

40. Carell, p. 217.

41. Martin Blumenson, *Breakout and Pursuit*. U.S. Army in World War II, The European Theater of Operations, Office of the Chief of Military History (Washington, D.C.: United States Government Printing Office, 1961), p. 148.

42. Ibid., pp. 53, 57, 78–84, 119; Montgomery, p. 71.

43. Blumenson, p. 63.

44. The 15th Parachute Regiment was normally part of the 5th Parachute Division but was attached to the 17th SS Panzer Grenadier Division during the Battle of Normandy (Tessin, Volume 4, p. 19).

45. Blumenson, pp. 78–101.

46. Carell, p. 215. The 16th Luftwaffe Field Division was officially dissolved on August 4, 1944. Most of its survivors were incorporated into the 21st Panzer Division, although some were transferred to the reconstituted 16th Infantry Division.

Karl Sievers (who had previously led the 321st Infantry Division on the Eastern Front) was not held responsible for the poor performance of the 16th Luftwaffe Field. He was given command of the 719th Infantry Division in the Netherlands on July 30 and was promoted to lieutenant general on October 1, 1944. He was living in Goettingen in the late 1950s (Keilig, p. 324).

47. McKee, pp. 175–79.

48. Ibid., p. 179.

49. Montgomery, pp. 73–74.

50. McKee, pp. 179–81.

51. Blumenson, pp. 123–27; McKee, pp. 128–33.

52. Ibid., pp. 102–17.

53. Carell, pp. 218–19.

54. McKee, pp. 191–92.

55. In his memoirs Montgomery stated that the preparatory air strikes were launched from 9:50 P.M. to 10:30 P.M. on July 7, and the ground attack began at 4:20 A.M. on July 8. He explained that the bombers struck this far in advance of the ground attack because weather conditions were forecasted as unfavorable for air activity on the morning of July 8 (Montgomery, pp. 72–73).

56. McKee, pp. 197–201; Montgomery, pp. 72–73.

57. Carell, pp. 215–16.

58. Ibid.

59. Foster, p. 338.

60. Montgomery, p. 75.

61. Irving, pp. 339–40, 406.

62. McKee, pp. 205–11.

63. Ibid., pp. 212–17. Herbert Fuerbringer, *9.SS-Panzer-Division* (Editions Heimdal, 1984).

64. Montgomery, p. 78; McKee, pp. 212–17.

65. McKee, p. 227.

66. Ibid., pp. 227–28.

67. Montgomery, pp. 74–75.

68. Eugen Meindl, who was as brave as he was arrogant, was born in Donaueschingen, Baden, on July 16, 1892, the son of a forestry official. He joined the 67th Artillery Regiment in Hagenau (then part of the German

Alsace) in 1913 and was commissioned in 1914. He fought in World War I, rising to the posts of battery commander and regimental adjutant. He remained in the Reichsheer, mainly in the artillery, and was a battalion commander in 1935. In November 1938 he became commander of the 112th Mountain Artillery Regiment, which he led in the Polish campaign. In the Norwegian campaign he made a combat jump at Narvik, despite the fact that he had had no parachute training. This no doubt impressed Goering. In November 1940 Meindl transferred to the Luftwaffe as a major general, commanding the Assault Regiment. He was seriously wounded in the airborne assault on Crete. After recovering, he fought on the Eastern Front and was instrumental in forming the first Luftwaffe Field divisions. In October 1942 he became commander of the XIII Air Corps, which organized some 22 Luftwaffe Field divisions. In November 1943 he assumed command of the II Parachute Corps; he was promoted to general of paratroopers on April 1, 1944.

Meindl was later involved in the breakout from the Falaise Pocket. He later fought at Cleve, Nijmegen, Venlo, and in the Wesel bridgehead against the British. He surrendered to the British in Schleswig-Holstein on May 8, 1945. Released from the POW camps in 1947, he died in Munich on January 24, 1951.

69. Blumenson, pp. 147–69.
70. Ibid., pp. 168–69.
71. MacDonald and Blumenson, "Recovery," p. 90.
72. Montgomery, p. 78; Ellis, I, p. 334.
73. Montgomery, p. 79; McKee, pp. 230–32.
74. Fuller, p. 300.
75. Ibid.
76. Ibid.
77. Friedrich-August Schack led his division in the breakout from the Falaise Pocket and was named commander of the LXXXI Corps on September 4. He was relieved on September 21 (during the Battle of Aachen) because he was suffering from nervousness and battle fatigue. After a rest of several weeks, he briefly commanded the LXXXV Corps and ended the war as a general of infantry, commanding the XXXII Corps on the Eastern Front. Schack, however, managed to surrender his command to the British. He retired to Goslar and was still alive in the 1950s.

Theodor "Teddy" Wisch was born in Wesselburener Koog, Schlesiwig-Holstein in 1907 and volunteered for the Leibstandarte Adolf Hitler in the spring of 1933. He rose rapidly—from private in 1933 to company commander in 1939 and divisional commander in 1944, succeeding Sepp Dietrich as commander of the Leibstandarte. A holder of the Knight's Cross with Oak Leaves and Swords, he was critically wounded on August 20 and apparently never reemployed.

78. Montgomery, p. 79.
79. Foster, p. 344.
80. Ruge, p. 344.
81. Carell, pp. 226–28; McKee, p. 256; Foster, p. 341.
82. The suggestion that Montgomery be relieved was allegedly made by the Deputy Supreme Commander, British Air Chief Marshal Sir Arthur Tedder, Eisenhower's second-in-command. Tedder later denied that he made the suggestion (Hart, II, pp. 553, 556).

CHAPTER 6

"A PITILESS DESTINY"

At 4:00 P.M. on July 17, 1944, Field Marshal Erwin Rommel left the headquarters of Sepp Dietrich's I SS Panzer Corps at St. Pierre-sur-Dives on his way back to La Roche-Guyon. He never reached it. What happened to him was not unusual: It happened to thousands of German soldiers on the Western Front in 1944 and 1945. On a secondary road from Livarot to Vimoutiers, his car was jumped by a pair of Allied fighter-bombers. His driver, Corporal Daniel, stepped on the accelerator and headed for a little side road about 300 yards ahead, which would have given them some protection. Before they could reach it, however, the leading aircraft—which was only a few feet above the ground—pulled to within 500 yards and opened fire. Rommel was hit in the temple and cheekbone, suffered a triple skull fracture, and lost consciousness immediately. Major Neuhaus was hit in the holster with such force that it broke his pelvis. Another shell from the Allied cannon shattered Daniel's left shoulder and arm, causing him to lose control of the car. As Captain Helmuth Lang (Rommel's aide) and Sergeant Holke (his spotter) jumped out, the car struck a tree stump on the left, skidded to the right, and turned over in the ditch. Rommel was thrown out and lay unconscious in the road, about 20 yards behind the car.[1]

The field marshal's left cheekbone was destroyed, he had numerous shell splinters and fragments in his head, his left eye was injured, his skull badly fractured in four places, and his temple penetrated. It was 45 minutes before Captain Lang and Sergeant Holke could get him to a French religious hospital. At first it was thought that there was no chance of him living through such serious wounds.

Later that night the Desert Fox, still unconscious, was transferred to the Luftwaffe hospital at Bernay, about 25 miles away. His driver, Corporal Daniel, also unconscious, was transported with him. That night, doctors operated on the driver but were unable to save his life. He never regained consciousness.[2]

The average 52-year-old man probably would have died from the wounds Rommel received on July 17. However, Field Marshal Rommel's years of physical training and his strong constitution worked for him, and within a few days he had recovered enough to be moved to the more sophisticated hospital of Professor Esch at Vesinet. A few weeks later he went home to Germany. He did not realize it yet, but he was as good as dead.

Up until Adolf Hitler interfered with his conduct of the Battle of El Alamein on November 3, 1942, Erwin Rommel had been completely loyal to him. On that day, the Fuehrer had issued a senseless "stand fast" order that led to the virtual destruction of Panzer Army Afrika. Rommel was never able to regain the initiative in North Africa after that. Even after El Alamein, the marshal continued to accord Hitler the respect due him as chief of state, even if the dictator pursued a military policy that no longer made sense. Only gradually did his attitude begin to change. He was bitter about the loss of so many men in North Africa, where Germany lost 130,000 men when Tunisia fell. Rommel could have overrun Egypt and captured the Suez Canal if he had been given only a small fraction of this army group just a few months before.

Exactly when Rommel learned of the mass murders of Himmler's SS, or who told him, is not known. We do have some clues, however. In December 1943 his 14-year-old son Manfred (who was attracted by the undeniably sharp looking uniforms of the SS) asked his father's permission to join the Waffen-SS. Rommel curtly rejected this idea as "out of the question." He would not allow his son to serve under the command of a man who carried out mass killings.

"Do you mean Himmler?" Manfred asked.

"Yes," the field marshal replied. At this time Rommel did not know how deeply Hitler was involved in this mass slaughter, or even if he knew about it at all.

It was only in the early months of 1944 that he learned of the magnitude of the Nazis' crimes and of the extent of Hitler's involvement in them. His son wrote later that from the moment Rommel learned of Hitler's involvement, all of his former inner loyalty to the Fuehrer vanished, and he decided to act against him.[3]

Although he did not realize it at the time, Rommel first became connected with the conspiracy to assassinate Adolf Hitler in February 1944. At that time he was visited by Doctor Karl Stroelin, the mayor of Stuttgart. Stroelin (who had served with Rommel in World War I and who was on friendly terms with Lucie) came to Rommel at the request of Dr. Carl Goerdeler, the former mayor of Leipzig and the leading civilian member of the conspiracy. They discussed the possibility of a legal change of government and the means to end the war.[4] Stroelin, however, initially moved too quickly for a man like Rommel, who was a straightforward soldier and was out of his element in the realm of power politics. With Rommel's wife, son, and friend Hermann Aldinger present, the Stuttgart mayor made a speech on the subject of the criminality of Hitler and the Nazis. He even had documentary proof that they were systematically committing genocide against the Jews and others. Finally he declared that if Hitler did not die, then everybody in Germany was lost. This was too much for Rommel, who asked Stroelin not to express such opinions in front of his young son.[5] Realizing that he had gone too far too fast, Stroelin immediately adopted a more moderate tone and confined himself to discussing the desirability of overthrowing Hitler and the Nazi regime. The Stroelin-Rommel discussions lasted for more than five hours,[6] and the mayor gradually won Rommel over. "You are our greatest and most popular general and more respected abroad than any other," he told the marshal. "You are the only one who can prevent civil war in the Third Reich."

Erwin Rommel was clearly agonizing. He recalled a statement once voiced by Hitler himself: "When the government of a nation is leading it to its doom, rebellion is not only the right but the duty of every citizen."

The Desert Fox made his decision. "I believe it is my duty to come to the rescue of Germany," he said.[7] From this day on, Rommel was in the conspirator's orbit, although he never advocated killing Hitler. He was afraid that the Fuehrer's death might create a great Nazi martyr and another "stabbed in the back" legend of the type that grew after World War I.[8] It would have no doubt surprised Rommel if the mayor had told him the whole truth: The conspirators' plans to assassinate the Fuehrer were already well advanced; and Stroelin and several other members of the resistance intended to make Erwin Rommel President of the Reich!

Other powerful or important Germans had already joined or were soon to join the secret resistance movement. They all realized that the war was lost and hoped to rid Germany of the madman in Rastenburg before he went down to final defeat and dragged the whole nation with him. General of Infantry Alexander von Falkenhausen, the Military Governor of Belgium and Northern France, cast his lot with the plotters. Rommel's chief of staff, Doctor Hans Speidel, was a longtime advocate of the removal of Adolf Hitler by whatever means necessary. General Carl-Heinrich von Stuelpnagel, the Military Governor of France, met Rommel at a country house near St. Germain early that spring. Stuelpnagel, his chief of staff Luftwaffe Lieutenant Colonel Dr. Caesar von Hofacker, and Rommel all agreed that the Nazi regime must be overthrown. Both Rommel and the military governor told Field Marshal von Rundstedt of their discussions. The aging marshal's reaction was typical of the senior German commanders of the time. He would not help them, but he would do nothing to stop them either. "You are young. You know and love the people. You do it!" were his exact words to the Desert Fox. Like far too many men who could have made a difference, he acquiesced. All too many generals in the top echelon, who had shown great physical courage in their lives, lacked the moral fortitude to stand up against their supreme commander, even when it became obvious that he was a madman. This was the true tragedy of the German officer corps in World War II.

Rommel's interest in the conspiracy increased as the time for the Allied invasion approached. Sometime after May 15 he met with General of Artillery Eduard Wagner, the First Quartermaster General of the Army. For the first time he was informed of the active resistance, the planned revolt, and of the previous attempts on Hitler's life. He learned that in 1943 a bomb had been placed aboard Hitler's airplane but had failed to explode. He learned that a certain Captain Alex von dem Bussche had been prepared to blow himself up to kill the Fuehrer but could not manage to get close enough to carry out his plan. Rommel, as always politically naive, objected to the idea of assassination. He wanted Hitler arrested and forced to stand trial for his crimes. He did not want to create a great Nazi martyr. Wagner's comments concerning Rommel's rather idealistic views are not recorded. It is known, however, that Rommel did not change Wagner's mind, nor the minds of his associates. Men with greater political vision were in charge of the plot, and Rommel's notions could not divert them from their course. With great courage and strength of character, they plotted to blow up Adolf Hitler.

The real leader of the conspiracy was Colonel Count Claus von Stauffenberg, the chief of staff to the Commander-in-Chief of the Replacement Army, headquartered in Berlin. Stauffenberg had served briefly in Rommel's Army Group Afrika, and although they had met only professionally, Stauffenberg considered Rommel "a great leader."9 While acting as operations officer of the 10th Panzer Division in April 1943, von Stauffenberg, like Rommel a year later, fell victim to an Allied fighter-bomber. His left arm was now useless, and one of his eyes was gone, but he soldiered on. This human dynamo became the catalytic agent for the conspiracy. Around himself he rallied the best men still alive in Nazi Germany. They included Colonel General Ludwig Beck, the former chief of the General Staff and Prussia's last philosopher-in-uniform; Admiral Wilhelm Canasis, the former chief of the Abwehr; and Julius Leber, the former Socialist member of the Reichstag, who was so tough that not even the Gestapo could get a single word out of him despite weeks of prolonged torture. Other members of the resistance included Count Helmuth von Moltke, a diplomat and a descendant of the field marshal who defeated and captured Napoleon III at Sedan;

Major General Helmuth Stieff, the chief of the Organization Branch at OKH; Ernst Juenger, a friend of both Rommel and Speidel and perhaps the leading German author of his day; Albrecht Haushofer, the son of Professor Karl Haushofer and a noted geopolitical thinker in his own right; Field Marshal Erwin von Witzleben, the former Commander-in-Chief West, now retired; Count Wolf von Helldorf, police president of Berlin; Colonel General Erich Hoepner, former commander of the 1st Panzer Army, who had been sacked by Hitler for failing to obey a senseless "hold at all costs" order in January 1942; Ulrich von Hassell, former German ambassador to Rome; Count Friedrich Werner von Schulenburg, former ambassador to Moscow; Father Alfred Delp, a Jesuit leader; Major General Henning von Treschow, the chief of staff of 2nd Army, which was now fighting for its life on the Eastern Front; and dozens of others.

The addition of Rommel as a sympathizer apparently provided new momentum to the conspirators. Generals Dollmann and von Salmuth both told Rommel that they were prepared to obey his orders, even if they were in direct contradiction to those issued by Adolf Hitler. Geyr von Schweppenburg also made a similar pronouncement. Lieutenant General Count Gerhard von Schwerin-Krosigk of the 116th Panzer Division and Lieutenant General Baron Heinrich von Luettwitz of the 2nd Panzer Division declared to the field marshal that their units were to be available for use against the Nazi regime.[10]

On July 9, Colonel von Hofacker visited Rommel at La Roche-Guyon. Hofacker had a great deal of personal influence with Rommel because his father had commanded Lieutenant Rommel on the Italian Front in World War I. Also, the military situation had deteriorated considerably since von Hofacker and his chief, General von Stuelpnagel, had first met with Rommel early that spring. The persuasive staff officer spoke of the growing German resistance to Nazism and urged independent military action to end the war in the West. He asked Rommel how long the Normandy Front could be held. They needed to know in Berlin, he said, in order to know how to proceed against Hitler. "At the most 14 days to three weeks," Rommel replied, with typical candor. "Then a break-through may be expected. We have no additional forces to throw into the battle." Hofacker departed to visit von Kluge but promised to meet with Rommel again on July 15.[11]

Before that date, Rommel conferred with all of his top commanders. It is obvious that he was sounding them out to determine what they would do if Hitler was arrested. Even SS Generals Dietrich and Hausser disagreed with Hitler's conduct of the war. Dietrich went so far as to demand "independent action if the front is broken." Finally, on July 17, just hours before he was wounded, the Desert Fox went so far as to ask Dietrich if he would obey his orders, even if they contradicted Hitler's orders. Dietrich extended his hand and replied that he would obey only Rommel—no matter what he was planning.[12] The conspirators could expect no resistance from the Waffen-SS in Normandy if Hitler was removed.

On July 12 Field Marshal von Kluge visited his most brilliant and most difficult subordinate at La Roche-Guyon. The two marshals discussed the deteriorating military situation and found themselves in complete agreement, for a change. Rommel suggested that the army and corps commanders forward an ultimatum to Hitler and take bilateral action against him if he rejected it, as expected. Kluge listened attentively and agreed in principle to Rommel's statements. However, "Clever Hans" would not commit himself to the hilt. He said he would make his final decision after discussions with the army commanders. After von Kluge left, Rommel told his chief of staff that he would take independent action against the Nazi dictator, no matter what Kluge decided.[13] Unlike Field Marshal von Kluge, Rommel was motivated solely by his sense of duty and morality and by his love for Germany. As always, since the first day he put on the uniform as a private soldier, he stood ready to sacrifice himself for his country.

Three days later Rommel sent the following message to Adolf Hitler. History has since labeled it the ultimatum of July 15, and it drove another nail into Rommel's coffin. In it, Rommel again summarized the deteriorating military situation in Normandy and pointed out that Army Group B was losing an average of 2,500–3,000 men a day, and had suffered 97,000 casualties to date, but had received only 10,000 replacements. It had also lost 225 panzers, but only 17 had been replaced. He concluded:

The troops are everywhere fighting heroically, but the unequal struggle is approaching its end. It is urgently necessary for the proper political conclusions to be drawn from this situation. As C-in-C of the Army Group I feel myself in duty bound to speak plainly on this point.[14]

Field Marshal von Kluge endorsed Rommel's ultimatum and stated that he agreed with the Desert Fox's opinions and demands. "I have given him [Hitler] his last chance," Rommel snapped. "If he does not take it, we will act!"[15]

The next day, July 16, Rommel made a rare visit to 15th Army's sector and looked up Lieutenant Colonel Elmar Warning, a former member of the operations staff of the Afrika Korps. The physically huge Warning, now operations officer of the 17th Luftwaffe Field Division at Le Havre, had been the one on whom Rommel had unburdened himself at El Alamein in early November 1942, when Hitler first sent him a senseless "stand-fast" order.

He told Warning that he and Kluge had sent Hitler an ultimatum, informing him that the war was lost and demanding that he draw the appropriate conclusions.

"What if the Fuehrer refuses?" Warning wanted to know.

"Then I'm going to open up the Western Front!" Rommel cried, "because there's only one thing that matters now—the British and Americans must get to Berlin before the Russians do!"[16]

As we have seen, Rommel did not have a chance to act. Two days after writing the ultimatum, and the day after his visit to Warning, an Allied fighter-bomber cut him down. Now it was up to Count von Stauffenberg. He would act, without Rommel's help.

"The blow that felled Rommel . . . deprived our plan of the only man strong enough to bear the terrible weight of war and civil war simultaneously—the only man with enough naivete to counter the frightful simplicity of those he was to attack." Ernst Juenger wrote later. Rommel's wounds "broke the only pillar that could have made such a venture feasible."[17]

Meanwhile, disaster struck Nazi Germany on the Eastern Front. On June 22 the Russians launched their summer offensive of 1944. They broke through the thinly held lines of Army Group Center with more than two million men and could not be stopped. Hitler fired the army group commander, Field Marshal Ernst Busch, even though he was a loyal Nazi, and replaced him with Field Marshal Walther Model. This change in leadership did no good, however, because both the 4th and the 9th armies (and much of the weakened 3rd Panzer Army) were already destroyed. The Russians penetrated 150 miles in a week, and the front on both sides of the Pripet Marshes collapsed. Army Group Center was done for as an effective combat force. Army Group North was cut off in Courland, its back to the Baltic Sea. By the end of July the surviving German soldiers had been driven back to the Vistula, near Warsaw. As was the case in the West, there was very little left to stop the enemy from pushing all the way to Berlin.

On July 20, 1944, the one-armed Chief of Staff of the Replacement Army arrived at Hitler's headquarters in East Prussia with a bomb in his briefcase. He placed it under Hitler's table, barely six feet from the Fuehrer, and then left. Unfortunately, Colonel Heinz Brandt bumped into the count's briefcase. Annoyed by the inconvenience, he moved it. He shifted it only a few feet, but in doing so he placed it on the other side of a thick oaken table support. When he did that he changed history. Moments later this support deflected the force of the explosion away from Adolf Hitler. Brandt had saved Hitler's life, though not his own. General of Fliers Guenther Korten, the chief of the General Staff of the

Luftwaffe, and several other important officers were killed or mortally wounded by the blast. Rommel's only real friend at Fuehrer Headquarters, Lieutenant General Rudolf Schmundt, was blinded and mortally wounded, dying in agony several weeks later. Colonel General Jodl was among those hurt; only Field Marshal Keitel was completely uninjured. The one for whom the exercise had been planned, however, escaped with only minor injuries. Stunned, Adolf Hitler emerged from the ruins of his bunker, half-supported and half-carried by Wilhelm Keitel. It took him some time to recover enough to react, but when he did his reaction was murderous. "I will smash and destroy these criminals who have presumed to stand in the way of Providence and myself!" he screamed in rage. "They deserve nothing but ignominious death! And I shall give it to them! This time the full measure will be paid by all who are involved, and by their families."[18] Erwin Rommel's fate was sealed, along with that of von Stauffenberg, Beck, von Hofacker, and hundreds of others.[19]

For several days after being wounded, the hero of North Africa lay in that gray world between life and death. He was not expected to survive his first night in the French hospital. Then he made some progress, slowly, as if by pure force of will. While he recovered, the Battle of Normandy reached its climax.

Despite his heavy losses in "Goodwood," Montgomery continued to slug it out in the Caen sector, pinning down the panzer reserves of Army Group B. Field Marshal von Kluge assumed personal command of the army group following Rommel's wounding and also retained command of OB West. His consolidation of power in his own hands did nothing to improve Germany's position, however.

On July 19 the armored divisions of the British VIII Corps continued to be held up by I SS Panzer Corps and Rommel's deep defensive obstacles, while the British I Corps remained bogged down near Troarn. The Canadian II Corps, however, gained some ground and cleared the Caen suburbs of Faubourg de Vaucelles and Colombes. The 1st SS, 9th SS, 10th SS, and part of the 2nd Panzer divisions were decisively engaged. The battle finally ended the next day when it rained and the battlefield turned into "a sea of mud."[20] The British offensive on the German right flank had been halted; meanwhile, however, the Americans were preparing to deliver the decisive blow miles to the west.

Shortly after the attempt on Hitler's life, the scales fell from the eyes of the High Command, and it began to grasp the fact that Normandy was really the site of the Great Invasion. At last infantry divisions from 15th Army started to march down to Normandy as fast as their feet or the ruined transportation system would carry them.

"The decision was made too late," Field Marshal Montgomery wrote later. "The divisions arrived so slowly and so piecemeal that they were to find themselves reinforcing failure."21 Most of them arrived just in time to be destroyed.

On July 24 a force of some 1,600 heavy and medium bombers was scheduled to obliterate Lieutenant General Bayerlein's Panzer Lehr Division in the 7th Army's zone. They were called back at the last minute because of the weather, but almost 100 of them dropped their bombs anyway. Most of these bombs fell within American lines, killing more than 100 men, including Lieutenant General Leslie J. McNair, the former chief of U.S. Army Ground Forces and now commander of the fictitious 1st U.S. Army Group, which Berlin believed would deliver the real invasion blow at Pas de Calais. McNair was secretly buried and replaced by Lieutenant General John L. DeWitt. Eisenhower, although upset by the premature bomb releases, decided to try again the next day.

On July 25, 1944, the heaviest tactical employment of strategic air power during World War II was concentrated against the Panzer Lehr Division, then defending a sector west of St.-Lô. From 9:00 A.M. until noon 1,600 Flying Fortresses dropped thousands of tons of high explosives on Bayerlein's units. They were followed by hundreds of medium bombers and Jabos. In all, the air forces dropped 12 bombs for every German soldier in the target area. Tanks were hurled into the air like so many plastic toys. Entire companies were buried alive and completely wiped out. The massive carpet bombing continued on an unprecedented scale until the entire area resembled the surface of the moon.22 Montgomery, still the supreme Allied ground commander, wrote later: "Enemy troops who were not casualties were stunned and dazed, and weapons not destroyed had to be dug out and cleaned before they could be used; communications were almost completely severed."23 By the end of the day, the U.S. troops had gained two miles, even though the remnants of Panzer Lehr and nearby units were resisting as best they could.

General Bayerlein himself was trapped in a regimental command post near La Chappelle-en-Juger. The CP was an old Norman chateau with walls 10 feet thick. Only this saved Rommel's former chief of staff from being killed, along with most of his men. Later he told of his adventure: "Again and again the bomb carpets rolled toward us. . . . The ground shuddered. Quick glimpses outside showed the whole area shrouded by a pall of dust, with fountains of earth spewing high in the air. For many hours we were unable to leave the cellar." It was afternoon before Bayerlein was able to leave the chateau. He hopped on a motorcycle and raced back to his command post. (He had long since given up traveling by car; six of his automobiles had been shot up by fighter-bombers since the invasion began, and several of his drivers had been killed.)

Back at HQ, the first reports of the American advance were coming in. Surviving battle groups offered scattered resistance, but they were soon overwhelmed. A few weak reserves tried to counterattack but were soon defeated or scattered by fighter-bombers. By the following morning the breakthrough was complete.[24]

On July 26, von Kluge sent a messenger to Bayerlein's headquarters, ordering him to hold his positions. The lieutenant general, whose division had been totally smashed, replied tartly and bitterly to Kluge's staff officer: "Out in the front every one is holding out, Herr Oberstleutnant. Every one. My grenadiers and my engineers and my tank crews—they're all holding their ground. Not a single man is leaving his post. Not one! They're lying in their foxholes mute and silent, for they are dead. Dead! Do you understand? You may report to the field marshal that the Panzer Lehr Division is annihilated."[25]

Bayerlein's shocking report was essentially correct. Panzer Lehr had not been wiped out, but it had been slaughtered and was no longer able to check the U.S. armor, which surged through its broken lines. The general himself was soon overtaken by the pursuing Americans and lay pinned down in a farmhouse until nightfall. Then he escaped and walked southward, a commander without a command. Bayerlein was luckier than most. A fleeing German vehicle picked him up about midnight and took him to safety. "But," he wrote, "the Americans were now pouring through into open country with nobody to stop them—just as Rommel had predicted."[26]

Only one regiment of the decimated 275th Infantry Division and the battalion-size Battle Group Heinz (from the same division) were left intact; they were thrown forward to plug the hole, where they had to face the entire U.S. VII Corps (1st, 4th, and 30th Infantry and 2nd and 3rd Armored divisions). By nightfall Battle Group Heinz had been wiped out, and the 275th's regiment was down to 200 men. "As of this moment," von Kluge reported, "the front has . . . burst."[27] Within the week, the U.S. 3rd Army Headquarters under Lieutenant General George S. Patton was activated and took command of the breakout forces.[28] Soon they were behind Hausser's German 7th Army—with nothing left to stop them. The headquarters of the 2nd SS Panzer Division was among the rear-area units that tried to delay them; it was overrun, and its commander, SS Lieutenant Colonel Christian Tychsen, was killed in the fighting. (Heinz Lammerding, the original divisional commander, had been seriously wounded on June 26.[29]) Patton's army surged southward, out of the confines of the Cotentin Peninsula. Kluge attempted to cut off Patton's spearheads by counterattacking at Avranches, but the U.S. and Royal air forces crippled his strike forces in their assembly areas. The Allies had broken free; the Battle of Normandy was lost.

Hitler kept the news of Rommel's wounds secret from the public and made it appear that he was responsible for Patton's Avranches breakthrough, which took place on July 30 and 31. This aggravated Rommel, who was meanwhile transferred from the Luftwaffe hospital at Bernay to the LeVesinet Military Hospital because the Caen sector had also begun to collapse. Rommel recovered rapidly. On July 24, one week after his injuries, he was able to write to his wife. He told her his left eye was still swollen shut, and that his head hurt him at night, but that he felt much better in the daytime.[30]

Rommel was an awful patient for the doctors and nurses to deal with. He was a man of action, and being confined made him cantankerous and short-tempered. Besides all this, he was too powerful for the medical personnel to give him orders or to treat without his approval. Despite the seriousness of his wounds, the Desert Fox repeatedly climbed out of bed when it suited him, until one day a surgeon came in with a human skull and proceeded to shatter it with a hammer. Then he told Rommel that that was how badly his skull had been crushed.[31] But not even this demonstration kept the field marshal cooperative for more than a few days.

About this same time Baron von Esebeck, the German war correspondent who frequently traveled with Rommel, visited him at the hospital. "I'm glad it's you," Rommel said when he saw the baron. "I was afraid it was the doctor. He won't allow me to sit up. I'm sure he thinks I'm going to die, but I haven't any intention of dying. You'd better take a picture of me," he said as he got out of bed and put on his uniform jacket. He made von Esebeck take a profile of the right (undamaged) side of his face. "The British will be able to see that they haven't managed to kill me yet," he remarked. Then he began discussing the military situation and again remarked that the war was lost.

"He was especially bitter about the complete failure of the Luftwaffe," the journalist remembered. He said nothing about the attempt on Hitler's life.

Speidel and Ruge also visited Rommel at Le Vesinet a few days later. They found that he was now shaving himself. A surgeon major general tried to keep him from moving about but only received a severe reprimand for his efforts. "Don't tell me what I must do or mustn't do," Rommel said. "I know what I can do."

After this, Admiral Ruge visited him almost daily and read to him from a book entitled *The Tunnel*. "It was about building a tunnel from Europe to the United States," Ruge recalled, "exactly the sort of thing he liked. We used to talk about 'after the war.' He had been very much impressed by the enormous rise and fall of tide on the coast of Brittany and said that he would like to be actively interested in a project for drawing power from the tides. Anyway, he wanted to do something technical and practical."

Ruge and Rommel also discussed the assassination attempt. The Desert Fox felt that murder was the wrong way to go about it. "The

Hitler legend will never be destroyed until the German people know the whole truth," he said.[32]

On July 30 he remarked that he was glad that he had been wounded; now, at least, he did not have full responsibility without full authority.[33] He had been concerned that his left eye would never be normal again, but it was healing better than expected.

Ruge feared for his chief's life. He wanted Rommel to surrender himself to the British, but he never quite worked up enough courage to suggest it.[34] For his part, all Rommel wanted to do was to go home to his family at Herrlingen. On August 8 he returned there and startled his wife, who was not prepared for the ugliness of his head wounds. Rommel grinned at her reaction.[35] He continued to receive constant medical care, for his condition was still not good. Upon examining Rommel, Doctor Albrecht, a noted German brain surgeon, declared, "No man can be alive with wounds like that."[36]

Rommel was not only alive but growing better each day. He arranged to have his son posted to his staff, so the family was again reunited by mid-August. The wounded Desert Fox spoke to his 15-year-old son about the war and the hopelessness of continuing the fighting. He told the young Luftwaffe antiaircraft gun crewman that Germany should allow the British and Americans to occupy all of Central Europe, to keep the Russians outside the borders of the Reich.[37] He never could believe that the British and Americans were seriously allied with the Russians or were as fully committed to them as they, in fact, were. He believed that a Third World War, between the Russians and the Western Allies, was only a matter of time. This war, however, would come only after the defeat of Nazi Germany. While Rommel continued to recover and engage in idle conversations with his family, the Gestapo inevitably closed in on him. True enough, he had opposed the actual assassination attempt, but he had been implicated in it and had advocated the arrest of Adolf Hitler and his henchmen on charges of high treason. He had planned to open independent negotiations with the Western powers after the overthrow of the Nazi regime. He was also on some of the conspirators' lists as the next President of the Reich.

Count von Stauffenberg and General Beck were executed just before midnight on July 20 by Colonel General Friedrich "Fritz" Fromm, the Commander-in-Chief of the Replacement Army. Fromm was an unscrupulous man who played on both sides of the conspiracy question. As one who was privy to the attempt, Fromm felt that the firing squad was the best way to cover his tracks, so he summarily liquidated five of the top conspirators. Although this piece of treachery did not save him, it did remove the top potential witnesses against Erwin Rommel. Major General von Treschow, the chief of staff of 2nd Army and a leading member of the resistance, blew his own head off with hand grenades on the Russian Front as soon as he was sure the attempt had failed. He realized that the Gestapo would eventually torture him into revealing the names of his coconspirators and, true to his code, he preferred death to this dishonor. Eduard Wagner, the quartermaster general of the army, felt the same way. After lunch on July 23 he sat at his desk, placed a pistol on each temple, and pulled the triggers. There were, however, other witnesses around who were less thorough than Treschow and Wagner when it came to suicide.

On July 21 General Heinrich von Stuelpnagel was summoned to Berlin to explain why he had arrested the SS and Gestapo members in Paris on the day of the assassination attempt.[38] That night the military governor of France drank heavily and carried on loud, irrational conversations with himself. The next day he set out by car for the German capital. At Verdun, where he had distinguished himself as a junior officer in the 1914–1918 war, he ordered his driver to stop. He waded into the Meuse Canal and shot himself in the head. Both of Stuelpnagel's eyes were destroyed by the bullet, but he lived. The general's driver and orderly found the badly wounded officer, and—thinking that he had been shot by partisans—dragged him out of the water before he could drown and rushed him to the hospital at Verdun. This attempted suicide was tantamount to an admission of guilt. According to Dr. Speidel, the Gestapo agents were already beside Stuelpnagel's bed when he woke up, crying "Rommel!" over and over again.

The blind soldier was taken to Berlin, where he was tortured by the Gestapo. Apparently they could get no further information out of him, but he had already said too much in his delirium: Rommel was incriminated. Eventually Stuelpnagel was hanged with piano wire, like dozens of others.

Dr. Carl Goerdeler, the former mayor of Leipzig and the civilian head of the conspiracy, was also captured and tortured by the Gestapo. Unfortunately, he was not as tough as Stuelpnagel or Julius Leber and soon incriminated everyone he knew. The brutal but efficient Nazi secret police learned of Rommel's involvement with the resistance and closed in on him, as they did on so many others during those dangerous and violent years.

Others went down first. Helmuth von Moltke was executed by the SS without benefit of trial. Albrecht Haushofer was arrested and later shot in the back of the head, and his father, Professor Karl Haushofer, was thrown into a concentration camp. Julius Leber was tried and executed, as was Field Marshal von Witzleben and Generals Stieff and Hoepner. On August 15 Field Marshal von Kluge was relieved of his commands, replaced by Walther Model, and summoned to Berlin. Realizing the implications of this order, Kluge took poison near Verdun and died almost within sight of the spot where Heinrich von Stuelpnagel had blinded himself.

On September 6 Hans Speidel visited his former chief at Herrlingen for what proved to be their last meeting. He had been suspended from his duties as chief of staff of Army Group B, despite Model's objections, and had been replaced by Lieutenant General Hans Krebs, a pro-Nazi veteran of the Eastern Front.[39] Speidel found his ex-commander in good health and in fine spirits. Already his left eye was half open. Naturally the two men discussed the events of July 20. Speaking of Hitler, Rommel said, "That pathological liar has now gone completely mad. He is venting his sadism on the conspirators of July 20, and this won't be the end of it. I am afraid that this madman will sacrifice the last German before he meets his own end."[40]

At 6:00 A.M. the next morning, the Gestapo arrested General Speidel. Rommel tried to obtain his release, but in vain. Remarkably—thanks mainly to the efforts of Heinz Guderian and Sepp Dietrich—Dr. Speidel survived both his imprisonment and the war. He became a professor of philosophy at Tuebingen University, where Manfred Rommel later studied law.[41] Speidel eventually became a full general (i.e., four-star general) in the Bundeswehr and was the first German to hold the post of Commander, Allied Land Forces Central Europe, in the North Atlantic Treaty Organization (NATO). He retired in 1963 and died in 1984.

Erwin Rommel would not survive the war, and he knew it. After Speidel's arrest, old friends and acquaintances stopped coming around. "The rats are leaving the sinking ship," he said with a bitter smile.[42] A few days later the local party chief, a man named Maier, visited the wounded field marshal. He asked Rommel if he could trust the servants and warned him that the SS leader in Ulm suspected that he was a defeatist. Rommel replied to this comment with characteristic bluntness. "Victory!" he snapped. "Why don't you look at a map? The British are here, the Americans are here, the Russians are here. What is the use of talking about victory?" When Maier said something about Hitler, Rommel denounced the Fuehrer as a "damned fool." "You should not say things like that, Field Marshal," the party boss warned. "You will have the Gestapo after you—if they are not after you already."[43]

Rommel and his son had gotten into the habit of taking daily walks through the woods near their home. One day the field marshal told his boy that there were "certain people" who might like to do away with him—perhaps on their daily walk. He, however, was not about to skip the enjoyable exercise with his son, so from then on they would both carry pistols. Manfred did not completely grasp the implications of these remarks until a few days later, when Rommel said, "Tell me, Manfred, what do you young chaps think when Hitler suddenly hangs a whole lot of people who have persuaded themselves—not wholly without reason—that the war is lost and we should make an end of it at last?"

Manfred replied that they were all pretty sick of the conflict, but most thought Germany would win it "somehow or other."

"But it's already lost," the Desert Fox replied. "What if I, too, had declared myself ready to end it, even against Hitler's will?"

"Why do you ask that?" the lad answered.

Perhaps to keep his son from learning too much, Rommel insisted that they drop the subject, but after that conversation Manfred also had a sense of approaching disaster.[44]

Rommel took steps to provide for his family after his death. He visited his old comrade Oscar Farny at his Durren estate, near Wangen. They had served in the same regiment as lieutenants and had been close friends for years. Farny had left the army and had entered politics as a member of the Centrist Party. He was eventually elected to the Reichstag, where he opposed the rising party of Adolf Hitler. Then he retired from the political arena and took up farming, which explains why he was still alive in 1944. Rommel said to Farny, "I am in grave danger. Hitler wants to do away with me. His reasons are my ultimatum to him on July 15th, the open and honest opinions I have always expressed, the events of July 20th, and the reports of the Party and the Secret Police. If anything should happen to me, I beg you to take care of my son."

When Farny protested in disbelief, Rommel replied, "You will see. He will have me put to death. You are a politician and should understand this criminal better than I. He won't be afraid to do this."[45]

His anxiety about the future of Germany, the premonitions of his own death, the unhealed head wounds, and the inactivity combined to give Rommel sleepless nights and restless days. He wrote his former artillery advisor, Colonel Lattmann, on September 27 that he was very dissatisfied at his slow physical recovery, that he still had headaches and tired easily, and it was very hard for him to remain inactive while Germany's military condition continued to deteriorate.[46]

On October 7 the expected summons to Berlin came. Field Marshal Keitel talked with Rommel's aide and requested Rommel's appearance at an important conference to be held three days later. A special train would pick him up at Ulm. As soon as he heard the news, Rommel declared that he would not go and privately told Admiral Ruge (who was there on a visit) that he would never reach Berlin alive.[47] The marshal telephoned Keitel but talked only to Schmundt's successor, Lieutenant General Wilhelm Burgdorf. He told the new personnel officer that he was still unfit to travel. Doctor Albrecht, the brain surgeon, immediately substantiated this assertion and certified Rommel as unfit to travel. He apparently also believed that the Gestapo was out to murder the Desert Fox, for he tried to persuade him to go to his clinic, where it would be harder for the Secret Police to get at him. Rommel thanked Albrecht and said that he would keep his offer in mind.[48] However, time was running out for the Desert Fox. His refusal to go to Berlin extended his life by less than a week.

On October 13 Rommel was out with his friend Captain Hermann Aldinger. He was another one of Rommel's old comrades from World War I, who had also served as his aide in 1941, when Rommel commanded the Afrika Korps. Aldinger's health had broken down in the harsh desert environment, but now he was again back with his old friend. Rommel told Aldinger that in the event of his death, he wanted to be buried in one of three places: Heidenheim (his birthplace), Heidelberg, or Herrlingen. While they were gone, a telegram arrived from Berlin. It told Rommel that Burgdorf and Major General Ernst Maisel would arrive from Berlin at noon the next day. Since July, Maisel, chief of the Legal Section of the Army Personnel Branch, had been engaged in investigating officers suspected of being involved in the attempt on Hitler's life. Rommel commented to Aldinger that the two men were doubtless coming to talk to him about the invasion or about a new assignment. However, he surely knew better and was unusually quiet the rest of the day.[49]

On October 14, 1944, the last day of his life, Field Marshal Erwin Rommel rose early. His son received leave that day, almost certainly owing to the influence of his father. They ate breakfast together at 7:00 A.M. and later took a walk in the garden. Rommel told Manfred that two generals from Berlin were arriving at noon that day to discuss his future employment. Soon he would know if he would be facing the People's Court or a new command on the Eastern Front.

After Manfred asked if he would accept such a command, Rommel took him by the arm and declared that their enemy in the East was so terrible that all other considerations were secondary. Of course he would go, he declared.[50]

Manfred knew that his father was worried. They walked for some time. The conversation centered around Manfred and his future. Rommel wanted him to be a doctor and not a soldier. The Desert Fox probably would have been surprised to learn that his son would become a lawyer and was mayor of Stuttgart, a city slightly larger than Milwaukee, in the 1990s.

At about 11:00 A.M. they returned home. Shortly before noon Rommel changed from his civilian clothes to his old African outfit, his favorite uniform. At precisely 12:00, the Army sedan arrived from Berlin. The two generals alighted and, after exchanges of courtesies, asked to speak to the field marshal alone. They talked for nearly an hour. Then Rommel went upstairs to see his wife.

Frau Rommel knew immediately that something was wrong. "There was so strange and terrible an expression on his face," she recalled later. "What's the matter with you?" she exclaimed. "What has happened? Are you ill?"

"I have come to say good-bye," he replied. "In a quarter of an hour I shall be dead. . . . They suspect me of having taken part in the attempt to kill Hitler. It seems my name was on Goerdeler's list to be President of the Reich. . . . I have never seen Goerdeler in my life. . . . They say that von Stuelpnagel, General Speidel, and Colonel von Hofacker have denounced me. . . . It is the usual trick. . . . I have told them that I do not believe it and that it cannot be true. . . . The Fuehrer has given me the choice of taking poison or being dragged before the People's Court. They have brought the poison. They say it will take only three seconds to act."

Frau Rommel begged her husband to stand trial. "No," replied the field marshal. He realized what would happen to his family if he tried to take this course. "I would not be afraid to be tried in public, for I can defend everything I have done. But I know that I should never reach Berlin alive."[51]

Frau Rommel felt faint, but she returned his last embrace. Then he left, and the tears came.

After speaking to Lucie, Rommel saw his son for the last time. "I have just had to tell your mother that I shall be dead in a quarter of an hour," he said in a calm voice. He explained that he had been given the choice of death by poison or a public trial. If he committed suicide, the Nazis would not molest his family or his staff, provided they remained silent about the cause of his death; otherwise, he could expect both Lucie and Manfred to share his fate. Naturally Rommel—always the exemplary family man—had opted for suicide.

Manfred tried to talk him out of it, but Rommel cut him off. The house was surrounded, he said, they had very little ammunition, and it was better for one of them to sacrifice himself than for all of them to die in a gunfight. This settled, they said their final good-byes.[52]

Last of all, Rommel said farewell to his old friend Hermann Aldinger. They had fought side by side during World War I, and in the first desperate and exciting days of the Afrika Korps. Like Manfred, Captain Aldinger wanted Rommel to shoot his way out. They had been in bad places before, he said, and had gotten out by this method.

"It's no good, my friend," Rommel answered. "This is it. All the streets are blocked with SS cars and the Gestapo are all around the house. We could never get back to the troops. They've taken over the telephone. I cannot even ring up my headquarters."

Aldinger wanted to at least shoot Maisel and Burgdorf. "No," Rommel said. "They have their orders. Besides, I have my wife and Manfred to think of." He explained that nothing would happen to them if he committed suicide. His family would receive a pension, and he would be buried in Herrlingen with full military honors.[53] It was all prepared in every detail, Rommel related. In 15 minutes, Aldinger would receive a telephone call from the Wagnerschule Reserve Hospital in Ulm, saying that Rommel had died of a brain seizure. The field marshal looked at his watch and said he had to go. They had given him only 10 minutes.[54]

Rommel, Aldinger, and Manfred walked down the stairs together. In the hall Rommel's dachshund puppy Elbo saw him and threw himself into a fit of joy. This sight must have made it even harder on the Desert Fox, who always loved dogs. "Shut the dog in the study, Manfred," he said. When the young man returned, the three of them walked out of the house together. The crunch of the gravel beneath their shoes sounded unusually loud, Manfred later recalled.[55]

As they approached the gate, Burgdorf and Maisel saluted and then stood to one side. The SS driver opened the back door and stood at attention. Rommel swung his marshal's baton under his left arm, and shook hands with Aldinger and Manfred one last time. His face was calm. Then he got into the car, followed by Burgdorf and Maisel. The car ascended the hill near the house and disappeared around a bend in the road. Erwin Rommel never looked back.[56]

A few hundred yards beyond the hill the car stopped in an open space at the edge of the woods. Maisel and the driver got out, leaving Rommel alone with Burgdorf. Five minutes later Burgdorf got out, leaving the field marshal alone. The Nazi general paced up and down alongside the sedan. In another five minutes he waved to Maisel and the driver. When they arrived, the SS driver later testified, they found Rommel doubled up and sobbing. He was practically unconscious and obviously in his death throes.

Burgdorf, who was called "the gravedigger of the German Officer Corps," committed suicide when the Russians overran Berlin in May 1945, so exactly what transpired in Rommel's last ten minutes is impossible to determine. One thing is certain: At 1:25 P.M. on October 14, 1944, Field Marshal Erwin Rommel was reported dead on arrival at the Wagnerschule Reserve Hospital in Ulm. The hospital doctors were obviously suspicious but said nothing. No postmortem was allowed. The body was to be cremated—no evidence of what really happened was to be left behind. One feature, however, struck all who saw the body of Germany's great military leader: the expression of deep contempt on his dead face. "It was an expression we had never seen on it in life," his widow recalled later. The expression may still be seen on his death mask.[57]

Soon the expressions of condolence came pouring in from the great and small. Among the most effusive were those from members of the Nazi hierarchy who were responsible for, or at least privy to, the cause of his death. On October 16 Hitler sent a message to Frau Rommel, expressing his "sincerest sympathy" and recalling Rommel's heroic service in North Africa.[58] Hitler did not mention the Battle of Normandy in his wire.

Seven months later the Nazi dictator was finished. Almost completely mad, he shot himself in the head. The Russians were a few hundred yards from his bunker. He had gambled everything and lost, becoming, in the end, not the creator of a Thousand Year Reich, but one of the most despised figures in the history of mankind.

Reichsmarschal Hermann Goering, the number two man in the Third Reich, also sent the widow of his bitter enemy his "heartfelt sympathy."[59]

Like the more honorable Rommel, "Fat Hermann" died of poison by his own hand. He committed suicide in the Nuremberg prison on October 16, 1946, two hours before he would have been hanged.

Minister of Propaganda Dr. Joseph Goebbels sent a telegram to Lucie Rommel, expressing his "deepest sympathy" and praising Rommel for his victories in the desert.[60]

A few months later, as Berlin fell, Goebbels and his wife murdered their six young sleeping children and then committed suicide themselves. They survived their Fuehrer by a few hours.

Field Marshal Model, who now commanded Rommel's old Army Group B as well as OB West, published an Order of the Day. In it he called Rommel "one of the greatest German commanders . . . with a lightning power of decision, a soldier of the greatest bravery and of unequalled dash. . . . Always in the front line, he inspired his men to new deeds of heroism by his example."[61]

Of all the top Nazis who privately or publicly expressed sympathy, Model was probably the only one who was sincere. It is reasonably certain that he never knew that Rommel's death was, in fact, murder. In the months ahead Walter Model led Rommel's old command to its final defeats. Then, surrounded in the Ruhr Pocket, he dissolved Army Group B and on April 18, 1945, hopelessly surrounded by the Americans, he shot himself in a wooded area north of Dusseldorf.

At least two of Rommel's worst enemies refused to take part in the farce. Field Marshal Keitel and Colonel General Jodl sent no letters of condolence. They might have been accomplices to murder, but, in this case at least, they were not hypocrites.

On October 16, 1946, both of these men were hanged by the Allies as major war criminals. They outlived Rommel two years, almost to the day. They were the last of his enemies to die, except perhaps for Martin Bormann, Hitler's party chief, who has variously been reported as killed in Berlin in May 1945 and as alive in South America in the 1970s. (Although Bormann's fate is still the subject of dispute, German journalist Joachim von Lang unearthed a body in the 1970s that was located almost exactly where he said Bormann's body would be. Later, he wrote a book about it and has convinced me that Bormann committed suicide during the night of May 1/2, 1945.)[62]

Heinrich Himmler sent a personal representative to Frau Rommel's home to express his regrets. The person he chose was none other than Captain Alfred Berndt, one of Rommel's aides from North Africa and now a member of the SS. Berndt had been an official in the Ministry of Propaganda but had been dismissed for repeating something Rommel had told him: that the war was lost. Now he was one of Himmler's personal assistants. According to Berndt, neither Hitler nor Himmler ordered Rommel's murder. The responsibility lay solely with Keitel and Jodl. This statement must be considered a lie. The two military lackeys would never have dared to perform such an audacious act without Hitler's permission.

As an SS major, Berndt was killed in action on the Eastern Front in the last days of the Third Reich. Himmler poisoned himself after being captured by the British in May 1945.[63]

Erwin Rommel's body lay in state at the Ulm town hall for two days. He was buried on October 18, 1944, with full military honors. Thousands of common people from miles around came to mourn the dead leader, and many of his surviving friends also attended the funeral. Admiral Ruge represented the German Navy. Stroelin, ex-Foreign Minister Baron Constantin von Neurath, Gause, Colonel von Tempelhoff, Colonel Freyberg, Captain Lang, and Frau Speidel were also present, as no doubt were Farny and Aldinger. Retired Field Marshal Ritter Wilhelm von Leeb and Colonel General Richard Ruoff (whom Hitler had sacked in 1943) were also present,[64] as were Rommel's two brothers and Baron von Esebeck, the war reporter, who gave a moving tribute and was the first to mention that Rommel's injuries had been due to a strafing attack. Many others who certainly would have attended could not do so. Bayerlein, for instance, was leading the remnants of Panzer Lehr out of France, while Walther Nehring, the former Afrika Korps commander, was leading the battered XXIV Panzer Corps out of Russia. Ludwig Cruewell, Rommel's deputy commander in Africa, was in an Allied prisoner-of-war camp, as were a host of his lieutenants: Gustav von Vaerst, Baron Johannes von Ravenstein, Reverend Wilhelm Bach, Ritter Wilhelm von Thoma, and dozens of others. Speidel was in a Gestapo cell, as were Goerdeler and von Hofacker, among others. Dollmann, Marcks, Witzleben, Wagner, von Stueplnagel, Daniel, Georg von Bismarck, von Stauffenberg, and dozens of others were already dead.[65]

Field Marshal von Rundstedt, now greatly aged, unwittingly performed the last act in the tragic farce. In his funeral oration, he spoke of Rommel as one whose "heart belonged to the Fuehrer" and claimed that the Desert Fox was "imbued with the National-Socialist spirit."[66]

As ironic as von Rundstedt's address was, it had one saving phrase: "A pitiless destiny," he said, "has snatched him from us, just at the moment when the fighting has come to its crisis."[67] A pitiless destiny indeed!

Rommel's coffin, draped in a huge swastika flag, was carried to the crematorium. He was escorted by an honor guard composed of former members of the Afrika Korps, two companies of infantry, a Luftwaffe company, and a company of Waffen-SS. Later his ashes were interred in a corner of the graveyard of the village church of Herrlingen, the pretty little village near Ulm. A small stream flows nearby, and the cemetery is said to be quite peaceful. Erwin Rommel was at rest at last.

NOTES

1. Young, pp. 170–71.
2. Ruge, *Rommel*, p. 240.
3. Rommel, p. 429.
4. Speidel, p. 65.
5. Irving, p. 328.
6. Law and Luther, *Rommel*, p. 258.
7. Breuer, *Cherbourg*, p. 24.
8. The "stab-in-the-back" legend began after World War I. It held that the German Army had not really been defeated but rather stabbed in the back by traitors at home, especially by the Jews, Social Democrats, and Bolsheviks. Hitler, Field Marshal Paul von Hindenburg, and General Erich Ludendorff were among the leading advocates of the legend, which was believed by most of the German people and was a major contributing factor to the rise of Nazism.
9. Forman, p. 72.
10. Speidel, p. 100. The Gestapo did not discover the involvement of either von Luettwitz or von Schwerin in the anti-Hitler plot. Both survived the war. Count von Schwerin surrendered the LXXVI Panzer Corps to the British after the 8th Army cut it off during the collapse of Army Group C in Italy, April 1945. He retired to Bonn.
11. Ibid, pp. 106–7.
12. Franz Kurowski, "Dietrich and Manteuffel," in Correlli Barnett, ed., *Hitler's Generals* (London: Weidenfeld and Nicolson, 1989), p. 418; Irving, pp. 417–18.
13. Speidel, pp. 108–9.
14. Rommel, pp. 486–87.
15. Speidel, p. 111.
16. Irving, pp. 413–14.
17. Ruge, *Rommel*, p. 249, citing Ernst Juenger, *Strahlungen*.

18. Forman, p. 216.

19. Count von Stauffenberg was executed shortly after midnight on July 21, on the orders of General Fromm, the Commander-in-Chief of the Replacement Army, who wanted to dispose of any inconvenient witnesses. Hitler—who suspected the truth—could not prove Fromm's involvement in the conspiracy, so he had him shot for cowardice instead. He was put to death on or about March 17, 1945. General Beck shot himself twice in the head during the night of July 20/21, but did not die, so Fromm had him executed as well.

20. Montgomery, p. 82.

21. Ibid., p. 85.

22. Rommel, p. 489.

23. Montgomery, p. 86.

24. Rommel, pp. 489–90.

25. Carell, p. 235.

26. Rommel, p. 490. Bayerlein escaped the Falaise debacle and led Panzer Lehr in the Siegfried Line battles and in the Battle of the Bulge. He was named commander of the LIII Corps in February 1945 and was captured in the Ruhr Pocket in April. He died in Wuerzburg of a kidney disease on January 30, 1970.

27. Blumenson, p. 240.

28. Third U.S. Army was under Lieutenant General Omar Bradley's U.S. 12th Army Group. Both were activated on August 1, 1944. Lieutenant General Courtney Hodges replaced Bradley as commander of the U.S. 1st Army. The Canadian 1st Army under Lieutenant General Sir Henry D. G. Crerar was activated on July 23 as part of Montgomery's 21st Army Group.

29. Blumenson, p. 273. Lammerding had been wounded in an air attack. Christian Tychsen was born on December 3, 1910, in Flensburg, Schleswig-Holstein, the son of a master carpenter. He was killed in action on July 28, 1944 (Kraetschmer, pp. 452–55). The 2nd SS Panzer lost two-thirds of its men during the Normandy fighting (Max Hastings, *Das Reich*, New York: Holt, Rinehart and Winston, 1981, pp. 217–18).

Hans Lammerding was born in Dortmund on August 27, 1905, and became a certified engineer. He served in the training office of the Reichswehr during the days of the Weimar Republic but joined the SS-VT as an engineer officer after the Nazis rose to power. He commanded the engineer battalion of the SS-Totenkopf Division (the "Death's Head" division, made up of concentration camp guards) during the campaign in Belgium and France and in the early stages of the Russian invasion. He became Ia of the Totenkopf (later 3rd SS Panzer) Division in the summer of 1941. In 1942 he commanded the division's motorcycle battalion and later led an SS battle group in Russia.

Lammerding served on the Eastern Front until early 1944 when, as an Oberfuehrer, he was appointed commander of the 2nd SS Panzer Division "Das Reich," then rebuilding in southern France. He was charged with murdering hundreds of French civilians in the town of Oradour-sur-Glane on June 9, 1944, during the division's approach march to Normandy. It now seems likely that the atrocity was the act of revenge on the part of a young battalion commander, whose good friend, SS Lieutenant Colonel Helmut Kaempfe, had been murdered in Oradour-sur-Glane the day before. In any case, Lammerding was nowhere near Oradour-sur-Glane at the time and later brought charges against the commander, but this man was killed during the Normandy campaign and never tried.

Lammerding led the "Das Reich" Division until he was wounded in Normandy. Later he was chief of staff to Heinrich Himmler in his capacity as Commander-in-Chief of Army Group Vistula, but Lammerding was apparently a better commander than a staff officer. He was sacked by Colonel General Heinrici in March 1945 and was not reemployed. After the war, the French government attempted to prosecute Lammerding, but the Bonn government refused to extradite him. He died a painful death (of cancer) in Bad Toelz on January 13, 1971 (Schneider, pp. 210–14).

30. Speidel, p. 140; Rommel, p. 493.

31. Irving, p. 427.

32. Young, p. 184. Admiral Ruge had been reassigned to the German naval headquarters in August 1944; he became chief of the naval construction office at OKM on November 1, 1944—a post he held until the end of the war. Here he was involved in facilitating the construction of the new Type XXI U-boat. He became a member of the West German Navy in 1956 and was inspector of the navy (1957–61). He retired in 1961, wrote prolifically about the German Navy in World War I and World War II, and died in Tuebingen on July 3, 1985 (Hildebrand and Henriot, Volume 3, pp. 164–65.

33. Ruge, *Rommel*, p. 240.

34. Young, p. 185.

35. Irving, pp. 431–32.

36. Young, p. 185.

37. Rommel, p. 497.

38. Stuelpnagel had been relieved of his duties as military governor of France by von Kluge during the night of July 20/21 and was temporarily replaced by General Blumentritt. On August 7 Dietrich von Choltitz (whom Kluge had sacked as commander of the LXXXIV Corps) was named Wehrmacht Commander, Paris. He surrendered the city to the Allies on August 24.

39. Irving, p. 430. Krebs, the last chief of the German General Staff, committed suicide in Berlin in May 1945.

40. Speidel, p. 141.

41. Speidel was sacked on September 5.

42. Rommel, p. 500.

43. Young, p. 188.

44. Rommel, p. 497.

45. Speidel, p. 142.

46. Irving, pp. 435–36.

47. Rommel, pp. 501–2.

48. Young, p. 190; Rommel, p. 502.

49. Irving, p. 439; Young, p. 190.

50. Rommel, p. 502.

51. Young, pp. 190–91.

52. Rommel, p. 503.

53. Young, p. 191.

54. Rommel, pp. 503–4.

55. Ibid.

56. Ibid., p. 504.

57. Young, pp. 193–94.

58. Rommel, p. 505.

59. Ibid.

60. Ibid., pp. 505–6.

61. Young, p. 195.

62. See Joachim von Lang, *The Secretary. Martin Bormann: The Man Who Manipulated Hitler*, Christa Armstrong and Peter White, trans. (New York: Random House, Inc., 1979. Reprint ed., Athens: Ohio University Press, 1981).

63. Young, pp. 195–96.

64. A gentleman of the old school and a product of the old Bavarian Army, Field Marshal Ritter Wilhelm von Leeb had commanded Army Group C (later North) in the campaigns in France and Russia. Fed up with Hitler's leadership since the 1930s, he resigned in January 1942 and was never reemployed. He died in 1956. A native of Wuerttemberg, Richard Ruoff led the V Corps (1939–42), 4th Panzer Army (1942), and 17th Army (1942–43), and distinguished himself on the Eastern Front. He nevertheless fell afoul of Hitler and was sacked on June 24, 1943. He was never reemployed and was living in Tuebingen in the late 1950s (Keilig, p. 288).

65. Georg von Bismarck commanded a rifle regiment in Rommel's 7th Panzer Division in France (1940) and led the 21st Panzer Division in the Afrika Korps in the Gazala Line battles, the Second Battle of Tobruk, and the Egyptian Campaign of 1942. Rommel valued him very highly. He was killed in action on the night of August 31/September 1, 1942, while he was leading his division through a British minefield in the first stage of the Battle of Alma Halfa Ridge.

66. Young, p. 197.

67. Ibid. Field Marshal von Rundstedt's third retirement lasted only two months. On September 4, 1944, he was recalled to duty and again named OB West. He was sacked again on March 9, 1945, two days after the U.S. 9th Armored Division captured the Rhine River bridge at Remagen. He was captured by the Americans on May 2, 1945, at the hospital at Bad Toelz, where he was undergoing treatment for arthritis. He was indicted for war crimes in 1948 but was released the following year due to ill health. He died in Hanover on February 24, 1953.

APPENDIX I

TABLE OF EQUIVALENT RANKS

U.S. ARMY	GERMAN ARMY	SS RANK
General of the Army	Field Marshal (Generalfeldmarschall)	Reichsfuehrer-SS (Himmler)
General	Colonel General; (Generaloberst)	Oberstgruppenfuehrer
Lieutenant General	General of (Infantry, Artillery, etc.)	Obergruppenfuehrer
Major General	Lieutenant General (Generalleutnant)	Gruppenfuehrer
Brigadier General	Major General (Generalmajor)	Brigadefuehrer
none	none	Oberfuehrer
Colonel	Colonel (Oberst)	Standartenfuehrer
Lieutenant Colonel	Lieutenant Colonel (Oberstleutnant)	Obersturmbannfuehrer
Major	Major (Major)	Sturmbannfuehrer
Captain	Captain (Hauptmann)	Hauptsturmfuehrer
First Lieutenant	First Lieutenant (Oberleutnant)	Obersturmfuehrer
Second Lieutenant	Second Lieutenant (Leutnant)	Untersturmfuehrer

GERMAN STAFF ABBREVIATIONS

Chief of Staff (Not present below the corps level)

Ia   Chief of Operations

Ib   Quartermaster (Chief Supply Officer)

Ic   Intelligence Chief (subordinate to Ia)

IIa   Chief Personnel Officer (Adjutant)

IIb   Second Personnel Officer (subordinate to IIa)

III   Chief Judge Advocate (subordinate to IIa)

IVa   Chief Administrative Officer (subordinate to Ib)

IVb   Chief Medical Officer (subordinate to Ib)

IVc   Chief Veterinary Officer (subordinate to Ib)

IVd   Chaplain (subordinate to IIa)

V   Motor Transport Officer (subordinate to Ib)

National Socialist Guidance Officer (added 1944)

Special Staff Officers (Chief of Artillery, Chief of Projectors [Rocket Launchers], etc.)

APPENDIX III

CHARACTERISTICS OF OPPOSING TANKS

Model[1]	Weight (in tons)	Speed (mph)	Range (miles)	Main Armament	Crew
BRITISH					
Mark IV "Churchill"	43.1	15	120	1 6-pounder	5
Mark VI "Crusader"	22.1	27	200	1 2-pounder	5
Mark VIII Cromwell	30.8	38	174	1 75mm	5
AMERICAN[2]					
M3A1 "Stuart"[3]	14.3	36	60	1 37mm	4
M4A3 "Sherman"	37.1	30	120	1 76mm	5
GERMAN					
PzKw II	9.3	25	118	1 20mm	3
PzKw III	24.5	25	160	1 50mm	5
PzKw IV	19.7	26	125	1 75mm	5
PzKw V "Panther"	49.3	25	125	1 75mm	5
PzKw VI "Tiger"	62.0	23	73	1 88mm	5

1. Characteristics of each tank varied somewhat from model to model.
2. All American tanks were also in the British inventory. The British Shermans were sometimes outfitted with a heavier main battle gun. These Shermans were called "Fireflies."
3. A reconnaissance tank.

ROMMEL'S SCHEDULE,
March 23–June 4, 1944

March 23–27:   five-day inspection of Belgium and the Netherlands with Meise, Lattmann, Tempelhoff, and Ruge. Met with General von Falkenhausen (a fellow conspirator) in Brussels. Also visited Calais and Abbeville.

March 29:   consulted with General Hermann Geyer, a highly respected general of infantry and acknowledged defensive expert, at La Roche-Guyon. Geyer had been relieved by Hitler on December 31, 1941—(for conducting an unauthorized retreat during the Battle of Moscow)—and was never reemployed. To the Desert Fox's delight, Geyer agreed with Rommel's concepts entirely.

March 30:   inspected the Bay of the Seine sector, including the 711th, 716th, 352nd, and 77th Infantry Divisions. Conferenced with Rundstedt in Rouen.

March 31:   lunch with Admiral Krancke. Again unable to convince him to mine the Bay of the Seine.

April 1:   in Paris, inspecting a plant manufacturing reinforced concrete and a revolving concrete turret.

April 2:   visit to 15th Army Headquarters.

April 3–5:   inspecting on both sides of the Seine.

April 6:   visited HQ, 19th Army.

April 7:   in the Dieppe area, inspecting 245th Infantry Division.

April 8:   at 15th Army Headquarters.

April 9:   conference with Blumentritt, then Geyr.

April 10:   meeting with Rundstedt to discuss the deployment of the panzer divisions.

April 11–14:   visited Brittany; conferred with General Staube at St.-Malo. Inspected the defenses at and in the vicinity of Brest, Lorient, Saint-Nazaire, and Le Mans. Also inspected the engineer school at Angers.

April 15–16:   at La Roche-Guyon. Met with Speidel, Stuelpnagel, von Luettwitz, von Falkenhausen, and von Schwerin. Topic: how to overthrow the Nazi regime and establish contact with the Western Allies.

April 17–19: inspected coastline between the Somme and the Schelde; inspected LXVII Corps, 348th, 344th, 49th, 47th, and 712th Infantry divisions and 18th Luftwaffe Field Division.

April 18–19: visited General von Gilsa's LXXXIX Corps at Breskens; inspected tetrahedrons, "nutcracker" mines, stakes, etc.

April 20: at La Roche-Guyon; farewell party for General Gause. Rommel gave a lengthy speech in his honor.

April 21: meeting with General Guderian.

April 24: inspected troops on both sides of the Seine, including the 84th Infantry Division, army coastal artillery units, fortifications, and the port defenses of Le Havre.

April 28: meetings with Guderian. Speidel met with Geyr. Rommel later met with Luftwaffe General Student.

April 29: covered 780 kilometers in one day. Inspected LXXX Corps, 158th Reserve Division, and 17th SS Panzer Division.

April 30: crossed the Gironde into Bordeaux and went almost to the Spanish border.

May 1: in southern France. Inspected IV Luftwaffe Field Corps (General Petersen) and the 277th and 271st Infantry divisions.

May 2: inspected 388th, 244th, and 242nd Infantry divisions. Dinner with General von Sodenstern, the commander of the 19th Army.

May 3: drove up the Rhone River Valley and back to La Roche-Guyon.

May 4–9: at La Roche-Guyon. Issued orders to improve the defense and met with a series of officers and officials, including State Secretary Gunzenmueller of the Reich Ministry of Transportation.

May 9: inspected LXXXIV Corps and Cotentin peninsula defenses.

May 10: spent the day at Cherbourg and St.-Lô.

May 11: Caen, Falaise. Inspected 21st Panzer Division. Also inspected coastal defenses, including what became Utah Beach.

May 12: at La Roche-Guyon. Called OKW and defended reinforcements for the Cotentin.

May 13: headed for the Somme; inspected 2nd Panzer Division at Courselles and the 85th (in the second line of defense at Abbeville). Then visited 348th Infantry Division sector and the tetrahedron plant at Cayeaux.

May 14: visited 326th Infantry and 191st Reserve divisions. Met with General von Salmuth, who greeted him with genuine affection. Visited 331st Infantry and 182nd Reserve divisions (the latter a training unit). Conference with LXXXII Corps senior officers.

May 15–16: at La Roche-Guyon. Dinner with Ambassador Abetz on the 16th.

May 17: back to Cotentin Peninsula. Met with Major General Falley and visited 91st Air Landing Division.

May 18: inspected 77th Infantry Division. Saw glass mines and inspected three plants manufacturing nutcracker mines. Met with Generals Meindl and Dollmann (commanders of II Parachute Corps and 7th Army, respectively) west of St.-Malo. Inspected the zone of XXV Corps and met with officers of the 5th Parachute Division. Detoured back to meet with officers of the 21st Panzer Division.

May 19–21:   caught up on work at GHQ. Interrogated two captured British commandos. According to Fuehrer orders, they were supposed to be handed over to the Sicherheitsdienst (the SS Security Service) for execution, but Rommel sent them to regular POW camps, and they survived the war.

May 22:   inspected alternate Army Group B command post at La Vernon. Lunch with General von Salmuth.

May 23:   series of conferences about increasing transport usage on inland waterways.

May 24:   inspected army ordnance depot, a machine gun with a periscope, and a smoke screen device factory.

May 25–29:   at GHQ. Met with Baron von Funck and his chief of staff (XXXXVII Panzer Corps). Met with General Pickert, General Student, and others. On the 29th, met with Generals Buhle and Jakob of OKW concerning multiple rocket launchers.

May 30:   attended demonstration of multiple rocket launchers and smoke projectors with Salmuth, Dollmann, Kuntzen, Admiral Krancke, Marcks, von Funck, and others. Spent the afternoon inspecting coastal positions with Generals Buhle and Jakob.

June 1:   met with Assistant Secretary Berndt of the Propaganda Ministry (a former aide from North Africa). Drove to Dieppe; inspected fortresses and the 245th and 348th Infantry divisions.

June 2:   at La Roche-Guyon.

June 3:   met with General Hans Cramer, the last commander of the Afrika Korps, who had just been exchanged; tried to get more multiple rocket launchers for the 21st Panzer Division; met with von Rundstedt in Paris and told him that he intended to go to Germany from June 5 to 8 to once again ask for the transfer of two panzer divisions, the III Flak Corps, and a mortar brigade to Normandy.

June 4 (6:00 A.M.):   departed for Germany.

BIBLIOGRAPHY

Absolon, Rudolf, comp. *Rangliste der Generale der deutschen Luftwaffe nach dem Stand vom 20. April 1945*. Friedberg: Podzun-Pallas-Verlag, 1984.

Ambrose, Stephen. *Pegasus Bridge, June 6, 1944*. New York: Simon and Schuster, Inc., 1988.

Barnett, Correlli, ed. *Hitler's Generals*. London: Weidenfeld and Nicolson, 1989.

Bates, Charles C., and John F. Fuller. *America's Weather Warriors, 1814–1985*. College Station: Texas A & M Press, 1986.

Bender, Roger James, and Hugh P. Taylor. *Uniforms, Organization and History of the Waffen-SS*. Mountain View, Calif.: R. James Bender Publishing, 1971.

Blumenson, Martin. *Breakout and Pursuit*. U.S. Army in World War II, The European Theater of Operations, Office of the Chief of Military History, U.S. Department of the Army. Washington, D.C.: United States Government Printing Office, 1961.

Blumentritt, Guenther. *Von Rundstedt: The Soldier and the Man*. London: Odham's Press, 1952.

Breuer, William B. *Hitler's Fortress Cherbourg*. New York: Stein and Day, Publishers, Inc., 1984.

_____. *Drop Zone Sicily*. Novato, Calif.: Presidio Press, 1983.

Carell, Paul. *Invasion: They're Coming!* Boston: Little, Brown and Company, 1965. Reprint ed., New York: Bantam Books, 1966.

Chandler, David G., and James Lawton Collins, Jr., eds. *The D-Day Encyclopedia*. New York: Simon and Schuster, 1993.

Chant, Christopher, Richard Humble, William Fowler, and Jenny Shaw. *Hitler's Generals and Their Battles*. New York: Chartwell Books, Inc., 1976.

Dietrich, Wolfgang. *Die Verbaende der Luftwaffe, 1935–1945*. Stuttgart: Motorbuch-Verlag, 1976.

Edwards, Roger. *German Airborne Troops, 1936–1945*. Garden City, N.Y.: Doubleday and Co., Inc., 1974.

Eisenhower, Dwight D. *Crusade in Europe*. Garden City, N.Y.: Doubleday and Co. Inc., 1949.

Ellis, L. E. *Victory in the West*. Volume I: *The Battle of Normandy*. London: Her Majesty's Stationery Office, 1968.

Esposito, Vincent J., ed. *A Concise History of World War II*. New York: Frederick A. Praeger Publishers, 1964.

FitzGibbon, Constantine. *20 July*. New York: W. W. Norton and Co., Inc., 1956.

Fleming, Gerald. *Hitler and the Final Solution*. Berkeley: University of California Press, 1984.

Forman, James. *Code Name Valkyrie: Count von Stauffenberg and the Plot to Kill Hitler*. New York: S. G. Phillips, Inc., 1973. Reprint ed., New York: Laurel-Leaf Library, 1975.

Foster, Tony. *Meeting of the Generals*. Toronto: Methuen, 1986.

Fuerbringer, Herbert. *9.SS-Panzer-Division*. Editions Heimdal, 1984.

Fuller, J.F.C. *The Second World War, 1939–45: A Strategical and Tactical History*. New York: Duell, Sloan and Pearce, 1949.

Galland, Adolf. *The First and the Last*. New York: Henry Holt and Co., Inc., 1954.

Geyr von Schweppenburg, Leo. "Panzer Group West (mid-1943–15 July, 1944)." Foreign Military Studies *MS # B-258*. Office of the Chief of Military History.

———. "Panzer Group West (mid-1943–15 July, 1944)." Foreign Military Studies *MS # B-466*. Office of the Chief of Military History.

———. "Panzer Tactics in Normandy." U.S. Army ETHINT 3. Interrogation conducted on December 11, 1947. U.S. National Archives.

Goebbels, Joseph. *The Goebbels Diaries*. Louis P. Lochner, ed. Garden City, N.Y.: Doubleday and Co., Inc., 1948. Reprint ed., New York: Universal-Award House, 1971.

Graber, Gerry S. *Stauffenberg*. New York: Ballantine Books, 1973.

Guderian, Heinz. *Panzer Leader*. New York: E. P. Dutton, 1957. Reprint ed., New York: Ballantine Books, 1967.

Harrison, Gordon A. *Cross-Channel Attack*. U.S. Army in World War II, European Theater of Operations. Office of the Chief of Military History, U.S. Department of the Army. Washington, D.C.: United States Government Printing Office, 1951.

Hart, B. H. Liddell. *History of the Second World War*. New York: G. P. Putnam's Sons, 1972. 2 Volumes.

———. *The Other Side of the Hill*. London: Cassell, 1951.

Hastings, Max. *Das Reich*. New York: Holt, Rinehart and Winston, 1981.

Haupt, Werner. *Das Buch der Panzertruppe, 1916–1945*. Friedberg: Podzun-Pallas-Verlag, 1989.

Hayn, Friedrich. *Die Invasion von Cotentin bis Falaise*. Heidelberg: Kurt Vowinckel Verlag, 1954.

Hildebrand, Hans H., and Ernst Henriot. *Deutschland Admirale, 1849–1945*. Osnabrueck: Biblio Verlag, 1990. 3 Volumes.

Hoehne, Heinz. *Canasis*. J. Maxwell Brownjohn, trans. Garden City, N.Y.: Doubleday and Co., Inc., 1979.

Hoffman, Peter. *The History of the German Resistance, 1933–1945*. Cambridge, Mass.: MIT Press, 1977.

How, J. J. *Hill 112*. London: William Kimber, 1984.

Huemmelchen, Gerhard. "Friedrich Ruge." In David G. Chandler and James L. Collins, Jr., eds. *The D-Day Encyclopedia*. New York: Simon and Schuster, 1993. p. 473.

Infield, Glenn. *The Big Week*. Los Angeles: Pinnacle Books, 1974.

Irving, David. *Hitler's War*. New York: The Viking Press, 1977.

———. *The Trail of the Fox*. New York: E. P. Dutton, 1977.

Jacobsen, Hans-Adolf, ed. *July 20, 1944*. Bonn: Federal German Government Press and Information Office, 1969.

Jacobsen, Hans-Adolf, and J. Rohwer, ed. *Decisive Battles of World War II: The German View*. New York: G. P. Putnam's Sons, 1965.

Keilig, Wolf. *Die Generale des Heeres*. Friedberg: Podzun-Pallas-Verlag, 1983.

Keitel, Wilhelm. *In the Service of the Reich*. Briarcliff Manor, N.Y.: Stein and Day, Publishers, 1979.

Kraetschmer, E. G. *Die Ritterkreuztraeger der Waffen-SS*. 3rd ed. Preussisch Oldendorf: Verlag K. W. Schuetz KG, 1982.

Krancke, Theodor. "Invasionabwehrmassnahnen der Kriegsmarine im Kanalgebiet, 1944." *Marine-Rundschau*. Volume 66 (1969). pp. 170–87.

Kriegstagebuch des Oberkommando des Wehrmacht (Wehrmachfuehrungsstab). Frankfurt-am-Main: Bernard and Graefe Verlag fuer Wehrwesen, 1961. 4 Volumes.

Kurowski, Franz. *Das Tor zur Festung Europa*. Neckargemuend: Kurt Vowinckel Verlag, 1966.

———. "Dietrich and Manteuffel." In Correlli Barnett, ed. *Hitler's Generals*. London: Weidenfeld and Nicolson, 1989. pp. 410–37.

Lang, Joachim von. *The Secretary. Martin Bormann: The Man Who Manipulated Hitler*. Christa Armstrong and Peter White, trans. New York: Random House, Inc., 1979. Reprint ed., Athens: Ohio University Press, 1981.

Law, Richard D., and Craig W. H. Luther. *Rommel*. San Jose, Calif.: R. James Bender Publishing, 1980.

Lucas, James. "17th SS Panzer Grenadier Division." In David G. Chandler and James L. Collins, Jr., eds. *The D-Day Encyclopedia*. New York: Simon and Schuster, 1993. pp. 504–5.

Luck, Hans von. *Panzer Commander*. New York: Praeger Publishers, 1989.

Luther, Craig W. H. *Blood and Honor: The History of the 12th SS Panzer Division "Hitler Youth," 1943–1945*. San Jose, Calif.: R. James Bender Publishing, 1987.

MacDonald, Charles B., and Martin Blumenson. "Recovery of France." In Vincent J. Esposito, ed. *A Concise History of World War II*. New York: Frederick A. Praeger, 1964.

McFarland, Stephen L. "Air Combat." In David G. Chandler and James L. Collins, Jr., eds. *The D-Day Encyclopedia*. New York: Simon and Schuster, 1993. pp. 10–12.

McKee, Alexander. *Last Round against Rommel*. New York: Signet Books, 1966.

Mehner, Kurt, ed. *Die Geheimen Tagesberichte der deutschen Wehrmachtfuehrung im Zweiten Weltkrieg, 1939–1945*. Osnabrueck: Biblio Verlag, 1984–90. 12 Volumes.

Mellenthin, Frederick Wilhelm von. *Panzer Battles: A Study in the Employment of Armor in the Second World War*. Norman: University of Oklahoma Press, 1956. Reprint ed., New York: Ballantine Books, 1976.

Messenger, Charles. *Hitler's Gladiator: The Life and Times of Oberstruppenfuehrer and Panzergeneral-Oberst der Waffen-SS Sepp Dietrich*. London: Brassey's Defence Publishers, 1988.

———. *The Last Prussian: A Biography of Field Marshal Gerd von Rundstedt, 1875–1953*. London: Brassey's Defence Publishers, 1991.

Mierzejewski, Alfred C. "Railroads." In David G. Chandler and James L. Collins, Jr., eds. *The D-Day Encyclopedia*. New York: Simon and Schuster, 1993. pp. 447–48.

Mitcham, Samuel W., Jr. *Rommel's Desert War*. Briarcliff Manor, N.Y.: Stein and Day, Publishers, 1982.

Mitcham, Samuel W., Jr., and Gene Mueller. *Hitler's Commanders*. Lanham, Md.: Scarborough House, 1992.

Montgomery, Bernard Law, The Viscount of Alamein. *Normandy to the Baltic*. London: Hutchinson and Company Publishers, Ltd., 1958.

Neumann, Peter. *The Black March*. New York: Bantam Books, Inc., 1960.

Perger, Mark C. *SS-Oberst-Gruppenfuehrer und Generaloberst der Waffen-SS Paul Hausser*. Winnipeg, Canada: J. J. Fedorowicz Publishers, 1986.

Perrett, Bryan. *Knights of the Black Cross*. New York: St. Martin's Press, 1986.

Price, Alfred. "Alfred Buelowius." In David G. Chandler and James L. Collins, Jr., eds. *The D-Day Encyclopedia*. New York: Simon and Schuster, 1993. pp. 130–31.

———. "IX Air Corps." In David G. Chandler and James L. Collins, Jr., eds. *The D-Day Encyclopedia*. New York: Simon and Schuster, 1993. pp. 390–91.

———. "II Air Corps." In David G. Chandler and James L. Collins, Jr., eds. *The D-Day Encyclopedia*. New York: Simon and Schuster, 1993. pp. 493–95.

———. "X Air Corps." In David G. Chandler and James L. Collins, Jr., eds. *The D-Day Encyclopedia*. New York: Simon and Schuster, 1993. pp. 545–47.

———. "Werner Junck." In David G. Chandler and James L. Collins, Jr., eds. *The D-Day Encyclopedia*. New York: Simon and Schuster, 1993. p. 325.

Ritgen, Helmut. *Die Geschichte der Panzer-Lehr-Division im Westen, 1944–1945*. Stuttgart: Motorbuch Verlag, 1979.

Rohwer, Juergen. "Theodor Krancke." In David G. Chandler and James L. Collins, Jr., eds. *The D-Day Encyclopedia*. New York: Simon and Schuster, 1993. pp. 334–35.

Rommel, Erwin. *The Rommel Papers*. B. H. Liddell Hart, ed. New York: Harcourt, Brace and Co., 1953.

Ruge, Friedrich. "The Invasion of Normandy." In H. A. Jacobsen and J. Rohwer, eds. *Decisive Battles of World War II: The German View*. New York: G. P. Putnam's Sons, 1965. pp. 317–49.

_____. *Rommel in Normandy*. San Rafael, Calif.: Presidio Press, 1979.

_____. "The Trail of the Fox: A Comment." *Military Affairs*. Volume XLIII, Number 3 (October 1979): 158.

Ryan, Cornelius. *The Longest Day*. New York: Simon and Schuster, Inc. 1959. Reprint ed., New York: Popular Library, 1959.

Scheibert, Horst. *Die Traeger des Deutschen Kreuzes in Gold: das Heer*. Friedberg: Podzun-Pallas-Verlag, n.d.

Schneider, Jost W. *Verleihung Genehmight!* Winder McConnell, ed. and trans. San Jose, Calif.: R. James Bender Publishing, 1977.

Seaton, Albert. *The Fall of Fortress Europe, 1943–1945*. New York: Holmes and Meier, Publishers, Inc., 1981.

_____. *The Russo-German War, 1941–45*. New York: Frederick A. Praeger, 1971.

Shirer, William L. *The Rise and Fall of the Third Reich*. New York: Simon and Schuster, 1960.

Shulman, Milton. *Defeat in the West*. London: Martin Secker and Warburg, Ltd., 1968. Revised ed., New York: Ballantine Books, 1968.

Speidel, Hans. *Invasion, 1944*. Chicago: Henry Regnery Co., 1950. Reprint ed., New York: Paperback Library, Inc., 1950.

Stahlberg, Alexander. *Bounden Duty: The Memoirs of a German Officer, 1932–1945*. Patricia Crampton, trans. London: Brassey's, 1990.

Stauffenberg, Friedrich von. "Panzer Commanders of the Western Front." Unpublished manuscript in the possession of the author.

Steinhoff, Johannes, Peter Pechel, and Dennis Showalter. *Voices from the Third Reich*. Washington, D. C.: Regnery Gateway, 1989.

Stoves, Rolf. *Die Gepanzerten und Motorisierten deutschen Grossverbaende: Divisionen und selbstaendige Brigaden, 1935–1945*. Friedberg: Podzun-Pallas-Verlag, 1986.

Stumpf, Richard. *Die Wehrmacht-Elite: Rang- und Herkunftsstruktur der deutschen Generale und Admirale, 1933–1945*. Boppard am Rhein: Harald Boldt Verlag, 1982.

Taylor, Hugh Page. *Uniforms, Organization and History of the Waffen-SS*. San Jose, Calif.: R. James Bender Publishing, 1982. 5 Volumes.

Terraine, John. "Allied Expeditionary Air Force." In David G. Chandler and James L. Collins, Jr., eds. *The D-Day Encyclopedia*. New York: Simon and Schuster, 1993. pp. 23–25.

Tessin, Georg. *Verbaende und Truppen der deutschen Wehrmacht und Waffen-SS im Zweiten Weltkrieg, 1939–1945*. Osnabrueck: Biblio Verlag, 1973. 15 Volumes.

Tippelskirch, Kurt von. *Geschichte des Zweiten Weltkrieges*. Bonn: Athenaeum Verlag, 1951.

Toland, John. *Adolf Hitler*. New York: Random House, 1976. Reprint ed., New York: Ballantine Books, 1977.

United States Army Military Intelligence Service. "Order of Battle of the
    German Army." Editions of October 1942, April 1943, and January
    1945. Washington, D.C.: Military Intelligence Service, 1942, 1943, and
    1945, respectively.
Warlimont, Walter. *Inside Hitler's Headquarters*. R. H. Barry, trans. London:
    Weidenfeld and Nicolson, 1964. Reprint ed., Novato, Calif.: Presidio
    Press, n.d.
Wedemeyer, Albert C. *Wedemeyer Reports!* New York: Henry Holt and Co.,
    1958.
Wilmot, Chester. *The Struggle for Europe*. New York: Harper & Row, Publish-
    ers, 1981.
Wilt, Alan F. *The Atlantic Wall: Hitler's Defense in the West, 1941–1945*. Ames,
    Iowa: Iowa State University Press, 1975.
Young, Desmond. *Rommel: The Desert Fox*. New York: Harper and Row, 1950.
    Reprint ed., New York: Perennial Library, 1965.
Zimmermann, Erich, and Hans-Adolf Jacobsen. *Germans against Hitler, July
    20, 1944*. Bonn: Federal German Government Press and Information
    Office, 1960.

INDEX

Rommel, Manfred, 3, 11, 180, 190,
192, 193, 194, 195, 196
Roosevelt, Franklin D., 37, 61, 62
Roosevelt, U.S. Brigadier General
Theodore, 74
Ruge, Vice Admiral Friedrich, 6, 10,
19, 21, 22, 23, 29, 30, 34, 35, 49,
133, 152, 173, 189, 193
Rundstedt, Field Marshal Gerd von,
4, 6, 7, 8, 11, 13, 20, 23, 25, 26,
29, 30, 31, 35, 38, 39, 41, 44, 47,
48, 57, 64, 66, 68, 77, 78, 94, 95,
97, 104, 112, 116, 118, 119, 120,
135, 142, 151, 152, 153, 154, 155,
181–82, 199, 202, 209, 211
Russian Front. *See* Eastern Front

St.-Lô, Battle of, 155–60, 161–63,
167–70
Salmuth, Colonel General Hans
von, 12, 18, 19, 20, 30, 49, 66, 67,
183, 210, 211
Sattler, Major General Robert, 137
Schellenberg, SS General Walter,
32
Schlieben, Lieutenant General Karl
Wilhelm, 19, 72, 73, 74, 89–90,
107, 122, 129, 130, 131, 132, 133,
134, 136, 140
Schmundt, General of Infantry
Rudolf, 79, 90, 165, 186
Schwerin-Krosigk, Lieutenant Gen-
eral Count Gerhard von, 183,
199, 209
Sievers, Major General Karl, 160,
177
Sodenstern, General of Infantry
Georg von, 27, 28, 30, 53, 210
Speer, Albert, 25, 43
Speidel, Lieutenant General Dovtor
Hans, 10, 11, 22, 24, 35–36, 41,
48, 64, 66, 67, 68, 78, 87, 95, 96,
150, 152, 153, 154, 181, 183,
189, 191, 192, 195, 198, 201,
209, 210
Sperrle, Luftwaffe Field Marshal
Hugo, 25, 28, 41, 55, 68, 103,
120

Staubwasser, Lieutenant Colonel
Anton, 10–11, 142
Stauffenberg, Colonel Count Claus
von, 10, 47, 63, 185, 186, 190, 200
Stegmann, Major General Rudolf,
130, 132, 133, 138, 192
Stieff, Major General Helmuth, 183,
191
Stoebe, Colonel Professor Walter, 63
Stroelin, Doctor, 180, 181, 198
Stuelpnagel, General of Infantry He-
inrich Karl von, 25, 52, 181, 183,
195, 201, 209

Talley, U.S. Colonel, 76
Tedder, British Air Chief Marshal
Sir Arthur, 178
Tempelhoff, Colonel Hans-Georg
von, 10, 122, 154, 169, 198, 209
Treschow, Major General Henning
von, 183, 190
Triepel, Colonel, 73
Tychsen, SS Lieutenant Colonel
Christian, 188, 200
Tzschoekell, Colonel, 175

United States Army
Army Groups
1st, 32, 141, 142, 187
12th, 200
Armies
1st, 60, 104, 141, 161, 169,
200
3rd, 138, 188, 200
Corps
V, 60, 68, 76, 106, 108, 156,
167, 168
VII, 68, 74, 99, 106, 108, 112,
130, 131, 137, 141, 156,
159, 161, 188
VIII, 60, 104, 132, 156, 158,
159, 161
XIX, 104, 156, 159, 162, 163,
167, 168
Divisions
1st Armored, 94
1st Infantry, 75, 93, 105, 106,
167, 188

OTHER COOPER SQUARE PRESS TITLES OF INTEREST

TRIUMPHANT FOX
Erwin Rommel and the Rise of the
  Afrika Korps
Samuel W. Mitcham Jr.
376 pp., 26 b/w photos, 8 maps
0-8154-1055-7
$17.95

HITLER'S FIELD MARSHALS
and Their Batttles
Samuel W. Mitcham Jr.
456 pp., 26 b/w photos, 9 tables, 22 maps
0-8154-1130-8
$18.95

HITLER'S COMMANDERS
Officers of the *Wehrmacht*, the
  ***Luftwaffe*, the *Kriegsmarine*, and**
  the *Waffen-SS*
Samuel W. Mitcham Jr. and Gene
  Mueller
354 pp., 51 b/w photos, 8 maps
0-8154-1131-6
$18.95

DEFEAT INTO VICTORY
Battling Japan in Burma, 1942–1945
Field-Marshal Viscount William Slim
New introduction by David Hogan
576 pp., 21 maps
0-8154-1022-0
$22.95

THE GI's WAR
American Soldiers in Europe During
  World War II
Edwin P. Hoyt
with a new preface
664 pp., 29 b/w photos
0-8154-1031-X
$19.95

GENERAL OF THE ARMY
George C. Marshall, Soldier and
  Statesman
Ed Cray
876 pp., 24 b/w photos
0-8154-1042-5
$29.95

CANARIS
Hitler's Master Spy
Heinz Höhne
736 pp., 21 b/w photos, 1 map, 2 diagrams
0-8154-1007-7
$19.95

THE MEDICAL CASEBOOK OF
  ADOLF HITLER
Leonard Heston, M.D. and Renate
  Heston, R.N.
Introduction by Albert Speer
192 pp., 3 b/w photos, 4 graphs
0-8154-1066-2
$17.95

Available at bookstores; or call 1-800-462-6420
COOPER SQUARE PRESS
150 Fifth Avenue
Suite 817
New York, NY 10011